Popular
Music Perspectives

Popular Music Perspectives:
Ideas, Themes, and Patterns in Contemporary Lyrics

B. Lee Cooper

Bowling Green State University Popular Press
Bowling Green, Ohio 43403

To the late, great 45 rpm record...
that magic vinyl carpet
to the land of rock 'n' roll.

Contents

Acknowledgments

Essayists, like songwriters, are keenly aware that their products usually have very short life spans. The three month run of a scholarly quarterly somewhat parallels the ninety-day celebrity of a hit tune. Just as tunesmiths long for entire record albums which display the breadth of their commentaries, writers of essays crave anthologies. I am grateful to Pat Browne, Editor of Bowling Green State University's Popular Press, for her advice, support, and generosity in assembling this volume. Her ability to compel focus, continuity, and meaning in essays that originally appeared in ten different journals over the past fourteen years was marvelous. Her personal warmth and kindness to a long-time popular culture colleague has always been greatly appreciated.

Writers rely upon friends, colleagues, and professional acquaintances for ideas, assistance, stimulation, criticism, and companionship during the I-can't-make-this-project-work stage of scholarly production. While reviewing their superb books, articles, and conference papers, I encountered several exceptional thinkers: Mark Booth, Ray B. Browne, Gary Burns, Ronald Butchart, George O. Carney, Norm Cohen, Ron Denisoff, Howard A. DeWitt, Colin Escott, Reebee Garofalo, Steve Gelfand, Archie Green, Charles Gritzner, Peter Hesbacher, Frank W. Hoffmann, David Horn, Hugo Keesing, Stephen Kneeshaw, David Leaf, John Litevich, Dennis Loren, J. Fred MacDonald, Jon McAuliffe, Hugh Mooney, Russel B. Nye, David Pichaske, Lawrence Redd, Jerome Rodnitzky, Roger B. Rollin, Fred E. H. Schroeder, Tom Schultheiss, Larry Stidom, Warren Swindell, Joel Whitburn, and Brett Williams. Through record collecting and correspondence concerning audio tapes I have also established beneficial contacts with many shrewd, helpful persons: James A. Creeth, Frank Scott, and Chas "Dr. Rock" White. Finally, my work as both a college professor and a chief academic officer has enabled me to develop a cadre of professional friendships which are sustaining and supportive during research doldrums: Sue Ayotte, Thomas Behler, Stuart and Teresa Blacklaw, David Boyd, Tommy Brewington, K. David Brown, Donna and Terry Brummett, Roger C. Buese, Dan and Emily Byrens, Dolores Chapman, Neil and Karen Clark, Colby Currier, Charles Ericson, Vicki Gallas, Charles Graessle, Susan Gray, Mary and Wayne S. Haney, Jerrilyn Holcomb, Joe and Mary McDonald, Donald and Zella Morris, Jack and Anne Patterson, Roland Patzer, Todd and Connie Reynolds, Kenn Robbins, Donald and Sue Rowe (and Jessi, too), Mary Schroth, Linda Jo Scott, Jeff and Rande Smith, Steen and Jane Spove (and young Steen, too), John and Linda Sukovich, David Thomas, Todd Trevorrow, Stewart Tubbs, Don and Louise Tuski, Donald Walker, Cliff Warnken, Gary Wetheimer, James Wilson, Dirk G. Wood, and especially Wayne A. Wiegand.

Authors also benefit from the loving, uncritical support of wives, children, parents, and other relatives. This indispensable sustenance was provided by Jill Cooper, Michael Cooper, Laura Cooper, Julie Cooper, Kathleen M. Cooper, Charles A. Cooper, Patty Jo Cooper, Robert Douglas, Larry W. Cooper, Angie Cooper, Dustin Cooper, Elizabeth Cunningham, Herb Jones, and Judy Jones.

The final type of support that made this study possible was financial. Two agencies provided economic assistance. I wish to thank the division of fellowships of seminars of The National Endowment For The Humanities (NEH) for awarding me a Travel To Collections Grant during 1985. I also acknowledge similar research funding provided by the Grants Committee and Board of Directors of The Association For Recorded Sound Collections (ARSC) in 1990. This special financial support permitted me to gain lengthy periods of research access to both literary and audio materials at the Sound Recording Archive in the William T. Jerome Library at Bowling Green State University. I was also able to consult directly with long-time friend and discographic expert William L. Schurk as a result of NEH and ARSC funding. Although only one of the essays in this collection was originally published with Professor Schurk as the co-author, I must assert that every essay contained in this collection was enhanced from conversations with the effervescent, knowledgeable, indefatigable archivist.

In conclusion, I wish to express my appreciation to the following editors and scholarly journals for granting me permission to reprint original portions or revised versions of the articles listed below:

"Perceptions Of Education In Lyrics Of American Popular Music, 1950-1980," *American Music*, V, No. 3 (Fall 1987), pp. 31-41. Reprinted with permission of co-author Ronald E. Butchart and © 1987 by The Board of Trustees of The University of Illinois.

"Controversial Issues In Popular Lyrics, 1960-1985: Teaching Resources For The English Classroom," *Arizona English Bulletin*, XXIX (Fall 1986), pp. 174-187. Reprinted with permission of Editor Suzanne Bratcher.

"Death" (pp. 49-55) and "Political Protest And Social Criticism" (pp. 183-189) originally published in *A Resource Guide To Themes In Contemporary American Song Lyrics, 1950-1985* (Westport, Connecticut: Greenwood Press, 1986). Copyright © 1986 by B. Lee Cooper. Reprinted by permission.

"Human Relations, Communication Technology, And Popular Music: Audio Images Of Telephone Use In The United States, 1950-1985," *International Journal Of Instructional Media*, XIII, No. 1 (1986), pp. 75-82, "Food For Thought: Investigating Culinary Images In Contemporary American Recordings," *International Journal Of Instructional Media*, XIV, No. 3 (1987), pp. 251-262, and "Images From Fairy Tales And Nursery Rhymes In The Lyrics Of Contemporary Recordings," *International Journal Of Instructional Media*, XV, No. 2 (1988), pp. 183-193. Reprinted with permission of co-author William L. Schurk, Editor Phillip J. Sleeman, The Baywood Publishing Company, and The Westwood Press, Inc.

"Record Revivals As Barometers Of Social Change: The Historical Use Of Contemporary Audio Resources," *JEMF Quarterly*, XVI (Spring 1978), pp. 38-44 and "Nothin' Outrun My V-8 Ford: Chuck Berry And The American Motorcar, 1955-1979," *JEMF Quarterly*,

XVI (Spring 1980), pp. 18-23. Used through the courtesy of Director Paul F. Wells in The Center For Popular Music At Middle Tennessee State University in Murfreesboro.

"The Image Of The Outsider In Contemporary Lyrics," *Journal Of Popular Culture*, XII (Summer 1978), pp. 169-178. Reprinted with permission of The Popular Press and Editor Ray B. Browne.

"Mick Jagger As Herodotus And Billy Joel As Thucydides? A Rock Music Perspective 1950-1985," *Social Education*, XLIX, No. 7 (October 1985), pp. 596-600 and "Popular Records As Oral Evidence: Creating An Audio Timeline to Examine American History, 1955-1987," *Social Education*, LIII, No. 1 (January 1989), pp. 34-40. Reprinted with permission of Editor Salvatore J. Natoli and The National Council For The Social Studies.

"Oral History, Popular Music, and American Railroads, 1920-1980," *Social Studies*, LXXIV (November/December 1983), pp. 223-231, "Social Concerns, Political Protest, And Popular Music, *Social Studies*, LXXIX (March/April 1988), pp. 53-60, and "Christmas Songs: Audio Barometers Of Tradition And Social Change In America, 1950-1987," *Social Studies*, LXXIX (November/December 1988), pp. 278-280. Originally published by Heldref Publications at 4000 Albemarle Street, N.W. in Washington, D.C. 20016. Reprinted with permission of The Helen Dwight Reid Educational Foundation.

Introduction

Popular recordings are pieces of oral history. Written accounts that attempt to communicate reactions to social situations, technological change, political events, and economic conditions are inevitably incomplete. So, too, contemporary lyrics offer only partial visions of American society. This limited perspective provided in popular song is magnified by several factors. First, the physical nature of sound recordings restricts the duration of a singer's commentary to an extremely brief time. The average song is less than three minutes long. Second, the achievement of "popularity" for a single recording indicates broad levels of public acceptance for a particular song. This market-oriented reality tends to limit extremes of lyrical deviance. Third, the radio-play life span for most songs is quite brief. A particular tune may be a frequently played, much discussed commodity for six-to-ten weeks, and then disappear from the music charts forever. Finally, songs may either consciously or unconsciously address significant historical conditions or personal concerns. Various listening publics may accept, reject, ignore or be totally unaware of the lyrical commentary being presented. This means that intent, content, and influence via recorded music are rarely synonymous.

Recognizing these limitations in assessing the impact of sound recording communications, why should songs be considered valuable oral history resources? As a communication medium, lyrics do not systematically propagandize listeners. Likewise, they do not function as flawless historical mirrors. Such polarized indictments of songs ignore the inherent pluralism of contemporary lyrics, a pluralism that is a logical by-product of the intellectual (and sometimes anti-intellectual) variety of modern U.S. society. Popular songs replicate in unsystematic, segmented fashions a multiplicity of ideas and values; in contemporary culture they form an unpredictable, ever-changing audio collage. The oral history that lyrics present resembles the historical remnants available in an Indian burial mound. Just as an archeologist must reconstruct cultural reality from innumerable fragments of a former civilization—pieces of pottery, projectile points, tools for building, stone drawings, ancient toys and games, eating utensils, religious tokens, and death masks——the contemporary soundscape researcher must examine many, many recordings produced within a defined time span in order to identify persistent ideas, themes, and patterns.

Some subjects of rock lyrics are overwhelmingly available for scrutiny. For example, the standard courtship theme—boy meets girl, boy dates girl, love blooms, marriage beckons and a wedding occurs—is predominant in all popular music. However, there are also numerous variations to the typical love-and-marriage scenario. Women's liberation, birth control, social mobility, economic independence, the sexual revolution, and dozens of other trends and situations in post-1950 U.S. history have dramatically altered and complicated the previously simple courtship theme. These same social and political activities have generated an enlarged spectrum of lyrical commentary within many popular tunes.

Between 1950 and 1990, U.S. society has been verbally photographed by innumerable itinerant tunesmiths and displayed in audio galleries across this continent and throughout the world. Radios, jukeboxes, cable television (M-TV), cassette recordings, motion picture sound tracks, compact discs, and millions and millions of records sound a clarion call to prospective oral historians. The irony is that so few teachers have utilized these recorded history resources. But just as armies of archeologists have successfully reconstructed the fabric of ancient Indian cultures by carefully examining buried relics, it is vital that modern historians and teachers apply their logical analyses and reasoned perspectives to the vinyl remnants of the American music industry.

Is popular music really a legitimate resource for investigating contemporary society? For Dick Clark, Wolfman Jack and Casey Kasem, maybe so; but what about for the thousands of teachers and millions of students in secondary schools and college classrooms across the country? The answer should be a resounding— "Yes!" This does not mean that rock music is either the *only* or the *best* resource for examining contemporary social and political events. Televised speeches, printed articles from newspapers and magazines, lectures by teachers, scholars, politicians, and businessmen, and innumerable other oral and written communication vehicles can stimulate student thought, reflection, decision making and action. But rock lyrics are "ear candy" to most youngsters, offering both audio gratification and the challenge of being "different" from the bland pabulum served in traditional textbooks.

The 1950-1990 period is blanketed with significant lyrical commentary. Because so few teachers consider rock to be "serious music"—let alone "serious history"—very few classes have explored the sociopolitical imagery contained in songs by Elvis Presley, Chuck Berry and The Coasters. Beyond these early rockers, though, the idea of Mick Jagger, John Lennon, Burton Cummings, Pete Townshend, Carole King, Bob Dylan, Elvis Costello and John Cougar Mellencamp making political and social statements is not nearly as unexpected. Popular music is, after all, the rhythmic voice of the young. Obviously, love themes, dancing, partying, and other less-than-polemic ideas dominate rock's frantic media message. Yet individuals like Bruce Springsteen, Paul Simon, David Bowie and Billy Joel and groups like The Beatles, The Rolling Stones, The Who, The Cure and Culture Club defy traditional society and explain modern history with statements of meaning and substance in their hit recordings.

The most productive approach to examining the past forty years of U.S. history through popular music is to focus on specific ideas, themes, and patterns. Obviously, this text is designed to be illustrative rather than comprehensive. It is impossible to devise a subject classification system, let alone a series of essays, that will establish the bounds of recorded commentary. The selectivity exercised in the following thirteen chapters is indicative of the author's interests and insights. Social change, human interaction, technology, and intellectual development constitute major points of interest that translate into audio examinations of public education, railroads, death, automobiles, and rebels. These ideas and themes are prominent in contemporary lyrics. Patterns in recordings that go beyond mere imagery are also significant in depicting American society. Humor, tradition, and historical events can be discerned through answer songs, cover recordings, nursery rhyme adaptations, and novelty tunes.

The goal of these essays is to stimulate thought among students, teachers, and popular culture researchers. A wealth of audio and literary resources are provided in the following pages for two purposes: to support the studies presented, but also to offer gateways for additional investigation. This book will not have fulfilled its mission unless each reader concludes that the soundscape of American life is a worthy field for further study.

Ideas

Chapter One
Education (I)

Teenagers have always had some distaste for school, and their defiant spirit has frequently been captured in the lyrics of rock 'n' roll songs. In the mid-1970s, Alice Cooper's "School's Out (Forever)" topped the charts; in the 1960s it was Gary U.S. Bonds' "School's Out (At Last)." Anti-education sentiments in rock run back to the very earliest days of the music when Chuck Berry frequently compared the frustrations of the classroom to the satisfaction of fast cars and music.

> —William Sievert
> "The New Youth Anthem"
> *Boston Sunday Globe*
> July 20, 1980

Music plays a highly visible role in American public education. Every secondary school has an athletic fight song and an alma mater, a choral director or a music teacher, a marching band and glee club, and usually several other organized vocal or instrumental musical activities. In addition, lunch-time record hops, piped-in cafeteria music, post-game sock hops, disc jockey dances, proms, and homecoming or spring formal big band extravaganzas are common elements at most high schools. What is particularly intriguing to the student of popular culture, though, is the focus on the nature of American public education which abounds in the lyrics of rock era songs. Not only are specific attitudes about schools, teaching, and peer relations frequently depicted in contemporary tunes, but a great deal of critical commentary surfaces regularly in the lyrics about the means and ends of all formal learning activities.

I.
"School days, school days,
Dear old golden rule days,
Readin' and writin' and 'rithmatic,
Taught to the tune of a hickory stick."

The sentiments of good times, firm discipline, and the inculcation of basic communication and computation skills contained in the traditional tune "School Days" represent perceptions of an earlier era of learning. Whether accurate or inaccurate, realistic or idealistic, this song symbolized public education during the first half of the twentieth century. But as Bob Dylan observed early in the 1960s, the times they are a-changin'. In 1954 the Supreme Court ordered that American education cease to be a racially segregated, "separate but equal" learning area. But the integration of public schools, a concept yet to be fully realized

9

in practice throughout the nation, wasn't the only revolution occurring in America during the mid-1950s. The currents of popular music were also beginning to flow more swiftly. The floodtide of rock 'n' roll occurred when country music tunes and rhythm 'n' blues songs found such synthesizing spokesmen as Bill Haley, Otis Williams, Elvis Presley, Chuck Berry, Carl Perkins, and Jerry Lee Lewis. This popular music explosion, aided by influential disc jockeys, several technological recording inventions, motion picture hype ("Blackboard Jungle"), and improved record company promotional techniques, launched a fundamental change in America's musical tastes.

As the Rock Era evolved, it enlisted more and more singers and songwriters who were drawn from and remained committed to the values of youth. The observations, ideals, and images contained in their songs were uncompromisingly youth-oriented. This meant that public schools, the physical environment of so much teenage involvement, were inevitably scrutinized, analyzed, and depicted in more and more song lyrics. The meaning of this audio examination of American schooling is eminently clear—and staggering. Internal verification of educational practices replaced external expectations and historic ideals concerning the nature of the public learning enterprise. Neither truth nor reality could be guaranteed by this change in perspective and commentators. However, the viewpoint of current student experience is undeniably sharper in assessing the behavior of principals, teachers, P.T.O.'s, student groups, and individual learners than the more philosophical observations offered by Sidney Hook, Hyman Rickover, Paul Goodman, William Bennett and other public school analysts.

No systematic, comprehensive statement of public school criticism can be found in the grooves of popular recordings. Nevertheless, several key ideas are present. Between 1950 and 1980 the previously dominant preachment and pretense images of schooling have been directly challenged. Lyrical idealism is not totally absent, of course. Admiration for the teacher who is bright, deeply committed to learning, concerned about his or her pupils, and engaged in a constant battle to overcome ignorance is warmly eulogized in a few tunes like "To Sir With Love" and "Welcome Back." But a much more critical tone dominates the majority of lyrical commentary about schooling. Teachers are generally condemned for being ignorant of student feelings ("Bird Dog"), for pursuing irrelevant classroom topics ("[What A] Wonderful World"), for corrupting student idealism ("The Logical Song"), and for intentionally stifling the development of their pupils' social and political awareness ("Another Brick In The Wall"). It is difficult to imagine a more blatant denunciation of entire public educational system than Paul Simon's introductory lines in "Kodachrome" (1973):

> "When I think back on all the crap I learned in high school,
> It's a wonder I can think at all.
> And though my lack of education hasn't hurt me none,
> I can see the writing on the wall."

II.

In order to illustrate the image of American public education present in popular music lyrics since 1950, it is necessary to isolate and define several key elements within the schooling process. The following definitions govern the use of terminology in this study:

School—the physical building (classrooms, hallways, cafeteria, restrooms, library, teacher lounges) and the total potential learning environment available to students (special meetings and ceremonies, organization of school personnel, and historical heritage)

Students—a group of young people ranging in age from 14 to 18 years, both male and female, predominantly American, in all physical shapes, sizes, and psychological dimensions, consisting of different races, religious, and socio-economic groups

Teachers—a group of adults ranging in ages from 22 to 65 years, both male and female, predominantly American, in all physical shapes and sizes, and psychological dimensions; primarily middle class, mostly white and Protestant, possessing at least four years of college education

Principals—the chief administrative officers in the schools possessing at least five years of college education and several years of classroom teaching experience; a group of adults ranging in age from 35 to 65 years, predominately white, male, middle class, Protestant, and American; in all physical shapes, sizes, and psychological dimensions

Parents—adult men and women, mostly married, ranging in age from 32 to 55, of different races, religions, and social and economic conditions, political persuasions, and personal interests

Community—the geographic area which constitutes the dwelling place for the parents and students, and the majority of teachers and principals; it is also the site of the school.

Education—the primary goals of public education are transmitting factual knowledge, fostering socialization, and preparing students for democratic citizenship; the teachers conduct a variety of learning activities under the administrative supervision of principals, with community involvement by individual parents and parent-teacher organizations

Beyond the identification of these seven elements in American public education, it is necessary to note three perceptual perspectives in order to depict and to assess the activities within the defined learning environment:

Preachment—the ideals or highest goals of a particular social organization or of any person associated with that organization.

Pretense—the act of attempting to justify specific activities within a particular social organization which are not functionally appropriate to furthering the ideas of that organization; a shadowy dimension of personal attitude and physical behavior located between the more easily defined zones of preachment and practice.

Practice—the actual activities which constitute the hour-by-hour, day-to-day-operations of a social organization.

All seven elements of the schooling process—schools, students, teachers, principals, parents, the community, and education—are frequently depicted in popular songs. Most lyrical comments are directly related to personal involvement in real (practice) rather than ideal (preachment) school situations. This means that interpretation and interpolation is required to establish the more ephemeral perspectives of preachment and pretense. Although practice may be more visible and more individually identifiable, many songs do contain lyrical segments which allude to all three dimensions. Based upon an impressionistic lyrical review and analysis, Table 1-A illustrates the broad perspectives on public education which exist in popular recordings. The radical divergence between preachment/pretense and actual practice is so sharp (according to most contemporary lyrical commentaries) that one wonders if the American public school system may not be malfunctioning.

Table 1-A

Terms Illustrating the Preachment, Pretense,
and Practice Imagery about American Public Education
Contained in the Lyrics of Popular Songs, 1950-1980

Area of Lyrical Commentary	Preachment Images	Pretense Images	Practice Images
1. School	human development cultural repository knowledge resource civic center	alma mater school loyalty commencement honor code	separation from life isolation from peers irrelevance social interaction
2. Students	inquiry reflection rationality	questioning participation investigating	friends, dancers clowns, romancers victims, gangs
3. Teachers	mentors models	friends counselors	baby-sitters fools arbitrary actors
4. Principals	learning leader experienced educator	chief administrator responsibility	authoritarian irresponsible
5. Parents	loving concern family stability	guiding hands mature guides	misunderstanding interference
6. Community	democracy participation	due process socialization	conformity hypocrisy
7. Education	wisdom knowledge understanding freedom creativity diversity	information citizenship decision-making communication stability cooperation	regimentation indoctrination illiteracy cynicism fear hostility

The lyrical images of American public education are lively, colorful, direct, and generally critical. A brief review of the recorded commentaries on each of the seven elements of the schooling process follows.

Images of School

"School" is depicted in contemporary lyrics as a state of mind as well as a physical entity. A few songs beckon students to recall "(The Days Of The) Old School Yard." Cat Stevens' nostalgic reverie is echoed by the spirited 28-versions of "High School U.S.A." recorded by Tommy Faceda, by The Beach Boys' loyalty hymn "Be True To Your School," and by The Arbors' nostalgic

"Graduation Day." But these tunes are atypical of the genre. The majority of lyrics portraying school life portray the buildings and grounds as a sinister series of segregated compartments which dictate varying kinds of student behavior.

The classroom is generally depicted as the domain of a teaching tyrant. "Gee, she don't know how mean she looks," notes Chuck Berry in "School Day." Activities which occur in classrooms are conducted in lock-step, intimidating, teacher-directed fashion. A student like The Coasters' "Charlie Brown" may walk into the classroom cool and slow, but then he'd better be quiet, orderly, and without guile. By contrast, the hallways are always alive with noise. Rigidly enforced classroom silence and cerebral irrelevance give way to cacophonous peer chatter and delirious social interaction. Discussions of cars, sex, smokes, food, movies, and immediate wants and needs occur in the jostling, locker-slamming hallway atmosphere. The school's corridors also lead to freedom— "...down the hall and into the street;" to a secret cigarette break in the restroom ("Smokin' In The Boys Room"); to a luncheon record hop ("High School Dance"); to more private activities in outdoor recreation areas ("Me and Julio Down In The Schoolyard"); and to the parking lot filled with cars and vans. The key word to describe most lyrical observations about the school building is *escape*. Even the songs which laud memories of by-gone secondary school experiences—such as Adrian Kimberly's "Pomp and Circumstance"—praise the senior commencement as the relief of alma mater status felt by all alumni. This escapist theme is most clearly delineated in numerous songs that depict the annual freedom period from June through August: Gary "U.S." Bonds' "School Is Out," The Jamies' "Summertime, Summertime," and Alice Cooper's "School's Out."

Images of Students

Lyrical images of students vary greatly. Clear recognition of both peer pressures and the dominance of special interest groups within school is illustrated in The Beach Boys' "I Get Around," Dobie Gray's "In Crowd," and Connie Frances' "Where The Boys Are." The isolation of non-conforming individuals and out-groups is depicted in The Crystals' "He's A Rebel," The Dixie Cups' "Leader Of The Pack," Carol Jarvis' "Rebel," and Janis Ian's "At Seventeen" and "Society's Child." Although they comprise the most heterogeneous group within the public educational system, students are lyrically characterized as the least franchised ("Summertime Blues"), most harassed ("Yakety Yak"), most regimented ("Another Brick In The Wall"), least trusted ("Smokin' In The Boy's Room"), most humorous ("Charlie Brown" and "My Boy Flat Top"), most victimized ("My Generation" and "Society's Child"), and least understood ("It Hurts To Be Sixteen" and "You And Me Against The World").

Students are usually described as extremely active and singularly non-contemplative. In fact, as Sam Cooke declared in his 1960 hit "(What A) Wonderful World," the typical romantic high school youth

> Don't know nothin' 'bout history,
> Don't know any biology,
> Don't know nothin' 'bout a science book
> Don't remember the French I took...

Nearly two decades later, Art Garfunkel, Paul Simon, and James Taylor revived Cooke's "(What A) Wonderful World" with an additional anti-intellectual refrain:

> Don't know nothin' bout the Middle Ages,
> Look at the book and turn the pages,
> Don't know nothin' bout no Rise and Fall,
> Don't know nothin', nothin' at all...

This sense of educational futility is a dominant element in popular lyrics. Paul Simon's 1973 song "Kodachrome," which begins with a stunning indictment of academic irrelevance, was followed three years later by an even more negative analysis of post-high school life in "Still Crazy After All These Years." This self-assessment was shared with a former high school girlfriend. Several songs capture poignant vignettes of post-high school reflections. Tunes like Bob Seger's "2 + 2 = ?" question the meaning of a school friend's senseless death in Vietnam; Alice Cooper's "Eighteen" examines the "I'm a boy, but I'm a man" predicament of a recent high school graduate; and Bob Dylan's "Subterranean Homesick Blues" presents an image of an illogical, mean-spirited society which awaits a formally educated, but non-street wise youth.

Images of Teachers and Principals

Adults who control the environment within public schools are neither admired nor respected. Even those few songs which praise teachers—"Mr. Lee" by The Bobbettes, "To Sir With Love" by Lulu, and "Abigail Beecher" by Freddie Cannon—offer sharp, derogatory contrasts between the caring behavior and independent actions of their *favored* instructors and the general demeanor of the majority of teachers who are boobs, bumpkins, and boors. Chuck Berry, The Coasters, The Who, Janis Ian, Paul Simon, and dozens of other singers acknowledge in simple tones the message so directly chanted by Pink Floyd: "Teacher, leave them kids alone!"

If teachers are fools, antiquarians, babysitters, arbitrary actors, and persons generally out-of-touch with reality, principals are outright villains with malevolent motives and totalitarian drives. Although very few lyrical commentaries are assigned solely to the chief administrative officers of the schools, the implications of their rule-making authority and harsh methods of enforcement abound. The jangling bell system of lock-step, class-to-class routine, the de-personalized hall passes, the regimented class changes, the overly-brief lunch periods ("School Days"), and dozens of other system-defining annoyances are attributed to the principal, though usually enforced by teachers.

Most distressing is the fact that teachers are universally defined in antithetical images to their students. They lack common sense ("Bird Dog"), are cynical ("The Logical Song"), humorless ("School Days" and Charlie Brown"), out of touch with personal problems ("Don't Stand So Close To Me"), and represent a system of thought and action that hides from rather than confronts genuine social problems ("Another Brick In The Wall"). Even John Sebastion's laudatory "Welcome Back"—a tribute to a teacher's responsibility—carefully notes an exception to the norm.

Images of Parents and the Community

Students regard the public school system as an extension of the policy-making power and educational goals of parents and other members of the local community. The lyrics of many contemporary songs depict the parental/ principal/community nexus as the primary source of conformity, authoritarianism, hypocrisy, and frustration. At best, students dwell in a world where they are "Almost Grown." But parents and the community seem unwilling to accept the occasional mistakes that are a normal part of personal maturation and social development. Schools do not function as experimental stages for the reflective consideration of alternative social, political, economic, and personal ideas and behaviors; instead, they are cloisters, cells and societal buffers. Deviant behavior is harshly labelled ("I'm Not A Juvenile Delinquent," "The Rebel," and "Leader Of The Pack") by a unified adult population ("Town Without Pity," "Sticks And Stones," and "Society's Child"). Insensitivity to growing pains ("At Seventeen") is compounded by intense social pressure to conform in thought, in word, and in deed ("Fortunate Son" and "The Free Electric Band"). Despite occasional public lapses between preachment and practice among community members ("Harper Valley P.T.A.") and parents ("That's The Way I Always Heard It Should Be"), schools remain bastions of patriotic ("Okee From Muskogee"), local ("Be True To Your School"), and moral ("Me And Julio Down By The Schoolyard") direction. Such a strong parental/community stance obviously renders democratic processes, instructional independence, intellectual objectivity, and open communication among students and teachers impossible. The smothering hand of community control is lyrically chided in the Simon and Garfunkel ballad "My Little Town."

The Image of Education

"Please tell me who I am?" This question seems to paraphrase Socrates' more positively stated dictum, "Know Thyself." But the question is part of the lyrical criticism of formal education posed by the British rock group Supertramp in their 1979 hit tune "The Logical Song." Echoing Rousseau's naturalistic educational premise, the lyric depicts an untutored youngster who views life as wonderful, a miracle, beautiful, and magical. Then he is sent away to school where he learns to be clinical, logical, cynical, sensible, responsible, and practical. Also in 1979, Pink Floyd's "Another Brick In The Wall" challenged the formal educational system with a stinging, chanting attack:

> We don't need no education.
> We don't need no thought control,
> No dark sarcasm in the classroom,
> Teacher leave them kids alone.

The Supertramp/Pink Floyd assertions seem far more deep-rooted and radical than the humorous, exasperated commentaries of Chuck Berry and The Coasters. Yet they are logical extensions of lyrical critiques presented by Janis Ian, Paul Simon, and several others who are understandably appalled by the failure of American education to meet—or even to approach in practice—its oft-repeated ideals. The laudable goals of fostering human dignity, creativity, freedom, individualism, knowledge, diversity, and objectivity are submerged in public schools beneath a miasma of regimentation, indoctrination, illiteracy, cynicism, arbitrariness, authoritarianism, local morality, and cultural bias. The disembodied voice of American youth—popular recordings—chant a consistent, sad tale.

It would be easy to argue, in defense of enlightened teaching, that few popular songs could appropriately detail the virtues of an inspired history lecture, the potential delight of analyzing Shakespeare's sonnets, or the feeling of confidence gained by conducting a successful chemistry experiment. However, the weight of contemporary lyrical evidence is conclusive. Good teaching is an exception; inept classroom performance is expected and received. Similarly, belittling ridicule rather than praise is the norm for dealing with students—from principals, from parents, from instructors, and (not infrequently) from insensitive, conforming peers as well. The public school arena is a polity that Aristotle would probably label an "unjust society"—where the "just" person (logical, creative, sensitive, democratic) will either become or be perceived as alienated and rebellious. What is even more regrettable, though, is the apparent success of this system in sustaining itself.

III.

If public schools are *not* effective sources of learning, then how do young people gain knowledge? Although contemporary tunesmiths provide a variety of answers, they concur on one point. Most valuable ideas, information, social contacts, feelings, beliefs, and personal values are secured through individual experience outside of the classroom. Recorded commentaries argue "I Gotta Be Me," "My Way," "Just The Way You Are," and "You May Be Right." The individualistic road through life is not necessarily solipstic, nor alienating, nor narcissistic. Once again, the lyrical images of community pressures ("Town Without Pity"), peer criticisms ("Sticks and Stones"), parental restraints ("Yackety Yak" and "Summertime Blues"), church irrelevance ("Only The Good Die Young"), political skulduggery ("Won't Get Fooled Again"), and wage labor meaninglessness ("Wake Me, Shake Me," "Get A Job," "Take This Job And Shove It," and "Workin' At The Carwash Blues") tend to hinder personal development through outside-of-school contacts.

This study does not intend to suggest that contemporary songs are devoid of paens to the joy of intellectual growth and discovery. Abundant examples illustrate constructive personal experiences. Some are humorous, such as "Spiders And Snakes," "Mr. Businessman," and "Dead End Street"; some are serious, such as "Question," "Who Will Answer," and "Eve of Destruction"; and some are poignant such as "Color Him Father," "Son Of Hickory Holler's Tramp," and "Patches." In each of these instances the learning is directly connected to individual perceptions of random, but personally meaningful life events. No organized, administered, routinized system can replace authentic human experience. Rousseau may not be correct about man's natural bent toward goodness; however, Thoreau's concept of simplifying in order to enrich each man's life might serve as a guiding principle to revise and reshape American public education. Real learning, if the messages communicated by popular songs are to be believed, is intrinsically personal. Therefore, the bureaucratic public education system of the United states is antithetical to the process of individual growth. Is it any wonder that school consolidation, classroom and curriculum regimentation, computerization, teacher unionization, and other facets of mass education have alienated so many students? The images of schools as minimal security detention centers ("Smokin' In The Boy's Room" "School Day," and "Charlie Brown") are more depressing than comic. The hard work of good principals, creative and caring teachers, and concerned parents to improve community schools may be futile because their efforts fail to take into account certain fundamental educational prerequisites. Learning is intrinsically personal. The needs and experiences of contemporary American students defy the factory-like organizational patterns which may have worked during former decades. The shifting technology of American society—a car culture, a television culture, a computer culture—is dramatically altering the lives of young and old alike. Similarly, events of the past forty years ranging from the launching of Sputnik and the prolonged Vietnam conflict to the attempted assassination of Ronald Reagan and the rise of Japanese economic dominance have altered the collective psyche of students in dramatic fashions. Several formal attitudinal surveys demonstrate this fact. But the primary audio barometer of America's youth culture—popular music—illustrates even more clearly the expectations, observations, assumptions, and goals of school-age people.

IV.

The conclusions of this study are undeniably as impressionistic and subjective as the lyrical evidence compiled to support it. Public education is clearly not respected in contemporary songs. Worse than that, it is openly ridiculed and condemned. Singers and songwriters openly attack the narrowness of hypocritical community norms ("My Little Town") and praise the survival of individuals beyond the pace of the classroom ("Kodachrome"). Contemporary performers are, to no small extent, the minstrels and balladeers for America's youth. This indicates that they offer sprightly, rhythmic entertainment as well as admittedly fictionalized, sometimes over-dramatized ("Subterranean Homesick Blues") pictures of life in a complex, confusing, highly industrialized, urbanized nation. Their messages should be heeded. The current problems of student illiteracy and in-school violence are indicative of the chronic mismatch of person and place. As Warren Bennis wrote in 1970 about the confusion of contemporary life, "Perhaps only a Homer or Herodotus, or a first folk-rock composer, could capture the tumult and tragedy of the last five years and measure their impact upon our lives.

Table 1-B

An Alphabetical List of 45 and 33-1/3
Records Featuring Education-Related
Titles, Illustrations, and Themes,
1950-1980

45 R.P.M. Records

The recordings listed below were released as 45 r.p.m. discs between 1950-1980. Each song achieved *Billboard* magazine's "Hot 100" chart during this period.

Song Title (Record Number)	Recording Artist	Date of Release
"Abigail Beecher" (Warner Brothers 5409)	Freddy Cannon	1964
"After School" (Decca 29946)	Tommy Charles	1956
"Almost Grown" (Chess 1722)	Chuck Berry	1959
"Another Brick In The Wall" (Columbia 11187)	Pink Floyd	1979
"At Seventeen" (Columbia 10154)	Janis Ian	1975
"Back To School Again" (Cameo 116)	Timmie Rogers	1957
"Be True To Your School" (Capitol 5069)	The Beach Boys	1963
"Bird Dog" (Cadence 1350)	The Everly Brothers	1958
"The Blind Man In The Bleachers" (MCA 40474)	Kenny Starr	1975
"Charlie Brown" (Atco 6132)	The Coasters	1959
"Department of Youth" (Atlantic 3280)	Alice Cooper	1975
"Dialogue (Parts I and II)" (Columbia 45717)	Chicago	1972
"Don't Be A Drop-Out" (King 6056)	James Brown	1966
"Don't Stand So Close To Me" (A&M 2301)	The Police	1980
"From A School Ring To A Wedding Ring" (ABC-Paramount 9732)	The Rover Boys	1956
"Graduation Day" (ABC-Paramount 9700)	The Rover Boys	1956
"Graduation Day" (Capitol 3410)	The Four Freshmen	1956
"Graduation Day" (Date 1561)	The Arbors	1967
"Graduation's Here" (Dolton 3)	The Fleetwoods	1959
"Harper Valley P.T.A." (Plantation 3)	Jeannie C. Riley	1968
"He's A Rebel" (Philles 106)	The Crystals	1962
"Hey Little Girl" (Abner 1029)	Dee Clark	1959
"Hey, School Girl" (Big 613)	Tom and Jerry	1958
"High School Confidential" (Sun 296)	Jerry Lee Lewis	1958

"High School Dance"		
(Capitol 4405)	The Sylvers	1977
"High School Dance"		
(Specialty 608)	Larry Williams	1957
"High School Romance"		
(ABC-Paramount 9838)	George Hamilton IV	1957
"High School U.S.A."		
(Atlantic 51-78)	Tommy Facenda	1959
"(I Wanna) Dance With The Teacher		
(Demon 1512)	The Olympics	1959
"I wish"		
(Tamla 54274)	Stevie Wonder	1977
"I'm Going Back To School"		
(Vee Jay 462)	Dee Clark	1962
"Kodachrome"		
(Columbia 45859)	Paul Simon	1973
"The Leader Of The Pack"		
(Red Bird 014)	The Shrangli-Las	1964
"The Logical Song"		
(A&M 2129)	Supertramp	1979
"Lonely School Year"		
(Rocket 40464)	The Hudson Brothers	1975
"Me And Julio Down By The Schoolyard"		
(Columbia 45585)	Paul Simon	1972
"Mr. Lee"		
(Atlantic 1144)	Bobbettes	1957
"My Boy Flat Top"		
(King 1494)	Boyd Bennett and His Rockets	1955
"My Generation"		
(Decca 31877)	The Who	1966
"My Little Town"		
(Columbia 10230)	Simon and Garfunkel	1975
"My Old School"		
(ABC 11396)	Steely Dan	1973
"New Girl In School"		
(Liberty 55672)	Jan and Dean	1964
"Pomp And Circumstance"		
(Calliope 6501)	Adrian Kimberly	1961
"Queen Of The Senior Prom"		
(Decca 30299)	The Mills Brothers	1957
"Question"		
(Threshold 67004)	The Moody Blues	1970
"Rebel"		
(Dot 15586)	Carol Jarvis	1957
"Remember The Days Of The Old Schoolyard"		
(A & M 1948)	Cat Stevens	1977
"Rose And A Baby Ruth"		
(ABC-Paramont 9765)	George Hamilton IV	1956
"School Boy Crush"		
(Atlantic 3304)	The Average White Band	1975

"School Day" (Chess 1653)	Chuck Berry	1957
"School Is In" (LeGrand 1012)	Gary "U.S." Bonds	1961
"School Is Out" (LeGrand 1009)	Gary "U.S." Bonds	1961
"School Teacher" (Reprise 1069)	Kenny Robers and The First Edition	1972
"School 's Out" (Warner Brothers 7596)	Alice Cooper	1972
"Seventeen" (King 1470)	Boyd Bennett and His Rockets	1955
"Smokin' In The Boy's Room" (Big Tree 16011)	Brownsville Station	1974
"Society's Child (Baby I've Been Thinking)" (Verve 5027)	Janis Ian	1967
"Spiders And Snakes" (MGM 14648)	Jim Stafford	1974
"Still Crazy After All These Years" (Columbia 10332)	Paul Simon	1976
"Stood Up" (Imperial 5483)	Ricky Nelson	1958
"Subterranean Homesick Blues" (Columbia 43242)	Bob Dylan	1965
"Summertime Blues" (Liberty 55144)	Eddie Cochran	1958
"Summertime Blues" (Philips 40516)	Blue Cheer	1968
"Summertime Blues" (Decca 32708)	The Who	1970
"Summertime, Summertime" (Epic 9281)	The Jamies	1958
"Swingin' On A Star" (Dimension 1010)	Big Dee Irwin	1963
"Swingin' School" (Cameo 175)	Bobby Rydell	1960
Teach Your Children" (Atlantic 2735)	Crosby, Stills Nash, and Young	1970
"To Sir With Love" (Epic 10187	LuLu	1967
"Town Without Pity" (Musicor 1009)	Gene Pitney	1962
"Waitin' In School" (Imperial 5483)	Ricky Nelson	1958
"Wake Up Little Susie" (Cadence 1337)	The Everly Brothers	1957
"Welcome Back" (Reprise 1349)	John Sebastian	1976
"White Sport Coat (And A Pink carnation)" (Columbia 40864)	Marty Robbins	1957

"Wonderful World" (MGM 13354)	Herman's Hermits	1965
"Wonderful World" (Keen 2112)	Sam Cooke	1960
"(What A) Wonderful World" (Columbia 10676)	Art Garfunkel, with James Taylor and Paul Simon	1978
"Woodstock" (Atlantic 2723)	Crosby, Stills, Nash and Young	1970
"Yackety Yak" (Atco 6116)	The Coasters	1958
"You Never Can Tell" (Chess 1906)	Chuck Berry	1964
"Young School Girl" (Imperial 5537)	Fats Domino	1958
"Young World" (Imperial 5805)	Ricky Nelson	1962
"Your Mama Don't Dance" (Columbia 45719)	Loggins and Messina	1973
"Young Blood" (Atco 6087)	The Coasters	1957

33-1/3 R.P.M. Records

The recordings listed below were released as 33-1/3 r.p.m. discs between 1950-1980. Each album achieved *Billboard's* "Top LP's " chart during this period.

Song Title and Album Title (Record Number)	Recording Artist	Date of Release
"Alma Mater" *School's Out* (Warner Brothers BS 2623)	Alice Cooper	1972
"Back To School Days" *The Parkerilla* (Mercury 2-100)	Graham Parker and The Rumor	1978
"Beauty School Dropout" *Grease* (RSO 2-4002)	Frankie Avalon	1978
"Chemistry Class" *Armed Forces* (Columbia 35709)	Elvis Costello	1979
"The Dean And I" *10 CC* (UK/London 53110)	10 CC	1975
"Education" *Schoolboys In Disgrace* (RCA 5102)	The Kinks	1975
"Getting Better" *Sgt. Pepper's Lonely Heart's Club Band* (Capitol 2653)	The Beatles	1967

"Goin' Through School And Love"		
Rock On		
(Arista 4212)	Raydio	1979
"The Happiest Days Of Our Lives"		
The Wall		
(Columbia PC 2-36183)	Pink Floyd	1979
"Headmaster"		
Schoolboys In Disgrace		
(RCA 5102)	The Kinks	1975
"High School"		
Back In The U.S.A.		
(Atlantic SD 8247)	MC 5	1970
"I Was Educated By Myself"		
The End Of The Beginning		
(A & M 4598)	Richie Havens	1976
"Jack The Idiot Dunce"		
Schoolboys In Disgrace		
(RCA 5102)	The Kinks	1975
"Maxwell's Silver Hammer"		
Abbey Road		
(Apple 383)	The Beatles	1969
"Rock And Roll High School"		
Rock And Roll High School		
(Sire 6070)	The Ramones	1979
"School"		
Crime Of The Century		
(A & M 3647)	Supertramp	1974
"School Days"		
The Runaways		
(Mercury 1090)	The Runaways	1976
"School Days"		
Explore Your Mind		
(Hi 32087)	Al Green	1974
"School Days"		
Schoolboys In Disgrace		
(RCA 5102)	The Kinks	1975
"School Days"		
Home, Home On the Road		
(Columbia 32870)	New Riders of The Purple Sage	1974
"School Is Out"		
Matthew And Son		
(Deram 18005)	Cat Stevens	1967
"School Is Out"		
Show Time		
(Warner Brothers 3059)	Ry Cooder	1977
"School Punks"		
School Punks		
(Big Tree 89500)	Brownville Station	1974
"Student Demonstration Time"		
Surf's Up		
(Reprise 6453)	The Beach Boys	1971
"Teacher"		
Benefit		
(Reprise 6400)	Jethro Tull	1970

"Teacher I Need You"		
Don't Shoot Me, I'm Only		
The Piano Player		
(MCA 2100)	Elton John	1973
"Teenage Jail"		
The Long Run		
(Asylum 508)	The Eagles	1979
"What Did You Learn In School		
Today?"		
We Shall Overcome		
(Columbia 2101)	Pete Seeger	1963
"(What A) Wonder World"		
Watermark		
(Columbia 34975)	Art Garfunkel	1978
"Wonderful World"		
We Remember Sam Cooke		
(Motown 629)	The Supremes	1965
"Wonderful World"		
Otis Blue		
(Volt 412)	Otis Redding	1965

Works Cited

Books

Simon Frith, *Sound Effects: Youth, Leisure, And the Politics Of Rock 'N' Roll.* New York: Pantheon Books, 1981.

Linda Martin and Kerry Segrave, *Anti-Rock: The Opposition to Rock 'N' Roll.* Hamden, Connecticut: Archon Books, 1988.

Articles

Robert D. Barr, "Youth And Music," in *Values And Youth: Teaching Social Studies In An Age Of Crisis—No. 2* (Washington, D.C.: National Council For The Social Studies, 1971), pp. 88-103.

Barbara Brittingham and Richard Katzoff, "The Life And Times Of The Class Of 1984," *The Chronicle Of Higher Education,* XXI (September 22, 1980), p. 48.

Ray B. Browne, "Popular Culture: Medicine For Illiteracy And Associated Educational Ills," *Journal Of Popular Culture,* XXI (Winter 1987), pp. 1-15.

Ronald E. Butchart and B. Lee Cooper, "Perceptions Of Education In The Lyrics Of American Popular Music, 1950-1980," *American Music,* V (Fall 1987), pp. 31-41.

George W. Chilcoat, Laurence I. Seidman, Sheldon Brown, and B. Lee Cooper, "Studying U.S. History Through Songs," *Social Education,* XLIX (October 1985), pp. 579-603.

B. Lee Cooper, "Foreward," in *Popular Culture And Libraries,* compiled by Frank W. Hoffmann (Hamden, Connecticut: Library Professional Publications By The Shoe String Press, Inc., 1984), pp. VIII—XV.

B. Lee Cooper and Larry S. Haverkos, "The Image Of American Society In Popular Music: A Search For Identity And Values," *Social Studies,* LXIV (December 1973), pp. 319-322.

B. Lee Cooper, "Popular Music: A Creative Teaching Resource," in *Nonprint In The Secondary Curriculum: Readings For Reference*, edited by James L. Thomas (Littleton, Colorado: Libraries Unlimited, Inc., 1982), pp. 78-87.

———— "Youth Culture," in *A Resource Guide To Themes In Contemporary American Song Lyrics, 1950-1985* (Westport, Connecticut: Greenwood Press, 1986), pp. 265-337.

Lawrence Grossberg, "The Politics Of Youth Culture: Some Observations On Rock an Roll In American Culture," *Social Text*, VIII (Winter 1983/84), pp. 104-126.

Steven A. Hilsabeck, "The Blackboard Bumble: Popular Culture And Recent Challenges to The American High School," *Journal Of Popular Culture*, XVIII (Winter 1984), pp. 25-30.

Phil Jochem, "Some Popular Songs Rip Into Teachers, "*Instructor*, LXXXV (October 1975), pp. 40-42.

Anne W. Lyons, "Creative Teaching In Interdisciplinary Humanities: The Human Values In Pop Music," *Minnesota English Journal*, X (Winter 1974), pp. 23-31.

Thomas J. Meyer, "In This Course 'Dare To Be Stupid' Can Be The Route To Intellectual Growth," *The Chronicle Of Higher Education*, XXX (November 6, 1985), pp. 1, 35.

David E. Morse, "Avant-Rock In The Classroom," *English Journal*, LVIII (February 1969), pp. 196-200 ff.

Chapter Two
Railroads

Introducing oral resources as teaching materials is not a simple task. Nevertheless, the use of non-print items to illustrate social change is steadily gaining academic support as television shows, motion pictures, and other forms of popular media become more and more dominant in depicting and reflecting American culture. The following pages suggest that sound recordings should be utilized by social studies teachers to demonstrate shifting public images about railroads in the United States since the end of the First World War. Vinyl discs of oral history—33-1/3, 45, and 78 r.p.m. records—offer fascinating glimpses into the meaning and evolution of American transportation technology. The lyrics of train songs, when structured in chronological patterns, offer revealing social, economic, and personal commentaries which can be examined by high school students to assess the cultural impact of one significant mode of transportation.

"How would you describe the American railroad system to a Martian?"

The boy wiggled uncomfortably in his classroom chair, looking intently at his desktop and only slowly raising his gaze to meet the teacher's eyes.

"Well, Michael? If a traveler from outer space asked you to explain railroads to him, how would you begin?"

Although the question seemed absurd to him, Mike finally tackled the topic. "I'd tell the Martian that trains were transportation vehicles for people and freight. I'd also say that people still sing about them even if they are vanishing."

The high school teacher was obviously surprised by the second part of this answer. The entire class, seeing her sudden bewilderment, giggled. Mike turned red in embarrassment. Then he took the offensive. "You guys know what I mean. The good old days of railroading are long gone. There's no more John Henry or Casey Jones, no more smoke belching steamers, and no train-riding hobos or gamblers. But for some reason guys like Kenny Rogers and Johnny Cash keep singing songs about railroads as if they were still around."

Despite this young man's assertion to the contrary, railroads are still around. But social, economic, and technological changes during the past sixty years have greatly diminished their functions in American life. What should be of particular interest to students and their teachers, however, is the continuing use of train-related images in modern song lyrics. From the Civil War until the end of World War II steam-powered engines played an integral role in the transportation, industrialization, and urbanization of the United States. An array of popular stories and social images emerged depicting the exploits of engineers, other trainmen, and railway travelers during this 80-year period. However, since 1945 the railroad world has changed dramatically. Employee unionization, the use of diesel engines, and the introduction of interstate highway systems and jet-propelled aircraft have drastically altered the scope of railroading activities. Yet the images of earlier transportation experiences still persist. Nowhere is this more evident than in the field of popular music. Social studies students can benefit by exploring the varying images of trains and train-related incidents in song lyrics.

Although the automobile has undeniably received a tremendous amount of lyrical attention, composers and crooners have also focused their roving commentaries on steamboats ("Proud Mary"), airplanes ("Jet Airliner"), trucks ("Convoy"), sailing vessels ("Wreck Of The Sloop John B"), buses ("Thank God And Greyhound"), and spaceships ("Jupiter C"). Yet no area of public and commercial transportation has a longer or richer tradition of melodious eulogy than the American railroad system. For several decades bluegrass pickers, country and western performers, folk singers, and bluesmen (and blueswomen, too) have sung about railroads. The country tunes of Jimmie Rodgers ("Waitin' For A Train," "Hobo Bill's Last Ride," "Brakeman's Blues," and "Old Number Five") and Hank Snow ("Golden Rocket," "Fireball Mail," and "City of New Orleans") have been echoed in the blues realm by Big Bill Broonzy ("This Train"), Howlin' Wolf ("Smokestack Lightnin' "), Leadbelly ("Rock Island Line"), and Son House ("Empire State Express"). Nearly all early twentieth-century folk, bluegrass, country and western, and blues performers recorded lyrical commentaries about trains. In fact, the variety of singers (Pete Seeger, Lester Flatt and Earl Scruggs, Mississippi John Hurt, Blind Willie McTell, Woody Guthrie, Bukka White, and others) who have dealt with railroading themes is exceeded only by the contrasting images which they presented concerning America's train culture. On the one hand, locomotive transportation has been lauded as scenic, cheap, readily available, romantic, individualistic, and a constant source of personal freedom and geographical mobility. On the other hand, the same trains have been condemned as noisy and ugly, prone to crashes and untimely delays, physically dangerous to humans and animals, sources of choking smoke and fire hazards, and potential vehicles for familial separation and human misery.

Between 1946 and 1980 drastic changes occurred in railroad technology and public involvement with railway transportation. Singers and songwriters reflected these changes in their postwar tunes. In order to present railroad songs as teaching resources, several specific thematic categories depicting train-related images must be established. Oral history, like its literary counterpart, requires focal points to accompany investigative resources related to those points. In order to illustrate the spectrum of lyrical opinions from more than three hundred train songs, the accompanying thematic guideline was created. Seven basic image categories—historical perspectives, social mobility, geographical mobility, employment situations, heroes and heroic achievements, metaphors for life situations, and rhythm patterns—are outlined below. Each category lists specific identifying characteristics and is accompanied by a brief descriptive explanation.

A. Historical Perspectives
1. Report of a Train Wreck or Railroad Accident
2. Biographical Review of a Prominent Railroading Figure
3. Recognition of the National or Regional Significance of a Specific Railroad Line

4. Nostalgic Yearning for the Conditions of an Earlier Age of Either Railroad Life or Social Style
5. Comment on the Social Implication or Economic role of a Railroad Within a Community
6. Observation About the Evolution of Transportation Technology

The high profile of railroads in commercial recordings prior to World War II can be partially attributed to a high frequency with which dramatic songs lyricized actual historical incidents. One of the most popular kinds of railroad songs was the train-wreck ballad. Numerous recordings capture other elements of train-related history. Construction of railway lines ("John Henry," "Nine Pound Hammer," and "Drill, Ye Tarriers, Drill"), reports of train robbers ("Let Jesse Rob The Train" and "Railroad Bill"), and even stories denouncing the practice of interstate toll charges ("Rock Island Line") are presented as historical observations, although the songwriters and singers occasionally embellish the heroics of laborers, bandits, or engineers. Perhaps the most humorous popular recording to recount a two-rail social furor was The Kingston Trio's revival of the 1948 protest song "M.T.A." The melody for this song was borrowed from "The Wreck Of Old 97." Beyond America's northern border, the historical development of locomotive transportation has been skillfully depicted in Gordon Lightfoot's "Canadian Railroad Trilogy."

B. Social Mobility
1. Shift from Poverty to Wealth
2. Personal Sense of Social Change
3. Desire to Increase Personal Opportunity
4. Expansion of Freedom
5. Interest in New Relationships and Novel Socio-Economic Setting
6. Decline in Social Status
7. Escape from Domineering Parents or from a Nagging Wife

Hank Snow, Bukka White, and dozens of other singers wrote and performed songs which depicted trains as vehicles providing avenues of escape from rural poverty; from nagging parents, bossy wives or interfering mothers-in-law; from prisons of the mind, body, or spirit; and from the drudgery of a boring job. Although the majority of railroad wanderers reported in popular lyrics tend to be male, it is undeniable that women in search of new lives were also frequent users of steam or diesel-driven transportation. The movement toward greater personal freedom, a new social status, more income potential, and other positive gains are depicted in: "Me And Bobby McGee," "I'm Movin' On," "Folsom Prison Blues," "Midnight Train," "The Gambler," and "Train, Train."

C. Geographical Mobility
1. Movement from Rural Setting to Urban Environment
2. Shift from East Coast to West Coast
3. Migration from Southern States to Northern States
4. Return to Southern Home from Northern Area
5. Return from West Coast to the South or East Coast
6. Flight from Complex City Life to a More Simple Rural Existence
7. Departure from a Loved One

8. Return to a Loved One

It is difficult to differentiate geographical from social mobility. The links, real and potential, between vertical shifts in status and horizontal moves from one region to another are obvious. The railroad functioned as a highly visible, available, inexpensive, and frequently used source of migration by rural dwellers to the centers of urban life in New Orleans, Chicago, Detroit, New York, and elsewhere throughout the United States. Among the songs which illustrate geographical mobility are: "The Atlanta Special," "Trains And Boats And Planes," "Freight Train," "Cannon Ball," "City Of New Orleans," and "Long Twin Silver Line." But Americans also used the train to return home—either in triumph or as a worldly wise, but financially disabled prodigal son (or daughter). This theme shows up in: "Homeward Bound," "Midnight Train To Georgia," "I'm Coming Home," and "Hey Porter."

D. Employment Situations
1. Search for New Employment Opportunities and Challenges
2. Explanation of the Occupational Roles of Engineers, Brakemen, Porters, Ticket Agents, and Other Railroad Employees
3. Escape from Unproductive Job Situations or Feelings of Occupational Boredom
4. Migration from Place-to-Place, from Job-to-Job
5. Runaway from Home to Seek Economic Opportunity and Personal Independence

Numerous songs contain references to railroad employees; some describe their occupational functions in great detail. Most of the time, however, the porter, ticket agent, engineer, or other train workers serve as sympathetic ears for a troubled traveler or as a source of frustration for a would-be rider. As long as railroads were viewed as functional sources of geographical relocation and social mobility, the gatekeepers of locomotive life were central figures in the process of departure. Migrants were uneven in their assessment of railroad personnel. However, whether the commentator is an unconcerned observer of railroad life, a potential or enroute passenger, or a railroad employee, the descriptions of railroad roles are informative. These songs include: "Hey Porter," "The Wreck Of Old 97," "Brakeman's Blues," "Conductor Took My Baby To Tennessee," "Crazy Engineer," "Drill, Ye Tarriers, Drill," "Good Conductor," "Hey Mr. Porter," "Hold That Train Conductor," "I've Been Workin' On The Railroad," "Mr. Brakeman, Let Me Ride Your Train," "Spike Driver Blues," and "Ticket Agent Blues."

E. Heroes and Heroic Achievements
1. Models of Behavior for Hard Work and Responsible Social Demeanor
2. Examples of Extreme Heroism in Difficult (or Apparently Impossible) Situations

Heroic images often emerge from the commission of anti-social or illegal activities. In the realm of railroad songs, Buck Owens' recent tribute to a premier 19th century outlaw—"Let Jesse Rob The Train"—illustrates this situation. This kind of salute has also been accorded to "Railroad Bill." On the other hand, the two most noted heroic figures of lyrical railroad lore are the brave but doomed engineer "Casey Jones" and the steam drill-hating powerhouse track liner "John

Henry." Other examples of heroism or actions of heroic dimensions in lyrics are illustrated in "Ben Dewberry's Final Run" and "The Wreck of Old 97."

F. Metaphors for Life Situations
1. Journey from Life to Death or from Earth to Heaven
2. Transformation from Evil and Captivity to Good and Freedom
3. Achievement of Wealth and Success
4. Trains as Women, Nations, Or Living Legends
5. Railroads as Paths to Freedom for Prisoners, Lost Souls, Youngsters, Henpecked Husbands, Mistreated Women, and Other Wanderers
6. Symbols of National Prominence, Individual Courage, or Historic Development

The most prominent illustrations of train metaphors are found in songs which portray escapes to freedom from either physical or spiritual captivity. These songs include: "Midnight Special," "Folsom Prison Blues," "Friendship Train," "Love Train," and "Peace Train." Transformations from earthly existence to heavenly afterlife are illustrated in: "People Get Ready," "This Train," "Hobo On A Freight Train To Heaven," "If I Got My Ticket, Lord," and "Slow Train." The complex nature of human relations is metaphorically depicted in: "Train Of Thought" and "Heart Like Railroad Steel." American Studies scholar Brett Williams has noted with particular interest the tendency of musicians to portray both positive (motherhood, loving wife, beautiful bride, stable family center) and negative (flighty female, cheating tramp, prostitute, unfaithful wife, and nagging mother-in-law) female images in railroad song. Among the tunes illustrating this trend are "Empire State Express," "Brakeman's Blues," "Train Of Thought," and "Train Of Love."

G. Rhythm Patterns
1. Source of Musical Cadence in a Song
2. Element in Human Pulse and Rhythm of Life
3. Sound Which Beckons an Individual to Escape from Drudgery of Current Existence in Search of a New Life

Trains are sound machines. Numerous singers allude to engine bells, whistles, clanging wheels, and other distinctive audio elements. In 1980 South Carolina native Jim Eleazer complained to a railroad company about the switchyard cacophony outside of his motel room. He described the sound produced by a slow-moving switcher and its endlessly shifting boxcars as follows:

Why is it that your switch engine has to ging and dong and fizz and spit and clang and bang and buzz and hiss and bell and wail and pant and rant and howl and yowl and grate and grind and pull and bump and click and clank and chug and moan and hoot and toot and crash and grunt and gasp and moan and whistle and squeak and squak and blow and jar and jerk and rasp and jingle and twange and rumble and jangle and ring and clatter and yelp and howl and hum and snarl and puff and growl and thump and boom and clash and jolt and jostle and screech and snort and slam and throb and crink and quiver and rumble and roar and rattle and yell and smoke and smell and shriek like hell all night long? (p.6)

Other examples of railroad sounds converted to rhythm sources and audio stimuli for human reactions include: "Wabash Cannonball," "I Heard That Lonesome Whistle," "Folsom Prison Blues," "Train Whistle Blues," and "Lonesome Whistle Blues." The rhythm of a train's drivers helped to shape the guitar-playing study of Chuck Berry's "Johnny B. Goode," while the distant screech of a locomotive whistle tempts both men and women to wander and roam.

The seven train-related themes identified here are illustrated in the songs listed in Table 2-A. In order to establish historical perspective, the tunes are divided into three unequal time periods during the past sixty years. These periods are: 1920-1945, 1946-1960, and 1961-1980. Some songs originating in the twenties, thirties, and early forties, were successfully revived by artists during succeeding decades. Such cultural transmission suggests either the strength of folk images contained in a particular lyric or the commercial acuity of a modern singer (or a manager, arranger, or producer). In some cases, both elements functioned simultaneously to generate song revivals. The extended Table 2-A offers a selected list of train songs and recording artists divided chronologically into the three periods identified above.

Table 2-A

A Selected List of Commerical Recordings
Featuring Train-Related Titles and
Railroad-Oriented Themes and Illustrations,
1920-1980

Year of Release	Song Title (Record Number)	Recording Artist
	1920-1945	
1927	"Ben Dewberry's Final Run" (Bluebird 5482)	Jimmie Rodgers
1923	"Casey Jones" (Okeh 40038)	Fiddlin' John Carson and His Virginia Reelers
1941	"Chattanooga Choo Choo" (Bluebird 11230)	Glenn Miller
1923	"Chicago Bound Blues" (Paramount 12056)	Ida Cox
1942	"Fireball Mail" (Okeh 6685)	Roy Acuff
1938	"Freight Train Blues" (Paramount 12211)	Trixie Smith
1929	"Hobo Bill's Last Ride" (Victor 22421)	Jimmie Rodgers
1929	"John Henry" (Vocalion 1474)	Furry Lewis
1929	"Long Train Blues" (Brunswick 7205)	Robert Wilkins
1926	"Mail Train Blues" (Okeh 8345)	Sippie Wallace

1925	"New River Train" (Herwin 75506)	Vernon Dalhart
1945	"On The Atchison, Topeka, And The Santa Fe" (Decca 23436)	Judy Garland and The Merry Macs
1926	"Panama Limited Blues" (Vocalion 1009)	Ada Brown
1924	"Railroad Bill" (Okeh 45425)	Frank Hutchison
1925	"Railroad Blues" (Paramount 12262)	Trixie Smith
1938	"Railroadin' and Gamblin' " (Bluebird 8325)	Uncle Dave Macon
1931	"The Southern Cannon Ball" (Vicotr 23811)	Jimmie Rodgers
1928	"Spike Driver Blues" (Okeh 8692)	Mississippi John Hurt
1935	"Ticket Agent Blues" (Decca 7078)	Blind Willie McTell
1932	"Wabash Cannonball" (Victor 23731)	The Carter Family
1928	"Waitin' For A Train" (Victor V-40014)	Jimmie Rodgers
1945	"Waitin' For The Train To Come In" (Columbia 36867)	Harry James and Kitty Kallen
1927	"The Wreck Of The Virginian Train" (Champion 15467)	John Hutchens

1946-1960

1950	"Black Train Blues" (Vocalion 05588)	Bukka White
1958	"Click-Clack" (Swan 4001)	Dickey Doo and The Don'ts
1947	"The Devil's Train" (Columbia 37822)	Roy Acuff
1960	"Down By the Station" (Capitol 4312)	The Four Preps
1957	"Down Home Special" (Check 850)	Bo Diddley
1958	"Fast Freight Blues" (Josie 828)	Sonny Terry
1956	"Folsom Prison Blues" (Sun 232)	Johnny Cash
1957	"Freight Train" (Mercury 71102)	Rusty Draper
1952	"Harmonica Train" (Jackson 2302)	Sonny Terry and His Night Owls
1955	"Hey Porter" (Sun 221)	Johnny Cash
1950	"I'm Movin' On" (RCA Victor 21-0328)	Hank Snow
1958	"Johnny B. Goode" (Chess 1691)	Chuck Berry

1951	"Lonesome Train" (Modern 888)	Johnny Moore's Three Blazers
1956	"Throw Mama From The Train" (Mercury 70971)	Patti Page
1953	"Mean Old Train" (Gotham 515)	John Lee Hooker
1955	"Midnight Cannonball" (Atlantic 1069)	Joe Turner
1955	"Mystery Train" (Sun 223)	Elvis Presley
1956	"Rock Island Line" (London 1650)	Lonnie Donnegan
1956	"Smokestack Lightnin' " (Chess 1618)	Howlin' Wolf
1949	"Toot, Toot, Tootsie (Good-Bye)" (MGM 10548)	Art Mooney
1948	"Train Fare Home" (Aristocrat 1306)	Muddy Waters
1951	"The Wreck Of Old 97" (RCA Victor 20-4095)	Hank Snow

1961-1980

1978	"Chattanooga Choo Choo" (Butterfly 1205)	Tuxedo Junction
1972	"The City Of New Orleans" (Reprise 1103)	Arlo Guthrie
1965	"Engine Engine #9" (Smash 1983)	Roger Miller
1968	"Folsom Prison Blues" (Columbia 44513)	Johnny Cash
1969	"Friendship Train" (Soul 35068)	Gladys Knight and The Pips
1979	"The Gambler" (United Artists 1250)	Kenny Rogers
1966	"Homeward Bound" (Columbia 43511)	Simon and Garfunkel
1963	"I'm Movin' On" (Smash 1813)	Matt Lucas
1970	"King's Speical" (ABC 11280)	B. B. King
1966	"Last Train to Clarksville" (Colgems 1001)	The Monkees
1979	"Let Jess Rob The Train" (Warner Brothers 49118)	Buck Owens
1976	"Locomoive Breath" (Chrysalis 2110)	Jethro Tull
1973	"Long Train Running" (Warner Brothers 17698)	The Doobie Brothers
1980	"Long Twin Silver Line" (Capitol 4836)	Bob Seger
1973	"Love Train" (Philadelphia International 3524)	The O'Jays
1962	"Lover Please" (Mercury 71941)	Clyde McPhatter

1969	"Marrakesh Express" (Atlantic 2652)	Crosby, Stills, Nash and Young
1965	"Midnight Special" (Imperial 66087)	Johnny Rivers
1973	"Midnight Train To Georgia" (Buddah 383)	Gladys Knight and The Pips
1965	"Orange Blossom Special" (Columbia 43206)	Johnny Cash
1971	"Peace Train" (A & M 1291)	Cat Stevens
1965	"People Get Ready" (ABC-Paramont 10622)	The Impressions
1972	"Southbound Train" (Atlantic 2892)	Graham Nash and David Crosby
1978	"Took The Last Train" (Elektra-45500)	David Gates
1974	"Train Of Thought" (MCA-40245)	Cher
1979	"Train, Train" (Atco 7207)	Blackfoot
1966	"Trains And Boats And Planes" (Scepter 12153)	Dionne Warwick
1961	"Trouble In Mind" (Colpix 175)	Nina Simone

As students investigate and reflect upon the lyrics of numerous train songs, certain conclusions begin to emerge. Contrasting the images of lyrical trains from 1920-1945 with those in tunes of the 1961-1980 period demonstrates both technological and social change. While lyrics from the early period contain great emphasis on both personal experiences with railroad personnel and detailed knowledge of train-related activities, the words of the later era depict locomotives, engineers, and rail transportation as sources of nostalgia. Realism is superceded by myth and stereotype. Social and geographical mobility, both strongly linked to rail travel in the pre-war era, are more directly linked in contemporary songs to airplanes and automobiles. In fact, both train and bus travel are regarded in most modern lyrics as indicative of either declining social status or a sad return home in failure. Depictions of actual employment situations concerning railroads sink sharply in lyrics from 1920 until 1980, and the heroic endeavors of engineers and firemen fade from real life adventures into antique caricatures over the same period. These patterns are illustrated in Table 2-B.

Table 2-B

Shifting Patterns in Train-Related Themes
Featured in Commercial Recordings, 1920-1980

Three Historical Periods Under Study

Train-Related Themes	1920-1945	1946-1960	1961-1980
A. Historical Perspectives	Great emphasis on personal experiences and historical events	Reduced emphasis on reports of train wrecks and the activities of railroad characters	Historical railroad events and train personnel regarded as sources of nostalgia

B. Social Mobility	High degree of railroad travel	Moderate use of trains for cross-state or cross-country travel	Sharp decline in use of trains as personal travel vehicles
C. Geographical Mobility	Same as above	Same as above	Same as above
D. Employment Situations	Many illustrations of railroad-related jobs mentioned	Reduced number of train-related jobs mentioned	Greatly reduced number of railroad jobs mentioned
E. Heroes and Heroic Achievements	High number of heroes and heroic illustrations	Reduced number of heroic images and unique railroading achievements	Railroading heroes viewed as antique characters
F. Metaphors for Life Situations	Large number of metaphorical illustrations	Moderate number of metaphorical illustrations	High number of metaphorical illustrations
G. Rhythm Patterns	Acoustic guitar or harmonica sounds used to imitate trains	Continuing use of guitars and harmonicas to imitate trains	Electrified guitars, drums, and other instruments employed to imitate trains

Apart from noting the shifting cultural images of railroads over the past sixty years, what else can students be expected to gain from participating in this type of lyrical investigation? Several corollary ideas come to mind. First, the increase of private automobile travel on interstate highways and the growth of airline, bus, and other forms of relatively inexpensive commercial travel alternatives have escalated the decline of public contact with railroads over the past three decades. Second, despite the commercial decline in railroading, public interest in technological nostalgia continues to be reinforced by model trains and grandparents' stories of train-related incidents. Finally, traditional railroad songs like "Casey Jones" and "John Henry," along with new tunes which contain train-related images, will probably continue to be a staple of American popular music. Although automobile and trucking themes dominated the music of the 1970s, train songs continued to be played, sung, recorded, and sold. Habits of thought, manners of speech, visual and mental images, and a host of other historical resources and cultural activities will continue to keep locomotives, engineers, rail, and other train-related facts and ideas alive in the lyrics and rhythms of popular songs.

How can a social studies teacher translate sixty years of railroad songs into classroom activities? This task is simple. Students will gladly offer a variety of observations about trains—myths, stories, rumors, generalizations, hypotheses and predictions. Just as the young man at the beginning of this article surprised his instructor, so too other students are likely to bewilder, intrigue, and fascinate their teachers with their statements. If a class seems interested in specific railroad personalities such as Casey Jones, George Pullman, Cornelius Vanderbilt, and John Henry, then literary biographical studies supported by appropriate train songs will work well. However, if a class relates events of the railroad era to the rise of individual fortunes, then songs illustrating both social and geographical mobility can be fruitfully examined for historical meaning. In this same vein, employment opportunities provided by the railroad itself can be usefully illustrated in lyrics. Some students may suggest even more exotic ways of combining train song images with other social barometers. By examining other popular culture materials —comic books, postage stamps, and pictures in contemporary magazines (*Colliers, Saturday Evening Post, Life, Time,*and *Newsweek*)—a class can visually test the hypothesis that after 1945 railroads became more metaphorical and mythical in lyrics and popular publications.

Beyond the realm of student-originated ideas for employing railroad songs as learning resources, transportation technology and social change themes can be investigated as community oral history projects. The songs should not be played before students alone. If other personalities are introduced into the age-limited classroom setting, a new educational perspective on railroads can be generated. Retired railroad engineers, brakemen, and conductors can trace the actual evolution of the rail industry; local businessmen can relate the value of railroads to spawning urban growth, employment opportunities, and economic development; grandparents of students can enlarge upon the nostalgic descriptions of railroad heroes and train wrecks provided in popular songs; and finally, truckers, airline pilots, and auto dealers can speak with authority about the meaning of dynamic transportation technology—yesterday, today, and tomorrow. In all of these cases, though, the recorded resources are superb initial stimuli for deeper thinking, broader analysis, and increased understanding.

Works Cited

Books

B. A. Botkin and Alvin F. Harlow (eds.), *A Treasury Of Railroad Folklore: The Stories, Tall Tales, Traditions, Ballads* and *Songs Of The American Railroad Man*. New York: Bonanza Books, 1953.

James H. Beck (ed.) , *Rail Talk: A Lexicon Of Railroad Language*. Gretna, Nebraska: James Publications, 1978.

Norm Cohen, with music edited by David Cohen, *Long Steel Rail: The Railroad In American Folksong*. Urbana, Illinois: University of Illinois Press, 1981.

Katie Letcher Lyle, *Scalded To Death By The Steam: Authentic Stories Of Railroad Disasters And The Ballads That Were Written About Them*. Chapel Hill, North Carolina: Algonquin Books, 1983.

James Alan McPherson and Miller Williams (eds.), *Railroad: Trains And Train People In American Culture*. New York: Random House, 1976.

Brett Williams, *John Henry: A Bio-Bibliography*. Westport, Connecticut: Greenwood Press, 1983.

Articles

Ann Miller Carpenter, "The Railroad In American Folksong, 1865-1920," in *Diamond Bessie And The Shepherds*, edited by Wilson M. Hudson (Austin, Texas: Texas Folklore Society, 1972), pp. 103-119.

Gerald C. Carter, "The Real John Henry Stands Up," *Michigan Academician*, XVIII (Summer 1986), pp. 329-337.

B. Lee Cooper, "Oral History, Popular Music, And American Railroads, 1920-1980," *Social Studies*, LXXIV (November/December 1983), pp. 223-231.

———— "Shifting Images Of Transportation Technology And American Society In Railroad Songs, 1920-1980," *International Journal Of Instructional Media*, X (1982/83), pp. 131-146.

———— "Transportation Systems," in *A Resource Guide To Themes In contemporary American Song Lyrics, 1950-1985* (Westport, Connecticut: Greenwood Press, 1986), pp. 235-252.

Lee A. Dew, "The Locomotive Engineer: Folk Hero Of The 19th Century," *Studies In Popular Culture*, I (Winter 1977), pp. 45-55.

J.M. Eleaser, "Boys Are That Way," *Living In South Carolina*, XXII (September 1980), p. 6.

Archie Green, "John Henry Revisited," *JEMF Quarterly*, XIX (Spring 1983), pp. 12-31.

Ambrose Manning, "Railroad Work Songs," *Tennessee Folklore Society Bulletin*, XXIII (June 1966), pp. 41-47.

Arthur H. Miller, Jr., "Trains And Railroading," in *Handbook Of American Popular Culture—Volume Three*, edited by M. Thomas Inge (Westport, Connecticut: Greenwood Press, 1981), pp. 497-515.

Paul Oliver, "Railroad Bill," *Jazz And Blues*, I (May 1971), pp. 12-14.

Paul Oliver, "Rock Island Line," *Music Mirror*, IV (January 1957), pp. 6-8.

Jack Parks, "The Lure Of The Railroad," *Country Music*, II (February 1974), pp. 32-34, 68-71.

Eric Townley, "Jazz, Blues, And U.S. Railroads," *Storyville*, No 68 (December 1976/January 1977), pp. 55-58.

Unpublished Materials

B. Lee Cooper, "Sounds Like a Train A-Comin': Audio Imitations Of Locomotives In Contemporary Songs, 1955-1980" (mimeographed paper and audio tape presentation at the 12th National Convention on The Popular Culture Association in April 1982).

Patricia Lucille Berger Porcello, "The Railroad In American Literature: Poetry, Folk Song, And The Novel" (Ph.D.: University of Michigan, 1968).

John W. Roberts, "'Railroad Bill' And The American Outlaw Tradition" (mimeographed paper presented at the 11th National Convention of The Popular Culture Association in March 1981).

Chapter Three
Rebels and Outsiders

Beyond the boundaries of tradition and the barriers of law lies the territory of the outsider. The success of the contemporary rebel in capturing public attention in the United States defies rational explanation. Perhaps the activities of outsiders provide necessary psychological relief to a modern populace frustrated by bureaucratic complexity, social stratification, political insensitivity, and personal feelings of inadequacy, anxiety, and apathy. The following pages suggest that the lyricized behavior of outsiders in popular songs serve as emotional outlets enabling individuals to vicariously overcome the pressures of living in an alienating, repressive society.

Violent, anti-social behavior has frequently aroused public interest in America. Popular fascination with acts of physical coercion and torture is as old as the tales of vigilante tar-and-feather parties for British tax collectors. Likewise, the Boston Tea Party, erroneously described as an act of "civil disobedience" by the Rev. Martin Luther King, Jr., was clearly an incident of overt violence and law-breaking in colonial Massachusetts. Even the traditional American heroes of history and fiction—Wyatt Earp, Billy the Kid, Jesse James, Mike Fink, John Dillinger, and Paul Bunyan—were anti-social men.

In recent times television and motion picture directors have spawned a new breed of hostile heroes. Billy Jack, Bullit, "Dirty Harry" Calahan, and Rambo have joined forces with a seemingly endless variety of roughnecks portrayed by such virile actors as Paul Newman, Steve McQueen, Sylvester Stallone, and Chuck Norris to titillate and intrigue the viewing public. Even the rise in popularity of professional football in what had been America's "Baseball Paradise" can be related to the emergence of individually identifiable renegades of the Mean Joe Green/Dick Butkus mold. It is hardly surprising, then, that the field of popular music should also contribute to the veneration of violent men.

Songs depicting the exploits of exceptional men are as traditional as the balladeer's trade. Prominence of the "folk ethic" in contemporary music has served to highlight the growing popularity of biographical themes. Tales of extreme courage are common. In contrast to the ancient hymns of valor, however, most of the characters described in modern lyrics are unattractive, unheroic, and unimaginatively violent in their expressions of hostility toward society. The audio image of the exceptional man is that of an outsider—a confused, arrogant, unstable individual with an established reputation for generating a particular style of mayhem and for surviving through a combination of charisma, luck, and brute force.

Why do records expounding the exploits of these undisciplined beings enjoy such success? What does public interest in songs which depict aggressive, anti-social behavior indicate about the American psyche? These questions are extremely difficult—if not impossible—to answer. Psychologists do not agree on the root causes of violent behavior. If a consensus can be established among behavioral theorists on issues related to human aggression, it may be found in the following generalizations: (a) hostility is generated by situations which create pain, boredom, or fear in the mind of an aggressor; (b) the major catalyst for violent actions is personal frustration; and (c) a frequent source of frustration is social and economic deprivation. The tendency for aggression to result from relative rather than absolute deprivation is an almost universally acknowledged phenomenon.

The question which arises from this situation is obvious: "How can the aggressive energies spawned by social frustration be harmlessly discharged?" Direct action—which may include lashing out at the source of frustration, biting, kicking, hitting, swearing, or killing—is both illegal and socially unacceptable. A more positive alternative is to attempt to substitute some alternative physical activity—running, jumping, punching a bag—as a release for pent-up psychic energy. A final choice in attempting to deal with hostile feelings might be found in the catharitic option of engaging in some form of fantasy aggression—dreaming of slugging an enemy, viewing a violent motion picture, or listening to a tale of malevolent action on the radio. Of course, none of these activities will totally resolve the basic problem. The only permanent solution is to find ways of reducing violence by reducing the injustice that produces the frustrations that eventually erupt as violent aggression.

II

The general term "outsider" was selected for this investigation specifically because it does not conform to any standard sociological characterization or psychological definition. In terms of behavioral patterns, the central figures being examined in this chapter display uneven combinations of the following traits or tendencies:

—They are front-runners in socially unacceptable practices and illegal activities;
—They are notoriously individualistic and egotistically arrogant about their personal reputations;
—They rarely take time to "sing the blues," to rationalize their plight, or to philosophize about their actions;
—They are invariably action-oriented and habituated to the practices of physical violence;
—They may be black or white, rich or poor, young or old, married or single, or from rural or urban areas;
—They are invariably prone to blatant exhibitionism in a variety of activities including dress, dance, and sexual behavior;
—They are accustomed to dealing in drugs (using and pushing), in alcohol (consuming, brewing, and distributing), and in various forms of gambling as keys to their personal well-being and economic existence;
—They are hostile to all forms of authority—from dictatorial high school principals to nagging wives—but reserve a special loathing for police officers;

—They reject all conventional forms of social courtesy, legal sanction, and intimate relationships.

These general characteristics used to identify the outsider must be supplemented with more specific information. Several distinctive lyrical cues can alert the listening audience that the individual being portrayed in a popular song is an outsider—a rugged beast prone to anti-social activities. Sometimes the title of the song reveals the character of the man in question. For instance, one would hardly expect songs entitled "Big Bad John," "Big Boy Pete," or "Bad, Bad Leroy Brown" to be performed by The Harry Simeone Chorale. But this system of judgement is not foolproof, since songs such as "A Boy Named Sue" or "Sunshine" might mislead a novice who is attempting to spot examples of lyric violence. Rather than relying strictly upon song title descriptions as keys to identifying aggressive behavior, a specific list of "tough guy indicators" was developed to delimit physical, behavioral, and attitudinal signs of rebellion against established social norms and legal sanctions. Although lyrical interpretation does constitute the backbone of this study, no attempt has been made to construct a rigid content analysis frame for the songs which were being investigated. The eleven qualities of personality selected to define an outsider are:

A. Physical Supremacy
—good/bad facial features
—strength
—size or stature
—peculiar physical traits (scars, amputated limbs, etc.)

B. Sexual Prowess
—potency and productivity
—endurance during intercourse
—experience with different females
—reputation among companions

C. Personal Courage
—fearlessness
—contentiousness
—arrogance among peers or in the face of enemies

D. Personal Vices
—murder
—sexual promiscuity or rape
—alcoholism
—gambling (cards, pool, or dice)
—drug abuse
—profane language

E. Personal Weapons
—guns
—knives or razors
—fists, feet, teeth

F. Companions
—motorcycle gang
—gambling buddies
—outlaw band
—none (loner)

G. Source of Reputation
—public media
—companions
—victims or enemies
—police officers

H. Cars, Clothing, and
—clothing

Other Personal Effects	—accessories (rings, jewelry)
	—automobiles
	—home or apartment furnishings
I. Nicknames	—among friends
	—among enemies
	—to self
J. Defiance of Authority	—unpatterned life style
and Assertion of	—hostility to law
Personal Independence	—failure to take orders
K. Assertion of Frustration	—attacks on social stratification
with the Existing Social	—hatred of police
or Political System	—cynicism toward politicians

The preceding characteristics provide a generalized skeleton to which the flesh of lyrical description can be added. For example, the area of physical supremacy is graphically depicted by lyrical phrases such as "stronger than a country horse" (Jim Croce), "bulldog mouth" (Carole King), "scar on his cheek and his evil eye" (Johnny Cash), and "muscle and blood and skin and bone" (Ernie Ford). The area of weapons is amply described in songs by references to guns ("Stagger Lee," "I Found the Law," "Smackwater Jack," and "Outlaw Man"), knives ("A Boy Named Sue," "Smokey Joe's Cafe," and "Mack The Knife"), and razors ("Bad, Bad Leroy Brown" and "High Heel Sneakers"). Retaining the same sequence of indicators developed above, specific records listed in Table 3-A illustrate the scope of outsider imagery between 1956-1976.

Table 3-A

Commercial Recordings Which Feature Various Thematic
Indicators Of Outsider Behavior In Lyrics,
1956-1976

A. *Physical Supremacy*

"A Boy Named Sue"
(Columbia 44944)
by Johnny Cash (1969)
"You Don't Mess Around With Jim"
(ABC 11328)
by Jim Croce (1972)
"Big Bad John"
(Columbia 42175)
by Jimmy Dean (1961)
"Sixteen Tons"
(Capitol 3262)
by Tennessee Ernie Ford (1956)
"Amos Moses"
(RCA 9904)
by Jerry Reed (1970)
"Ramblin' Gamblin' Man"
(Capitol 2297)
by The Bob Seger System (1968)

B. *Sexual Prowess*

"Medicine Man"
(Event 3302)
by The Buchanan Brothers (1969)
"Sixty Minute Man"
(Fame 250)
by Clarance Carter (1973)
"Light My Fire"
(RCA 9950)
by Jose Feliciano (1968)
"Superman"
(Warner Bothers 7403)
by The Ides of March (1970)
"Steamroller Blues"
(RCA 74-0910)
by Elvis Presley (1973)
"Hard To Handle"
(Atco 6592)
by Otis Redding (1968)

C. *Personal Courage*

"Trouble Man"
(Talma 54228)
by Marvin Gaye (1972)
"Saturday Night's Alright For Fighting"
(MCA 40105)
by Elton John (1973)
"Big Boy Pete"
(Arvee 595)
by The Olympics (1960)
"A Man And A Half"
(Atlantic 2575)
by Wilson Pickett (1968)
"Big Iron"
(Columbia 41589)
by Marty Robbins (1960)
"Jumpin' Jack Flash"
(London 908)
by The Rolling Stones (1968)

E. *Personal Weapons*

"Mack The Knife"
(Atco 6147)
by Bobby Darin (1959)
"Outlaw Man"
(Asylum 11025)
by The Eagles (1973)
"Smackwater Jack"
(Ode 66019)
by Carole King (1971)
"High Heel Sneakers"
(Smash 1930)
by Jerry Lee Lewis (1964)
"Stagger Lee"
(ABC-Paramount 9972)
by Lloyd Price (1958)
"Big Iron"
(Columbia 41589)
by Marty Robbins

G. *Source of Reputation*

"Goldfinger"
(United Artists 790)
by Shirley Bassey (1965)
"The Ballad of Bonnie And Clyde"
(Epic 10283)
by Georgie Fame (1968)
"Ringo"
(RCA 8444)
by Lorne Green (1964)
"Theme From Shaft"

(Enterprise 9083)

D. *Personal Vices*

"Folsom Prison Blues"
(Columbia 44513)
by Johnny Cash (1968)
"Desperado"
(Warner Brothers 7529)
by Alice Cooper (1971)
"Superfly"
(Curtom 1978)
by Curtis Mayfield (1972)
"The Ballad Of Thunder Road"
(Capitol 3986)
by Robert Mitchum (1958)
"(I Washed My Hands In) Muddy Water"
(Imperial 66175)
by Johnny Rivers (1966)
"Papa Was A Rollin' Stone"
(Gordy 712)
by The Temptations (1972)

F. *Companions*

"I Get Around"
Capitol 5174)
by The Beach Boys (1964)
"The 'In' Crowd"
(Charger 105)
by Dobie Gray (1965)
"Saturday Night's Alright For Fighting"
(MCA 40105)
by Elton John (1973)
"Stag-O-Lee"
(Atlantic 2448)
by Wilson Pickett (1967)
"Street Fighting Man"
(London 909)
by The Rolling Stones (1968)
"Leader Of The Pack"
(Red Bird 014)
by The Shangri-Las

H. *Cars, Clothing, and Other Personal Effects*

"Bad, Bad, Leroy Brown"
(ABC 11359)
by Jim Croce (1973)
"Dead Man's Curve"
(Liberty 55672)
by Jan and Dean (1964)
"The Ballad Of Thunder Road"
(Capitol 3986)
by Robert Mitchum (1958)
"Big Boy Pete"
(Arvee 595)

by Isaac Hayes (1971)
"(The Man Who Shot) Liberty Valance"
(Musicor 1020)
by Gene Pitney (1962)
"Soul Man"
(Stax 231)
by Sam and Dave (1967)

by The Olympics (1960)
"Stagger Lee"
(ABC 11307)
by Tommy Roe (1971)
"Hi-Heel Sneakers"
(Checker 1067)
by Tommy Tucker (1964)

I. *Nicknames*

J. *Defiance of Authority and Assertion*
of Personal Independence

"Super Bad"
(King 6329)
by James Brown (1970)
"Trouble Man"
(Talma 54228)
by Marvin Gaye (1972)
"Secret Agent Man"
(Imperial 66159)
by Johnny Rivers (1966)
"Seventh Son"
(Imperial 66112)
by Johnny Rivers(1965)
"Agent Double-O-Soul"
(Ric-Tic 103)
by Edwin Starr (1965)
"Sixty Minute Man"
(Buddah 321)
by The Trammps (1972)

"Ramblin' Man"
(Capricorn 0027)
by The Allman Brothers Band (1973)
"Midnight Rider"
(A & M 1370)
by Joe Cocker (1972)
"George Jackson"
(Columbia 45516)
by Bob Dylan (1971)
"Sunshine"
(Capricorn 8021)
by Jonathan Edwards (1971)
"A Natural Man"
(MGM 14262)
by Lou Rawls (1971)
"Born To Be Wild"
(Dunhill 4138)
by Steppenwolf (1968)

K. *Assertion of Frustration with the*
Existing Social or Political System

"Eighteen"
(Warner Brothers 1971)
by Alice Cooper (1971)
"Ninety-Nine And A Half (Won't Do)"
(Atlantic 2334)
by Wilson Pickett (1966)
"Indian Reservation (The Lament Of The
    Cherokee Reservation Indian)"
(Columbia 45332)
by The Raiders (1971)

"Dead End Street"
(Capitol 5869)
by Lou Rawls (1967)
"Big Boss Man"
(Vee Jay 380)
by Jimmy Reed(1961)
"Get Off My Cloud"
(London 9792)
by The Rolling Stones (1965)

It is also appropriate to note that several singers have achieved recording fame and fortune by eulogizing the activities of tough, mean bastards. Mick Jagger and The Rolling Stones, both before and since the terror and violence at Altamont, have fostered the rebellious images of "Jumpin' Jack Flash" and "The Street Fightin' Man." Alice Cooper's theatrical perversions are punctuated by songs of violent men, particularly "Killer" and "Desperado." And a particularly skillful cultivator of the outsider-image was the late Jim Croce. His villains of the peace paraded laughingly across a variety of discs—and found their way regularly to the top of the *Billboard* charts. In addition to his 45 r.p.m. hits featuring Big Jim Walker ("You Don't Mess Around With Jim") and "Bad, Bad Leroy Brown," Croce added to his menagerie of malefactors through album descriptions of an ex-marine bouncer named Gil ("Top Hat Bar and Grille") and a free-wheeling stock card driver called "Rapid Boy." Other popular singers who have frequently projected the image of rebellion in their lyrics include Johnny Rivers ("Secret Agent Man," "Seventh Son," and "(I Washed My Hands In) Muddy Water," Wilson Pickett ("A Man And A Half," "Born To Be Wild," and "I'm A Midnight Mover"), and Jerry Reed ("Amos Moses").

III

The audience which appreciates the simplistic, individualistic vigilanteeism in the motion pictures "Death Wish," "Lipstick," and "Taxi Driver" is also impressed with the easy solutions to complex problems offered by Marvin Gaye's "Trouble Man" and Isaac Hayes' "Shaft." The intellectual concepts and philosophical questions explored lyrically by The Beatles, Donovan, and Simon and Garfunkel are often too intricately structured to attract the general listening public. The audience that understands and internalizes the confrontations between a "Street Fightin' Man" and the law, or between Leroy Brown and Doris' jealous husband is not as likely to comprehend the subtle problems of a faceless/nameless "Nowhere Man" or an alienated Father MacKenzie, the seemingly senseless suicides of a "Richard Cory" or "A Most Peculiar Man," or an individual who declares "I Am A Rock." In the end, it is the power of personal presence that compels public attention. Action overrides contemplation; books and poetry give way to the fury of fists; suicide is rejected in favor of murder; the quest for being ceases to be mental and becomes the overt search for self through the humiliation or destruction of others. Through all of this dynamic action, the outsider emerges as an ultimately free man. He is uninhibited by law, custom, circumstance, or fear. He faces a society which demands his allegiance and compels his obedience; but he rises above the dehumanizing social order to shun all forms of authority and to denounce the humility of passive citizenship. Unfortunately, he also rejects all of the tender elements of Rousseau's uncivilized state of nature and turns his turf into a Hobbesian nightmare—sans Leviathan, sans justice. Self writ large dominates the scene. The outsider is at the center of the stage in a tragic drama that has only one logical or possible conclusion— his death.

In the context of popular music, as in other forms of mass media, the outlaw emerges as the purest statement of the audience's alter ego. Just as Aristotle noted that bad citizens were often good men trapped in an unjust society, so the universal dilemma of social entrapment is depicted in bold style through the actions of Stagger Lee, John Shaft, Willie McCoy, and The Trouble Man. Of course, few of the outsiders display Aristotlean nobility. In fact, while some of the renegades like "Smackwater Jack" are simply expressing nonrational responses to their surroundings, others are motivated by negative social objectives. In these latter cases, expressions of sexual dominance, attempts to amass material goods, or the wild pursuit of thrill-seeking system which they cannot penetrate by legal means. But all of the outsiders—from Aristotle's "just" rebels to the most amoral (if not immoral) outlaws—exist as active, self-motivated, functioning beings. Therein lies their public appeal.

The contemporary listening audience is saddled with a technologically-assisted, passive existence. Despite the momentary catharisis provided by football games, detective flicks, or frantic dancing, the listener is willingly swept up in the strength of an audio rebel's inner-directed dynamism. More than that, the audience revels in his quest for being, even when reality overtakes the badman, either in the form of legal vengeance (the Hangman's rope or a policeman's bullet) or in the currency of another form of anti-societal authority (gang vengeance, racing death, or murder).

The preceding explanation is neither startling nor particularly unique. What is significant, though, is the vast audio reservoir of recorded violence which is available to the public as a vicarious substitute for the real thing. Several scholars have speculated that the use of drugs and the loud playing of rock music by young people creates a kind of isolated shell of security from a larger world which alienates, represses, and is essentially unresponsive to individual needs and desires. Similarly, the rise of the outsider in contemporary music signals the general public's search for nonpassive images. A listener counteracts his own lack of personal authority by mentally associating with a violent character who responds to *every* frustrating situation openly and with force. From the depths of personal isolation, frustration, and failure, the Walter Mitty-fied audience can revel in the virility and power of an audio actor.

What specific images of contemporary American society cross the minds of listeners? The cruel world of the outsider is not totally fictional. It is based upon an Orwellian extension of reality. Listeners crystallize and translate the disc-world into their terms. They accept images of lovers in sexual competition—without joy, sensitivity, privacy, intimateness, or warmth; they find dancers challenging each other to be more creative, more skillful, more sensual; they note that law enforcement officers are isolated souls, driven by unspoken hatreds or unarticulated envy for the freedom of the outsider; they accept the violent man as a "hero"—an independent being who is frustrated by social complexity, technological change, universal materialism, and personal anxiety or betrayal. Human desires for honesty, naturalness, integrity, warmth, and other tender goals which make civilized life worth living are rarely considered or discussed. Typically, the outsider exhibits the marks of his environmental trap like the stripes of a jailed criminal. He may be able to rise above the pit of apathy long enough to "make his name known," but his notoriety is almost always short-lived. His independence and self-motivation are inevitably compromised by his emotional responses and his failure to comprehend the complexity of his plight. Like Butch Cassidy and The Sundance Kid, he chooses freedom in the end; but that choice of freedom leads to death, not life.

IV

If popular music is serving a therapeutic function with respect to easing the social tensions in American life, then why don't public officials praise this aspect of the audio media? The reason is obvious. It would be politically blasphemous to declare that contemporary U.S. society needs the charades of outsiders to pacify the public. To openly admit that frustration, isolation, and immobilization have been the result of technological advancement and social change in the United States would be sacrilegious in a progress-oriented technocratic society. The pariah label was publicly thrust upon those singers in the 1960s who chose to directly attack representatives of the military-industrial complex for warmongering in Vietnam. Bob Dylan, Stephen Stills, Joan Baez, and the other so-called "protest singers" who articulately challenged "the system" were openly denounced. It should be noted, however, that the feelings of personal frustration depicted in this essay are rarely grounded in unresolved international problems. The world scene with respect to civil rights, to war and peace, to pollution, and to other public concerns is inevitably structured as a secondary concern within each person's mind. The real "silent majority" consists of listeners and observers who rarely reflect upon concerns that are related to any issue beyond their personal security and welfare. Contemporary society has taught these people that the search for authentic heroes is universally frustrating, while the philosophical search for self is unrewarding. During the mid-1950s the balladeer of the outsider stepped into this vacuum. As stated earlier, the tale of a man bigger than life is not new. However, the mass availability of popular song praising outsiders has created a new barometer for measuring the magnitude of public alienation. The outsider has emerged as a mythical force to challenge that which listeners feel helpless to defeat—organized society, "the system."

Works Cited

Books

Ray B. Browne and Marshall W. Fishwick (comps), *The Hero In Transition.* Bowling Green, Ohio: Bowling Green State University Popular Press, 1983.

George Estey and Doris Hunter (eds.), *Violence: A Reader In The Ethics Of Action.* Waltham, Massachusetts: Xerox College Publishing, 1971.

William H. Friet and Price M. Cobbs, *Black Rage.* New York: Bantam Books, 1968.

Nelson George, *The Death Of Rhythm And Blues.* New York: Pantheon Books, 1988.

Hugh Davis Graham and Ted Robert Gurr (comps.), *Violence In America: Historical and Comparative Perspectives.* New York: Bantam Books, 1970.

Richard Hofstadter and Michael Wallace (eds.), *American Violence: A Documentary History.* New York: Vintage Books, 1970.

Jim Hougan, *Decadence: Radical Nostalgia, Narcissism, and Decline In The Seventies.* New York: William Morrow and Company, 1975.

James F. Kirkham, Sheldon G. Levy, and William J. Crotty, *Assassination And Political Violence.* New York: Bantam Books, 1970.

Robert M. Linder, *Rebel Without A Cause.* New York: Grune and Stratton, 1944.

Dave Marsh, with Lee Ballinger, Sandra Choron, Wendy Smith, and Daniel Wolff, *The First Rock And Roll Confidential Report: Inside The Real World Of Rock And Roll.* New York: Pantheon Books, 1985.

Dave Marsh, *Fortunate Son.* New York: Random House, 1985.

Joe Morella and Edward Z. Epstein, *Rebels: The Rebel Hero In Films.* Secaucus, New Jersey: The Citadel Press, 1971.

Robert Jay Nash, *Bloodletters And Badmen: A Narrative Encyclopedia Of American Criminals From The Pilgrims To The Present.* New York: M. Evan and Company, Inc., 1973.

David Pichaske, *A Generation In Motion: Popular Music And Culture In The Sixties.* New York: Schirmer Books, 1979.

Robert G. Pielke, *You Say You Want A Revolution: Rock Music In American Culture*. Chicago: Nelson-Hall, Inc., 1986.

Jerome L Rodnitzky, *Minstrels Of The Dawn: The Folk-Protest Singer As A Cultural Hero*. Chicago: Nelson-Hall, Inc., 1976.

Roger B. Rollin (comp.), *Hero/Anti-Hero*. New York: McGraw-Hill Book Company, Inc., 1973.

Arthur M. Schlesinger, Jr., *Violence: American In The Sixties*. New York: New American Library, 1968.

David P. Szatmary, *Rockin' In Time: A Social History Of Rock And Roll*. Englewood Cliffs, New Jersey: Prentice-Hall, Inc., 1987.

Articles

Werner G. Albert, "Dimensionality Of Perceived Violence In Rock Music: Musical Intensity And Lyrical Violence Content," *Popular Music And Society*, VI (1978) pp. 27-38.

Roy Blount, Jr., "Whiskey And Blood," *Journal Of Country Music*, VIII (August 1980), pp. 2, 15-28.

Richard C. Carpenter, "007 And The Myth Of The Hero," *Journal Of Popular Culture*, I (Fall 1967), pp. 79-89.

Norm Cohen, "Heroes And Badmen," in *Long Steel Rail: The Railroad In American Folksong* (Urbana, Illinois: University of Illinois Press, 1981), pp. 58-168.

Henry Steele Commager, "The Roots Of Lawlessness," *Saturday Review*, LIV (February 13, 1971), pp. 17-19 ff.

B. Lee Cooper, "The Image Of The Black Man: Contemporary Lyrics As Oral History," *The Journal Of The Interdenominational Theological Center*, V (Spring 1978), pp. 105-122.

_____ "The Image Of The Outsider In Contemporary Lyrics," *Journal Of Popular Culture*, XII (Summer 1978), pp. 168-178.

_____ "Political Protest And Social Criticism" and "Poverty And Unemployment," in *A Resource Guide To Themes In Contemporary American Song Lyrics, 1950-1985* (Westport, Connecticut: Greenwood Press, 1986), pp. 183-199 and 201-212.

_____ "Women's Studies And Popular Music: Using Audio Resources in Social Studies Instruction," *The History And Social Science Teacher*, XIV (Fall 1978), pp. 29-40.

Harris Friedburg, "Bob Dylan: Psycho-Historian Of A Generation," *The Chronical Of Higher Education*, VIII (January 28, 1974), pp. 15-16.

Peter Goldman, with Peter McAlevey, Shawn Doherty, John McCormick, and Frank Maier, "Rocky And Rambo," *Newsweek*, CVI (December 23, 1985), pp. 58-62.

Renatus Hartogs, "Who Will Act Violently: The Predictive Criteria," in *Violence: Causes And Solutions*, edited by Renatus and Eric Artzt (New York: Dell Publishing Company, 1970), pp. 332-337.

Columbus B. Hopper and Johnny "Big John" Moore, "Hell On Wheels: The Outlaw Motorcycle Gangs," *Journal Of American Culture*, VI (Summer 1983), pp. 58-64.

James A. Inciardi and Juliet L. Dee, "From The Keystone Cops To *Miami Vice*: Images Of Policing In American Popular Culture," *Journal Of Popular Culture*, XXI (Fall 1987), pp. 84-102.

Jim Leary, " 'Pretty Boy Floyd': An Aberrant Outlaw Ballad," *Popular Music And Society*, III (1974), pp. 215-226.

Gene Lees, "Rock: Symptom Of Today's Sociological Disturbances," *High Fidelity*, XVII (November 1967), pp. 57-61.

Ruth Ann Musick, "Murders And Cut-Throats In Song," *Tennessee Folklore Society Bulletin*, XIX (June 1953), pp. 31-35.

Ray Schultz, "I'll Stick My Knife Right Down Your Throat...: Rock And Violence— The Wave Of The '70s And The Legacy Of The '50s," *Rock*, XI (December 14,1970), pp. 16-17, 28-29.

Robert Warshow, "The Gangster As Tragic Hero," in *Things In The Driver's Seat: Reading In Popular Culture*, edited by Harry Russell Huebel (Chicago: Rand McNally and Company, 1972), pp. 97-102.

Unpublished Materials

Richard D. Ralston, "Bad Dude Or Common Criminal? The Interrelationship Of Contemporary And Folk Values In The Ballad Of Stagolee" (mimeographed paper presented at the 14th National Convention of The Popular Culture Association in March 1984).

John Oliver West, "To Die Like A Man: The 'Good' Outlaw Tradition In The American Southwest" (Ph.D.: University of Texas, 1964).

Chapter Four
Education (II)

(with Ronald E. Butchart)

Education has received more than its share of public criticism during the past three decades. From the conservative William Bennett to the radical Ivan Illich, spokesmen have assailed schooling and teachers from every angle. Politicians want schools to accomplish a variety of constructive societal goals. These include promoting unswerving patriotism, eliminating unemployment, curbing job dissatisfaction, ending social inequality, channeling young people into understaffed sectors of the job market, lessening drug and tobacco use, and stamping out teenage sexual promiscuity. Sociological theorists and educational researchers often fuel the fires of debate by suggesting additional social tasks, by exposing unhealthy relationships between the school and other social organizations, and by discovering that, after having been expected to do *everything*, schools do nothing particularly well. Parents also demonstrate their dissatisfaction through negative votes on school tax referenda or through the ubiquitous public opinion polls.

Despite the cacophony of criticisms from many pressure groups, observations from one key group—students, the subjects of the whole educational enterprise—continue to be ignored. But youth has not remained mute. Scholars simply have not applied their critical skills to a wide enough variety of resources on this issue. Popular music, a principle artifact of youth culture, gives a voice to a broad range of concerns, values, and priorities of young people. A careful analysis of scores of popular songs shows that lyrics consistently depict formal schooling as dehumanizing, irrelevant, alienating, laughable, isolating, and totally unworthy of any link with the Socratic tradition. To assess at least one measure of young people's perceptions of education, the authors surveyed over two hundred hit recordings that deal with some facet of public schools. We discovered strikingly clear images, few of which shift in emphasis over time.

Some would argue that popular music does not actually reflect subject perceptions per se. Most hit tunes, after all, are not written by students, and pop recordings are simply the products of market devices. But lyricists and singers are the troubadours of contemporary young people. To claim that they do not represent student perceptions because they are no longer students themselves is equivalent to arguing that the balladeers of medieval Europe did not reflect the culture of courtly society because they were not part of the aristocracy. Troubadours in any age are honored precisely because their musical messages resound with the values and imagination of their audience. Indeed, modern troubadours are better mirrors of the culture in whose name they sing than their feudal predecessors. Unlike the minstrels of old, modern rock musicians, although no longer students when they write or perform their music, have been in the classroom. Their medieval counterparts had never been aristocrats.

Those who contend that rock lyrics demonstrate the manipulative power of commodity culture rather than reflect student perceptions misperceive the power and control exercised by the rock music industry. Granted, popular music is not generated spontaneously like earlier forms of folk music. Granted, too, market mechanisms seek to manipulate taste, style, and even ideology. Popular songs are representative of the commodity forms of culture which are prevalent under advanced capitalism. But the logic of this contention does not inevitably lead to a conclusion that an attempt to analyze youth culture through its music is doomed to futility. Unlike many other monopoly sectors of the economy, the music industry remains surprisingly anarchic. Even strong efforts by the Federal Communications Commission to regulate lyrics have failed to impose boundaries on the diversified content of rock music. Further, if popular music reflected more closely the economic imperatives of the culture industry rather than the values of its consumers, a more moderate range of ideas and perceptions on such public topics as schooling would surface. Similarly, if youth culture embraced only an "accepted" range of images on a topic such as education, surely a similar range would appear in popular music. No middle-of-the-road situation exists here. In popular music, polarized myth systems often battle in lyrical arenas, but the messages on schooling lack diversity.

Popular music has not always portrayed schooling in a negative way. Education appeared less frequently as a theme in the pre-rock era, but when it did, lyrics were usually nostalgic as in Will D. Cobb's "School Days" or Al Wilson's "In The Little Red School House." In addition, earlier education themes were generally oriented toward college students, even though only a small proportion of young people attended college before the 1950s. From the 1906 recording of P.E. Browne's "College Life," through "Collegiate," "The Varsity Drag," "Betty Co-Ed," "The Sweetheart of Sigma Chi," to "The Whiffenpoof Song" in 1936, early popular music dealing with education emphasized the joys of campus social life. Ironically, in an age when university attendance has become the norm, very few rock era songs deal with college life. Most focus exclusively on public school experiences, particularly on secondary schooling. And with very few exceptions—The Arbors' "Graduation Day" and perhaps The Beach Boys' "Be True To Your School"—the sentiments communicated are anything but nostalgic.

One can best demonstrate the major thrust of rock music's view of schooling by focusing on three distinct issues: (1) images of teachers; (2) images of the formal content and process of schooling; and (3) images of the school as both a community and the center of youth activity.

In the world of rock music, just as in every real school, the good teacher, the memorable teacher, does exist. "Mr. Lee" and "Abigail Beecher" were the archetypes two decades age; "Welcome Back" and "To Sir With Love" also celebrate those outstanding teachers who took youngsters from crayons to perfume. But the last two songs were written under commission as theme songs for a television series and a motion picture, respectively; one could argue that they represent the least spontaneous examples of the genre. "Welcome Back," the only song in this study that truly celebrates conscientious teaching, probably owes much of its popularity to the success of the situation comedy that spawned it.

If one listens closely to those four tunes, however, one observes that these and other teachers are memorable not so much for their pedagogical prowess as for their imagined erotic appeal. During the 1950s Johnny Mathis and others crooned Al Stillman's "Teacher, Teacher," praying "Make me the teacher's pet" (1958), while The DeCastro Sisters asked, "Should the teacher stand so near, my love?" in "Teach Me Tonight" (1954). In 1980, Rockpile repeated the title "Teacher, Teacher" for a new wave hit that pleaded, "Teacher, teacher, teach me love/I can't learn fast enough...." Often in such songs the teacher is the sex object. Positive portrayals of teachers *as teachers* are rare. The few notable teachers portrayed in music stand in stark contrast to the implied mediocrity of the nameless, frowning educators depicted in so many negative rock lyrics. In "School Day" (1957) Chuck Berry complained of one teacher, "Gee, she don't know how mean she looks," More recent singers have put the matter more bluntly:

> I used to get mad in my school,
> The teachers who taught me weren't cool
> You're puttin' me down, turnin' me 'round,
> Filling me up with your rules.
>   ("Getting Better"—1967)

To underline that sentiment, The Beatles noted in their reprise that things *were* getting better—for they "can't get no worse." Alice Cooper's searing sarcasm was aimed directly at educators when he announced, "Well, we can' salute ya/ Can't find a flag/If that don't suit ya/That's a drag" ("School's Out"—1972). Pink Floyd put the matter even more succinctly: "Teachers, leave them kids alone!" The songwriter may have intended a universal denunciation of public school teachers when he wrote, "All in all, you're just another brick in the wall" (1979). Teachers, like formal education generally, simply function to wall in young people, to cut them off from reality.

What of the content and process of formal education? In earlier generations, school days may have been "dear old golden rule days." But today's rock lyrics generally reject formal education. Chuck Berry was sure that his teacher was teaching the golden rule; consequently, he would "work my fingers right down to the bone" ("School Day"—1957). Supertramp was more skeptical two decades later when they reminded students, "You know you've got to learn the golden rule" ("School"—1974). But recent attacks on the miserable content of schooling are even more direct:

> When I think back on all the crap I learned in high school,
> It's a wonder I can think at all.
>   ("Kodachrome"—1973)

> We don't need no education,
> We don't need no thought control.
> No dark sarcasm in the classroom—

> Teachers, leave them kids alone!
> ("Another Brick In The Wall"—1979)

> So you think your schooling is a phoney,
> I guess it's hard not to agree.
> You say it all depends on the money,
> And who is in your family tree.
> Right, right, you're bloody well right...
> ("Bloody Well Right"—1974)

Objections to the content of schooling are not limited to perceptions of irrelevance. Increasingly, rock lyrics protest the use of schooling to surreptitiously socialize young people to adult norms—norms that limit spontaneity and freedom. That is the dark message in Paul Simon's "My Little Town" (1975), the boisterous demand in "Smokin' In The Boys' Room" (1974) ("Teacher, don't you fill me up with your rules..."), and the focus of Supertramp's "School" (1974):

> They tell you not to hang around and know what life's about
> And grow up just like them—won't let you work it out
> And you're full of doubt.

> Don't do this and don't do that—
> What are they trying to do?
> Make a good boy of you.
> Do they know where it's at?

Although rock lyrics increasingly savage current educational practices, on occasion glimpses of alternative modes of educating can be found in the same music. They include expectations of greater relevance, as in Paul Simon's "Kodachrome," or of more critical self-assertion, as Supertramp suggests in "School." Graham Nash evoked a powerful image of learning in a supportive, integrative society in which teaching would be reciprocal between the generations. He portrayed a learning setting in which youths and elders would nurture one another with their dreams and ideals, and in which seeking truth would become the ontological vocation of all. The words of the first chorus, "Teach your children well," are answered by the second, "Teach your parents well..." ("Teach Your Children"—1970).

"The Logical Song" (1979) contains both the condemnation of traditional schooling and a prophetic vision of an alternative learning system. It reflects the continuing attraction of the Rousseauian ideal of a naturalistic education in which direct experience with nature reveals a world that is "wonderful, a miracle, ...beautiful, magical." Formal schooling strips away that sense of wonder, teaching instead "how to sensible, logical, responsible, practical." In place of a world of birds and trees, joy and playfulness, public school offers a dismal existence where one must be "dependable, clinical, intellectual, cynical." The point of the educational enterprise is to render people safe, to make them "acceptable, respectable, presentable. A vegetable!" As if to underline the descent from the Socratic dictum, "Know thyself," the Supertramp asks plaintively,

> Won't you please, please tell me what we've learned?
> I know it sounds absurd:
> Please tell me who I am.

Within popular music, the school is much more than teachers and classroom learning. It also serves as a social center for the youth culture. Numerous songs examine the social relations of school-based youth by focusing on the students themselves—the teacher's pet ("Bird Dog"), the class clown ("Charlie Brown"), the homocidal student ("Maxwell's Silver Hammer"), and the misfit ("Leader Of The Pack" and "He's a Rebel"). Janis Ian poignantly explores the darker side of social relations within secondary schools in both "At Seventeen" and "Society's Child."

Significantly, while popular music generally condemns teachers and formal education, the school as a youth-centered community is usually viewed more positively. Virtually no lyrics celebrate the drop-out, despite frequent musical protests against schooling. Rather the school is seen as a source of group loyalty ("Be True To Your School"), as youth's turf, as a place for autonomous (if sometimes illegal) behavior ("Me And Julio Down In The Schoolyard" and "Smokin' In The Boys' Room"), and as the context for general teenage activity and identity ("High School Dance," "Remember The Days Of The Old School Yard," "School Day," and "High School U.S.A.").

Some popular music celebrates escape from school, particularly the much-lauded three-month reprieve of summer vacation: Gary "U.S." Bonds' "School Is Out," Alice Cooper's "School's Out," and The Jamies' "Summertime, Summertime." The permanent reprive of graduation—The Arbors' "Graduation Day" and Adrian Kimberly's "Pomp And Circumstance"—is especially highly praised.

But even escape affirms the centrality of the school, for summer vacation leads back to school, while graduation leads either to more schooling, or to a world that (to judge from popular music) is beyond the pale of youth culture—uninteresting, frequently unsatisfactory ("Mrs. Robinson," "Mother's Little Helper," and "Dreams Of The Everyday Housewife"). Rockpile speaks from the post-school perspective with some wistfulness for the order and security of the public school community:

> Lesson one, just begun—
> We're old enough, ain't much fun.
> Growing up, out of school,
> Out of love and out of rules.
> No one there to tell me how,
> A different world—Teacher, teacher, teach me now.
>   ("Teacher, Teacher"—1980)

Youth culture, operating from its base within the public schools, is occasionally contrasted with adult culture. The tolerance and openness imputed to young people is frequently compared to the hypocrisy and bigotry of the adult community in songs such as "Society's Child," "Town Without Pity," and "Harper Valley P.T.A."

An important distinction can be made in rock music between the school as a place and schooling as a socializing process. The latter, along with its primary agent, the teacher, meets persistent resistance. By analyzing the shifting lyrical emphases over the last three decades, one notes that resistance to the process of schooling has been voiced with increasing frequency and intensity. Alienation from the process today dominates aritisic imagery. Two songs that chronologically bracket the rock era—Chuck Berry's "School Day" (1957) and Pink Floyd's "Another Brick In The Wall" (1979)—illustrate this shifting pattern. Berry portrayed the school as multifaceted: a place with teachers good and bad, a place of serious study and goofing off, a place for learning and fraternizing, a youthful continum ranging from books to juke boxes. In contrast, Pink Floyd pictures school as a one-dimensional, oppressive institution. Yet it is significant that "Another Brick In The Wall" continues to assume the inevitablility of school as a center for adolescent life. Deschooling is not on the agenda, for the school is the natural context for youth. Lyricists seem incapable of either imagining or depicting a contemporary youth culture without school.

Despite nearly ninety years in which popular music has fostered education themes, only during the last thirty years—the rock era—has a sustained, persistent image of public schools emerged. Within the 1950-1980 period, for instance, song lyrics consistently portray the schooling process and the agents of that process in increasingly negative images, while simultaneously accepting as a given the centrality of the school in the lives of American youth. This progression of images of schooling corresponds to, and appears to be symptomatic of, the history of youth in the twentieth century. One factor dominates that history: the progressive alienation of youth from integrative participation in the economic activity of family and community, as well as alienation from most other aspects of adult culture. Increasingly redundant socially and economically, increasingly warehoused for progressively longer periods in hierarchical structures, powerless to affect either the adult world or the asylums to which they are assigned, young people have turned to themselves for values and identities. In that process, the school as a physical place and a social context has become central to adolescent self-perceptions. It gives much more form and meaning to the lives of students than they themselves realize. It defines circles of friends; it provides a variety of pre-school and after-school activities; it promotes group loyalties; and it dominates social planning among young people for three-quarters of each year. Some major employers of youth consciously exploit school-based loyalties and friendships in their hiring practices, hoping to add stability to their workplace through peer pressure. As a result of such actions, even Hardees, McDonalds, and Burger King workplaces reflect the ubiquity of local school ties.

If the recent history of youth has raised the *school* to a position of centrality, *schooling*—the purpose for which formal education presumably exists—is facing more and more youthful resistance. This is symbolized by the anti-teacher, anti-education themes in rock music discussed above. Sources of this hostility are not difficult to find. The alienation of young women and men from adult community and from significant work roles has estranged them from knowledge, particularly that factual information featured in the classroom. The norms and mores taught in school are those of adult culture. Yet access to and participation in that culture is systematically postponed. Thus school values are irrelevant to, and often at odds with, the values and behavior patterns endorsed by the youth culture. The deeper this historical alienation becomes, the more fully we can expect young people to find the curriculum meaningless, and to resist formal schooling at least passively through their music.

Rock music expresses youthful disenchantment, at least with efforts to socialize young people to a world in contradiction and crisis. But nowhere in the music do we find attempts to understand this disenchantment. No analysis is ventured. Unlike the spate of politically oriented music during the late sixties, the legacy of folk protest music throughout American history, rock music generally is devoid of ideological comment. Rock lyricists content themselves with making the demand, "Teachers, leave them kids alone!" and featuring endorsements for the counter-cultural activities of youth, particularly in the realms of drugs and sex. Rock music, then, reflects not only attitudes toward education, but also contemporary youth's fatalistic, uncritical view of the future. That view, with its lack of perspective or sense of options, should give us pause. There is, ultimately, a beguiling nihilism in the observation contained in Sam Cooke's oft-recorded, "Don't know nothin' 'bout 'nothin' at all." (1960, 1965, and 1978).

The conclusions reached in this study are not invigorating. What is particularly sad, though, is that changes are unlikely to occur in a system dedicated to socialization rather than education, to increasing patriotism rather than objectivity, to establishing order rather than fomenting creativity, to molding passive citizens rather than enlivening renaissance thinkers, and to serving the goals of a capitalist economy rather than sponsoring searches for new, more humane, more productive economic systems. These same sentiments have been voiced by insightful educational critics. Is it so strange, then, that American popular culture's vinyl media should echo these themes? Obviously not. But there will undoubtedly be skeptics who will charge that the lyrics examined above and provided in the discography in Table 1-B are unrepresentative, unfairly selected, or quoted out of context. This charge cannot be proven. The immense weight of this oral evidence is unmistakable.

Works Cited

Books

David Pichaske, *A Generation In Motion: Popular Music And Culture In The Sixties.* New York: Schirmer Books, 1979.

Robert G. Pielke, *You Say You Want A Revolution: Rock Music In American Culture.* Chicago: Nelson-Hall, Inc., 1986.

Graham Vulliamy and Ed Lee (eds.), *Pop Music In School* (revised edition). Cambridge: Cambridge University Press, 1980.

Articles

Bill Barol, "The Eighties Are Over," *Newsweek*, CXI (January 4, 1988) pp. 40-48.

Ray B. Browne, "The Uses Of Popular Culture In the Teaching Of American History," *Social Education*, XXXVI (January 1972), pp. 49-53.

B. Lee Cooper, "Education," in *A Resource Guide To Themes In Contemporary American Song Lyrics, 1950-1985* (Westport, Connecticut: Greenwood Press, 1986), pp. 65-79.

_____ "Information Services, Popular Culture, And The Librarian: Promoting A Contemporary Learning Perspective," *Drexel Library Quarterly*, XVI (July 1980), pp. 24-42.

_____ " 'It's A Wonder I Can Think At All': Vinyl Images Of American Public Education, 1950-1980," *Popular Music And Society*, IX, No. 4 (1984), pp. 47-65.

_____ "Oral History, Popular Music, And Les McCann," *Social Studies*, LXVII (May/ June 1976), pp. 115-118.

_____ "Popular Culture: Teaching Problems And Challenges," in *Popular Culture And The Library: Current Issues Symposium* II, edited by Wayne A. Weigand (Lexington: University of Kentucky Press, 1978), pp. 10-26.

_____ "Social Change, Popular Music, And The Teacher," *Social Education*, XXXVII (December 1973), pp. 776-781, 783.

_____ "Sounds Of Schooling In Modern America: Recorded Images Of Public Education, 1950-1980," *International Journal Of Instructional Media*, XI, No. 3 (1983/84), pp. 255-271.

Paul Friedlander, "The Rock Window: A Systmatic Approach To An Understanding Of Rock Music," *Tracking: Popular Music Studies*, I (Spring 1988), pp. 42-51.

Andrew Greeley, "Agon And Empathos: A Challenge To Popular Culture," *Popular Culture Association Newsletter*, XV (April 1988), pp. 2-5.

Lawrence Grossberg, "Another Boring Day In Paradise: Rock And Roll And The Empowerment Of Everyday Life," in *Popular Music 4: Performers And Audiences*, edited by Richard Middleton and David Horn (Cambridge: Cambridge University Press, 1984), pp. 225-258.

Stephen Kneeshaw, " 'What If...': Alternative History, Or Teaching What Might Have Been," *The History And Social Science Teacher*, XVIII (Fall 1982), pp. 3-7.

John Shelton Lawrence, "A Critical Analysis Of Roger B. Rollin's 'Against Evaluation'," *Journal Of Popular Culture*, XII (Summer 1978), pp. 99-112.

Roger B. Rollin, "Against Evaluation: The Role Of The Critic Of Popular Culture," *Journal Of Popular Culture*, IX (Fall 1975), pp. 355-365.

_____ "Son Of 'Against Evaluation': A Reply To John Shelton Lawrence," *Journal Of Popular Culture*, XII (Summer 1978), pp. 113-117.

Robert L. Root, Jr., "A Listener's Guide to The Rhetoric Of Popular Music," *Journal Of Popular Culture*, XX (Summer 1986), pp. 15-26.

Gordon Stevenson, "The Wayward Scholar: Resources And Research In Popular Culture," *Library Trends*, XXV (April 1977), pp. 779-818.

Unpublished Material

Stephen Markson and Rob Rosentahl, "Music As Ideology: Opposition Themes In Punk Rock Lyrics" (mimeographed paper presented at the 16th National Convention of The Popular Culture Association in April 1986).

Themes

Chapter Five
Automobiles

Chuck Berry epitomizes the folk artist of the rock idiom. His style did not change because it did not have to; from the beginning it unconsciously expressed the responses of the artist and his audience to the ordinary realities of their world: to cars, girls, growing up, school, or music.

—Carl Belz
The Story Of Rock (1972)

The motorcar is omnipresent in contemporary American society. In 1974 David J. Neuman reported, "No mechanical convenience has so enthralled a jaded public as the automobile has the American masses. Certainly the television is used as often and for longer hours and the telephone is more plentiful, but the special relationship between an American and his/her car is based upon more than convenience..." (p. 123). What is even more unique than this elevated profile of the automobile is the ambivalent attitudes which characterize public opinion toward this enigmatic machine. An ironic love-hate relationship dominates the history of twentieth-century thought and writing about the motorcar. "The American automobile has traveled the whole circuit from hero to villain," notes Glen Jeansonne. "Once enshrined as a liberating and democratizing agent, it is now condemned as a major cause of pollution and congestion" (p. 125).

Since its initial appearance, the automobile has been a frequent subject of popular songs. From Billy Murray's "He'd Have To Get Under, Get Out And Get Under, To Fix Up His Automobile" to the Hot Rod/Surf Scene tunes of The Beach Boys ("409," "Shut Down," "Little Deuce Coupe," and "Fun Fun, Fun"), Jan and Dean ("Drag City," "Dead Man's Curve," and "The Little Old Lady From Pasadena"), and Ronny and The Daytonas ("G.T.O."), car-related songs have attracted record buyers. It is not peculiar, then, that the poet laureate of rock 'n' roll music—Chuck Berry—should be one of the foremost spokesman on the nature and impact of the motorcar on his fellow Americans. For the past quarter century no other songwriter has demonstrated more lyrical ingenuity in utilizing four-wheeled imagery to explore issues of freedom, mobility, sexual relationships, prosperity, and authority.

I

Chuck Berry emerged as a popular recording star for Chess Records of Chicago during the summer of 1955. His first hit release—"Maybellene"—rated as high as #5 on the *Billboard* "Top 100" charts. Despite the racist stigma which was often attached to rhythm-and-blues songs performed by black artists in the mid-

1950s, Chuck Berry produced hit after hit. "Roll Over Beethoven" rose to #29; "School Day" peaked at #5 after 26 weeks on the *Billboard* list; "Rock And Roll Music" and "Johnny B. Goode" both climbed to the #8 position in 1957 and 1958, respectively; and "Sweet Little Sixteen" closed at #2 during a 16-week period of popularity. The Chuck Berry hit song phenomenon stretches from 1955 to the present. During the 1960s his recording productivity slowed considerably, but no less than eight of his 45 rpm releases reached the *Billboard* "Top 100." And in early 1970, on the strength of praise by The Beatles and The Rolling Stones and during a surge of rock 'n' roll nostalgia, Chuck Berry reasserted himself with a revised version of his classic "Reelin' and Rockin'," and a new novelty song entitled "My Ding-A-Ling." In the 1980s induction into the Rock 'N' Roll Hall Of Fame, the publication of his autobiography, and the release of a feature-length film saluting his career have made Chuck Berry an authentic legend in his own lifetime.

Chuck Berry has always been a youth-oriented performer. His consistent popularity among record buyers and concert audiences, the fact that he has always been a *total* performer (singer, writer, dancer, and musician), and the dramatic effect of so many of his songs on the entire field of popular music make him a seminal figure in contemporary culture. The themes of his songs are manifestly personal. They demonstrate a minstrel's approach to depicting modern life. Chuck Berry's song-poems are pointed observations and commentaries about the life-styles of young people in urban-industrial America. He notes the lack of relevance in public school experiences ("School Day," "Too Much Monkey Business," and "Anthony Boy"); he depicts the universal reliance of young people on popular music as a means of communication and celebration ("Rock And Roll Music," "Round And Round," and "Go, Go, Go"); he capsules the invigorating, but confusing process of social maturation ("Almost Grown," "Sweet Little Sixteen," and "Sweet Little Rock and Roller"); he fabricates and breathes life into a series of twentieth-century Horatio Algers ("Johnny B. Goode," "Bye, Bye Johnny," and "You Never Can Tell"); he condemns the fickleness of the female heart ("Nadine" and "Little Queenie"); and he describes the simplistic image of America to teenagers everywhere ("Back In The U.S.A.").

The thematic consistency of Chuck Berry's lyrics constitutes only one aspect of his uniqueness, though. He is also a creative force in language usage. In addition to employing standard slang terminology in his songs—"machine" for automobile and "cruisin' " for driving, Chuck Berry initiates fascinating verbal images that have come to symbolize the characters or scenes which he is describing. For instance, Johnny B. Goode doesn't just sit beside the railroad track and play his guitar. Instead, he "strums to the rhythm that the (train's) drivers make..." And the young man chasing the fickle Nadine doesn't just call out her name; he is described to be "campaign shoutin' like a Southern diplomat..." Students at a dance don't just enjoy rock 'n' roll songs; they are "feelin' the music from head to toe..." And finally, the young women of Chuck Berry's lyrical world inevitably face the transition period called "the grown-up blues" when they begin to wear "tight dresses and lipstick" and start "sportin' high heel shoes..."

Recognizing Chuck Berry's orientation toward youth, his fascination with urban life and culture, and his folk-poet style of combining personal concerns with technological advances, it is hardly surprising that the automobile has emerged as a focal object in his lyrics. The following pages explore motorcar imagery in several songs written and performed by Chuck Berry.

"Maybellene"

Fast cars and fickle females have always sustained Chuck Berry's lyrics. "Maybellene" was the first. This 1955 tale illustrated two consistent themes in Chuck Berry's songs. First, the dude with the biggest, most elegant car will invariably capture the attention of *any* girl ("Maybellene, why can't you be true?"); and second, the pursuit of a wayward woman is never final ("You've started back doin' the things you used to do."). The driver of the Cadillac Coupe de Ville remains unidentified, although one suspects that his financial resources far exceed those of the singing hero driving the V-8 Ford. Fate, in the form of a sudden cloudburst, enables the over-heated Ford to catch the 110-mile-per-hour speeding Cadillac at the top of the hill. Then what happens? Chuck Berry doesn't depict a battle between the two drivers over the fair damsel. Instead, he returns to the original refrain—"Maybellene, why can't you be true?" Somehow, one senses that the man in the V-8 will be chasing her again in the near future.

"Come On"

This tune, both comic and tragic, finds a disabled automobile to be only one of a growing list of problems facing a young man. "Everything is wrong," he declares, "since me and my baby parted." It may be difficult to establish a causal relationship between lost love and failing technology, but Chuck Berry does it. The hero's car won't start. To further complicate matters, he loses his job and can't afford to hire a mechanic. Dolefully observing his immobilized vehicle, the hero expresses the frustrated wish that "...somebody'd come along and run into it and wreck it." One surmises that a token amount of insurance money might be gained from such an accident—although certainly not enough to resolve all of the problems detailed in this down-and-out song.

"Nadine (Is That You?)"

If dating a girl like Maybellene was a problem, having a fiancée like Nadine would be unbearable. Chuck Berry utilizes traffic congestion—crowded busses, loaded taxis, and endless lines of honking cars—to set the scene for this romantic chase. Nadine, who is reportedly always "...up to something new," is spotted doubling back from a corner and moving toward a coffee-colored Cadillac. As the hero calls out to gain her attention, she abandons the Caddie and gets into "...a yellow cab headin' up-town." The song provides no resolution since the pursuer is left at the mercy of his cab driver and must be content to be "leanin' out the taxi window tryin' to make her hear." Obviously, private transportation is superior to public vehicles—but courtship via buses, on foot, or in cabs is depicted by Chuck Berry as a losing battle.

"No Money Down"

A new Cadillac symbolizes power, sex, social mobility, notoriety, freedom, and ...the vehicular pot of gold at the end of the rainbow for the owner of a "broken down ragged Ford." The salesman in this tune is initially silent, but stands beneath a tempting "No Money Down" sign. When the prospective car buyer rolls onto the lot, however, the dealer offers to put him in a car "that'll eat up the road." The salesman soon learns that he is facing a young man who knows *exactly* what he wants. And the list of accessories requested for the yellow, four-door Cadillac Coupe de Ville staggers the mind—wire-chromed wheels and a Continental spare, power steering and power brakes, air conditioning and automatic heat, "a full Murphy bed in my back seat" (Maybellene and Nadine beware!), short-wave radio, television, telephone ("You know I gotta talk to my baby when I'm riding' alone."), four carburetors and two straight exhaust pipes, railroad airhorns, and a military spotlight. The values of the would-be buyer are clearly articulated. A peppy, ostentatious buggy to replace a tired, drab Ford— and the whole world will be fine.

"Too Much Monkey Business"

This song brings to mind Jim Croce's "Workin' In The Carwash Blues." The hero is *really* down on his luck. Too many bills and too much hard work. If it's not the antics of a woman trying to steal his freedom by forcing him to settle down, it's the mechanical thievery of a telephone operator stealing his dime, or the exile of Uncle Sam robbing him of physical autonomy and years of freedom through military service in Yokohama. The two automobile-related references in this song are brief. The first is a derogatory reference to the inferiority and sterility of military vehicles—"Army car! Arrgh..." The second is a negative attitude expressed about post-military employment at a local filling station— "Too many tasks: wipe the windows, check the tires, check the oil—dollar gas?!!!" There is no joyous speculation about owning the gas station, or driving a Coupe de Ville. Only frustration by being forced to endure too much monkey business.

"No Particular Place To Go"

This tune is Chuck Berry at his comic best. Initially, it appears to be a typical tale of automotive seduction. The boy is "cruising and playing the radio" with a sweet young thing seated close beside him. He steals a kiss, she whispers softly in his ear, and they continue "...cuddling more and driving low, with no particular place to go." The romantic mood is shaken, however, when the car is unexpectedly transformed from a lovers' chariot into a four-wheeled chastity belt. Just as the couple is ready to take a stroll in the moonlight, the young woman discovers that her safety harness will not release. The final verse is classic Berry: "Riding along in my calaboose, still trying to get her belt unloose. All the way home I held a grudge, for the safety belt that wouldn't budge." Here is the motorcar as entrapment, a classic example of technologically enforced morality in contemporary song that even Stephen King would applaud.

"Move It"

This upbeat tune contains two illustrations of Chuck Berry's creative automobile imagery. The cars mentioned here are utilized as symbols of sexual liberation and unthinking authority. In the first case, the singer yearns to possess a shapely disco queen who "...drives a mustang" and "let's her hair hang." The second case is more complex. The driver of a '55 Ford finds that his engine has mysteriously died on the freeway. Traffic begins to pile up behind him, despite that fact that he has rolled the disabled car toward that curb and raised the hood to indicate mechanical distress. When Officer Lamar arrives his only recommendation to resolve the automotive problem is a terse, "Move it!" The omission of any statement of sympathy, of an offer of direct aid, or even of a call for assistance is indicative of police mentality in high traffic areas. "You can't stop it here! Get it out of here!" is the authoritarian patrolman's heartless refrain. The stalled automobile symbolizes unexpected trouble (a personal difficulty) as well as an opportunity for someone to offer assistance. But everyone else on the highway ignores the potential Good Samaritan situation by simply "...tryin' to drive around." Only the policeman responds—unsatisfactorily.

"Almost Grown"

Coming-of-age, that anthropological combination of physical maturation and economic independence, is a common theme in Chuck Berry's songs. The automobile is frequently a focal point for youthful expenditures—purchase, the addition of personalizing accessories (as in "No Money Down"), the never-ending quest for gasoline ("I'm burnin' aviation fuel—no matter what the costs."), and pleasure-riding in the countryside. From the perspective of the young man in this tune, the acquisition of a car is a symbol of social stability. He's a reformed soul who's "...doing all right in school," "hasn't broken any rules," "...ain't never been in dutch" (with the police?), doesn't "...browse around too much," and doesn't "run around with no mob." In short, he's fairly respectable. But the undisguised sense of youthful uncertainty permeates the lyric. The "little car" he plans to buy will reportedly halt all his browsing and provide entry into the adult world.

"Wuden't Me"

This song features Chuck Berry's sardonic use of the automobile and a minor traffic violation to underscore social inequality which still exists in America. Instead of employing the make, model, and year of the car to identify the driver's personal background, the vehicle is introduced only to create the confrontation— "Oh boy, he ran a little stop sign in the South." The rest of the tale describes a quasi-legal incarceration in a Delta County jail, a fortunate escape, and the hot pursuit of the traffic offender by a K.K.K. Grand Dragon's posse and seven Alabama bloodhounds. In mock humor, the singer of the tune continues to insist, "Wuden't me."

"Carol"

"Come into my machine, so we can cruise on out," says Carol's would-be date. He wants to take her to a "swingin' little joint" that's located "not too far back off the highway, not so long a ride." The romantic approach is straight forward. No frills. The automobile is simply a source of horizontal mobility. But the slang term "my machine" which is utilized to describe the young man's vehicle hints that the engine may not be a stock variety, and that the car's body may have been artistically personalized. Nonetheless, Carol is an object of pursuit—not unlike the fickle Maybellene or the fleeing Nadine—and both the automobile and the dancehall figure prominently in the the lover's chase.

"If I Were"

This highly speculative song offers an automobile metaphor in which the desirable female is cast as a Mercedes Benz and the day-dreaming boy is a Cadillac Fleetwood Brougham. The idealized relationship is simple and straightforward: "...everytime I see you rollin' on the highway, I think I'd have to follow you home." There the Fleetwood longs to lodge in the Benz' double garage, bumper to bumper. Contentment is just settling down and living where there's "nobody home but the Benz and the Brougham, ready, rarin' to roll out together." This is truly a four-wheeled fairy tale.

"You Never Can Tell"

The message of this song—directed toward skeptical middle class parents— is clear. Don't make snap judgments about the failure of teenage marriages. The automobile once again functions in several sociological ways. First, it illustrates economic stability and personal independence from the older generation; second, it establishes the individualistic style of the young couple under observation ("They bought a souped-up jitney, 'twas a cherry red fifty-three"); and finally, it becomes a source of pleasure and geographical mobility ("They drove it down to New Orleans to celebrate their anniversary"). The skepticism of the "old folks" apparently is not totally overcome by this single instance of marital bliss, though, as the refrain—"It goes to show you never can tell"—indicates.

"Back In The U.S.A"

This is a paen to America, or more precisely, to the urban centers of the United States ("New York, Los Angeles, oh, how I yearn for you. Detroit, Chicago, Chattanooga, Baton Rouge. Let alone just to be at my home back in ol' St. Lou."). It is also punctuated by two automobile-related yearnings. The returning world traveler, who exudes love for his homeland, indicates that high on his list of things "missed" are freeways and drive-ins. It should be obvious that traffic congestion and greasy hamburgers are not considered to be social problems to this urban patriot; instead, lines of cars zooming along multi-lane highways and dozens of automobiles sandwiched together beneath the watchful eyes of highway patrolmen are signs of social progress, economic stability, and personal joy.

III.

Despite his numerous references to the automobile as a source of social mobility, Chuck Berry deviates from this prominent private transportation symbol in two of his most noted rags-to-riches tunes. For Johnny B. Goode ("Bye, Bye Johnny") it is the Greyhound bus which, funded by his mother's Southern Trust savings, whisks him from guitar playing beside a Louisiana railroad track to the gates of Hollywood. Similarly, the poor boy from Norfolk, Virginia is transported by Greyhound bus from his hometown to Birmingham, Alabama, from there by train to New Orleans, Louisiana, and finally by plane from Houston, Texas to Los Angeles, California—"The Promised Land." The only possibility of auto transportation in this quest for life is Hollywood occurs between New Orleans and Houston, but is depicted in lyrics which vaguely declare, "Somebody helped me get out of Louisiana, just to help me get to Houston Town." It might be that Chuck Berry is avoiding use of the automobile is these cases because his heroes are still unemployed and too young to have acquired even a used, battered Ford.

During the past thirty-five years Chuck Berry has chronicled the sociological impact of a particular segment of American technology faithfully and accurately. Undeniably, he is the oral historian, the balladeer of teenage life. In 1970 journalist Michael Lydon accurately described him in one sentence. "Serious and comic as only a genius can be; arrogant, beautiful, and demonically energetic, Chuck has indelibly marked our times." What is seldom recognized, though, is the cogent, efficient manner in which the master lyricist has adapted the most common physical element of the youth culture—the automobile—to his own poetic ends. Hopefully, this study will generate further investigation of Chuck Berry's expansive portfolio of tunes.

In the meantime, one cannot ignore the fact that the automobile will apparently remain a topic of sharply divided opinion and national attention during the coming decades. Just as Chuck Berry has explored the sociology and psychology of the motorcar for the younger generation, other poets will attempt to come to grips with the complex issues of traffic congestion, the energy crisis, environmental pollution, and the dozens of other concerns related to America's love-hate relationship with the automobile. As John L. Wright sagely noted in 1978,

Whatever the future holds for the automobile, it seems that for Americans the car is here to stay, in large part because it is a powerful iconic focus for the national ideals of individualism, freedom, and personal power. And the songs that celebrate this great American icon will continue to strike a responsive chord in the American psyche (p. 117).

This should mean Chuck Berry's tunes—old and new—will continue to be vital, valuable commentaries on youth and its favorite machine.

Works Cited

Books

Chuck Berry, *Chuck Berry—The Autobiography*. New York: Harmony Books, 1987.
Cynthia Golomb Dettelbach, *In The Driver's Seat: The Automobile In American Literature And Popular Culture*. Westport, Connecticut: Greenwood Press, 1976.
Howard A. DeWitt, *Chuck Berry: Rock 'N' Roll Music* (second edition). Ann Arbor, Michigan: Pierian Press, 1985.
James J. Fink, *The Car Culture*. Cambridge, Massachusetts: M.I.T. Press, 1975.
David L. Lewis and Lawrence Goldstein (eds.), *The Automobile And American Culture*. Ann Arbor, Michigan University of Michigan Press, 1983.
John B. Rae, *The American Automobile: A Brief History*. Chicago: University of Chicago Press, 1965.

―――― *The Road And The Car In American Life*. Cambridge, Massachusetts: M.I.T. Press, 1971.

Krista Reese, *Chuck Berry: Mr. Rock 'N' Roll*. London: Proteus Books, 1982.

Articles

Shana Alexander, "Love Songs To The Carburetor," *Life*, LVII (November 6, 1964), p. 33.

Roy Clifton Ames, "Cars In Song," *Special-Interest Autos*, (January/February 1977), pp. 40-45.

Warren Belasco, "Motivatin' With Chuck Berry And Frederick Jackson Turner," in *The Automobile And American Culture*, edited by David L. Lewis and Laurence Goldstein (Ann Arbor, Michigan: University of Michigan Press, 1983), pp. 262-279.

Carl Belz, "Chuck Berry: Folk Poet Of The Fifties," in *The Story Of Rock*, second edition (New York: Harper and Row, 1972), pp. 61-66.

B. Lee Cooper, "Chuck Berry And The American Motor Car," *Music World*, No. 86 (June 1981), pp. 18-23.

―――― " 'Crusin' And Playin' The Radio': Exploring Images Of The American Automobile Through Popular Music," *International Journal Of Instructional Media*, VII (1979-80), pp. 327-334.

―――― "Review of *Chuck Berry: Rock 'N' Roll Music* (second edition) by Howard A. DeWitt," *The Sonneck Society Newsletter*, XII (Summer 1986), pp. 69-70.

―――― "Review Of Chuck Berry's *Golden Decade* Albums," *The History Teacher*, VIII (February 1975), pp. 300-301.

―――― "Transportation Systems," in *A Resource Guide To Themes In Contemporary American Song Lyrics, 1950-1985* (Westport, Connecticut: Greenwood Press, 1986), pp. 235-252.

Frederick E. Danker, "Trucking Songs: A Comparison With Traditional Occupational Song," *Journal Of Country Music*, VII (January 1978), pp. 78-86.

Dr. Demento, " 'Check Out My Custom Machine': Vehicular Traffic Through The Ages," *Wax Paper*, II (April 29, 1977), pp. 16-19.

Maurice Duke, "The Automobile," in *The Handbook Of American Popular Culture—Volume One*, edited by M. Thomas Inge (Westport, Connecticut: Greenwood Press, 1978), pp. 27-48.

James V. Higgins, "Rock 'N' Cars Make Beautiful (?) Music Together," *Detroit News*, (October 15, 1986), pp. F-1, 2.

Tony Hossain, "A Rich Slice Of The American Pie," *Friends*, XXXVII (August 1980), pp. 26-28.

William Jeanes, "Doo-Wopping The American Dream," *Car And Driver* (March 1985), pp. 85-89.

Glen Jeansonne, "The Automobile And American Morality," *Journal Of Popular Culture* VIII (January 1974), pp. 125-131.

David L. Lewis, "Sex And The Automobile: From Rumble Seats To Rockin' Vans," *Michigan Quarterly Review*, XX (Winter 1981), pp. 518-528.

Michael Lydon, "Chuck Berry Lives!" *Ramparts*, VIII (December 1969), pp. 47-56.

H.F. Moorhouse, "Racing For A Sign: Defining The 'Hot Rod', 1945-1960," *Journal Of Popular Culture*, XX (Fall 1986), pp. 83-96.

David J. Neuman, "From Bumper...," *Journal Of Popular Culture*, VIII (Spring 1974), pp. 123-124.

Ralph M. Newman, "The Chuck Berry Story: Long Lives Rock And Roll," *Time Barrier Express*, No. 27 (April/May 1980), pp. 34-36.

Roger B. Rollin, *"Deus In Machina*: Popular Culture's Myth Of The Machine," *Journal Of American Culture*, II (Summer 1979), pp. 287-308.

Tom Wheeler, "Chuck Berry: The Interview," *Guitar Player*, XXII (March 1988), pp. 56-63.

John L. Wright, "Croonin' About Cruisin'," in *The Popular Culture Reader*, edited by Jack Nachbar, Deborah Weiser, and John L. Wright (Bowling Green, Ohio: Bowling Green University Popular Press, 1978), pp. 109-117.

Unpublished Materials

Richard Hawkins, "The Automobile As A Vehicle Of Engagement" (mimeographed paper presented at the 10th National Convention of The Popular Culture Association in April 1980).

George Lipsitz, " 'Living In The U.S.A!': Chuck Berry and St. Louis Rock And Roll, 1945-1960" (mimeographed paper presented at the 12th National Convention of The Popular Culture Association in April 1982).

William L. Schurk, "Unhurried Views Of Auto-Erotica: A Singalong" (mimeographed paper presented at the 11th National Convention of The Popular Culture Association in March 1981).

John Wright, "Car Tunes: Lyrics On The Automobile" (mimeographed paper and audio presentation at the 7th Annual Meeting of The Midwest Popular Culture Association in October 1979).

Chapter Six
Christmas

"Do you hear what I hear?"
  "What child is this, who laid to rest
on Mary's lap is sleeping?"
    "You better watch out,
    You better not cry,
    You better not pout,
    I'm telling you why...."
  "I'm dreaming of a White Christmas,
Just like the ones I used to know...."
    "Rudolph, the red-nosed reindeer,
    You'll go down in history...."
  "Although its been said many times, many ways,
Merry Christmas to you."
"Do you hear what I hear?"

American historians have been utilizing oral testimony and other audio resources for research, writing, and teaching purposes for several decades. However, most history classes continue to focus on wars, Presidents, and isolated social and economic events. This study suggests that students of contemporary American society can gain significant social understanding by investigating one recurring cultural event—Christmas—to determine how personal, commercial, religious, and artistic activities influence public thinking. Clearly, singular facts must take a back seat to more sweeping judgments about behavioral trends in such investigations. But sociologists and psychologists shouldn't be the only teachers to sail into uncharted, subjective waters. Historians owe it to their students—and to themselves—to speculate on the nature and meaning of popular events.

Christmas comes but once a year. But it comes *every* year. Nevertheless, few history teachers perceive learning opportunities in the holiday songs that dominate their students' lives each December. Traditional Christmas carols reflect the Gospel stories of the birth of Jesus Christ in Bethlehem. Thus comparisons of Biblical recitations, historical events, and lyrical depictions are always possible. Some history teachers worry, though, that the study of Christmas songs may infringe upon the beliefs of students raised in Hebrew, Moslem, or other religious traditions. They also worry that observations from Christian fundamentalist youngsters might clash with ideas presented by less conservative Christians. For these reasons, most high schools and colleges treat the Christmas Season strictly as a time of social ritual—with an assembly, a December Convocation, a few traditional carols sung in music classes, and two-week holiday vacation.

There is great potential in the study of Christmas songs. Approached objectively, tunes of the Yuletide season can provide valuable illustrations of historical information, cultural borrowing, and social change. Presented in this context, both Christian and non-Christian students can benefit from examining oral history resources of the holiday season.

History teachers should introduce the investigation of Christmas songs by noting the wide variety of holiday tunes that are played on radios, heard in downtown department stores, and broadcast throughout shopping malls. The initial instructional goal is to stimulate students to acknowledge that Christmas songs are really quite *different*—different in sound, different in lyric, and very different in meaning. Once the preliminary issues of "sound" have been discussed (rhythm and orchestration, vocal quality and instrumentation, individual singer and choirs), the classroom analysis should shift toward the varying Christmas messages being related. This latter activity will allow history instructors to involve students in vigorous, creative cultural analysis.

In order to structure discussions of Christmas song content, a teacher should ask students to examine the following format. Most students believe that all Yuletide songs can be divided into two clear-cut categories: traditional or non-traditional. That is, Bing Crosby's "Adeste Fideles" is a "traditional" hymn, while The Eagles' "Please Come Home For Christmas" is a "non-traditional" recording. Once this simple dichotomy is explored in detail, though, the class will note that the content of Christmas songs must be classified along more complex lines than the simple bi-polar traditional/non-traditional system. Lyrics fall into another dual system of sacred/secular themes. "Adeste Fideles" bids the faithful to come to Bethlehem to adore The King of The Angels; it presents a clearly sacred massage. In contrast, "Please Come Home For Christmas" beckons a wandering loved one to return to a lonely partner by December 25th (or January 1st at the latest), illustrating a secular holiday season concern. Key terms in this "sacred" vs. "secular" identification system are:

Sacred Images		*Secular Images*
Jesus Christ	_____	Santa Claus
Holy Night	_____	holiday
Blessed Child	_____	little children
Three Kings	_____	Alvin, Theodore and Simon
Mary and Joseph	_____	Currier and Ives
candles	_____	mistletoe
cradle	_____	sleigh
lambs	_____	reindeer
harps of gold	_____	tin horns and toy drums
straw	_____	Christmas tree
gifts of Gold, Frankincense, and Myrrh	_____	skates, sled and other presents
Blessed Angels sing	_____	Church choirs rejoice
cattle are lowing		chestnuts roasting
Heaven and Nature sing	_____	bells on bobtail ring
Emmanuel	_____	St. Nicholas

| good tidings | —— | cup of cheer |
| ox and ass | —— | Dasher, Dancer, Prancer, Vixen, Comet, Cupid, Donner, and Blitzen |

    In order to provide adequate recorded options for the four fields of analytical concern—traditional/non-traditional and sacred/secular—the following chart may be utilized.

Table 6-A

Selected Illustrations of Traditional and Non-traditional
Christmas Recordings, 1940-1988

Traditional Christmas Recordings		Non-Traditional Christmas Recordings	
Sacred Songs	*Secular Tunes*	*Sacred Songs*	*Secular Tunes*
1. "Adeste Fideles" by Bing Crosby (1960)	1. "Christmas Song" by Nat King Cole (1946)	1. "Child of God" by Bobby Darin (1960)	1. "Blue Christmas" by Elvis Presley (1957)
2. "Ave Maria" by Perry Como (1950)	2. "I'll Be Home For Christmas" by Bing Crosby (1943)	2. "Do You Hear What I Hear" by Bing Crosby (1963)	2. "The Chipmunk Song" by The Chipmunks (1958)
3. "Silent Night" by Bing Crosby (1957)	3. "Jingle Bell Rock" by Bobby Helms (1957)	3. "Go Tell It On The Mountain" by Mahalia Jackson (1962)	3. "Do They Know Its Christmas" by Band Aid (1984)
4. "Silent Night, Holy Night" by Mahalia Jackson (1962)	4. "Jingle Bells" by Perry Como (1957)	4. "Little Drummer Boy" by The Harry Simeone Chorale (1958)	4. "Donde Este Santa Claus" by Augie Rios (1958)
5. "Silent Night (Christmas Hymn)" by Sister Rosetta (1949)	5. "Rockin' Around The Christmas Tree" by Brenda Lee (1960)	5. "Little Drummer Boy" by Moonlion (1976)	5. "Grandma Got Run Over By A Reindeer" by Elmo 'N' Patsy (1981)
6. "Silent Night (Sleep In Heavenly Peace)" by Barbra Streisand (1966)	6. "Rudolph The Red-Nosed Reindeer" by Gene Autry (1949)	6. "Little Drummer Boy/Peace On Earth" by David Bowie and Bing Crosby (1982)	6. "Green Chritma" by Stan Freberg (1958)
	7. "Silver Bells" by Earl Grant (1967)	7. "Mary's Boy Child" by Harry Belafonte (1956)	7. "Please Come Home For Christmas" by The Eagles

(1978)

8. "The Twelve Days Of Christmas" by Burl Ives (1962)	8. "Mary's Boy Child" Oh My Lord" by Bony M (1978)	8. "Run Rudolph Run" by Chuck Berry (1958)
9. "White Christmas" by Bing Crosby (1942)	9. "What Child Is This?." by The Brothers Four (1962)	9. "Santa Claus Is Comin' To Town" by Bruce Springsteen (1985)
10. "Winter Wonderland" by Perry Como (1952)		10. "Snoopy's Christmas" by The Royal Guardsmen (1968)

What can students learn from this Christmas song categorizing exercise? Many things. First, church hymns and carols such as "Silent Night" are staples in numerous Christmas albums. Second, songs that only peripherally deal with the Bethlehem story have become traditional Christmas favorites over the past four decades because of their lyrical emphasis on humanitarian concern for others or on the special relationships among families and loved ones during the holiday period. Clearly, Bing Crosby's "White Christmas," Nat King Cole's "The Christmas Song," Earl Grant's "Silver Bells," and Dolly Parton's "Winter Wonderland/Sleigh Ride" are illustrations of this phenomenon. Third, there are no racist or sexist barriers in respect to recording artists that produce highly popular Christmas recordings. Similarly, neither religious nor ethnic barriers exist as illustrated by the hit recordings of "Silent Night (Sleep In Heavenly Peace)" by Barbra Streisand and "Donde Esta Santa Clause?" by Augie Rios. Fourth, a category of contemporary sacred Christmas tunes can be identified, with The Harry Simeone Chorale's "Little Drummer Boy" as the primary illustration. Fifth, the commercialism of Christmas-time and the materialism of the entire world is challenged in several recordings, especially Stan Freberg's "Green Chritma" and Band Aid's "Do They Know It's Christmas?" Sixth, a variety of holiday heroes and singing creatures have become synonymous with the modern Yuletide season. "The Chipmunk Song" featuring Theodore, Simon, and Alvin, "Rudolph, The Red-Nosed Reindeer," and "Frosty The Snowman" illustrate this trend. Seventh, the adaptation of traditional Christmas symbols into secular activities is demonstrated in Bobby Helms' "Jingle Bell Rock," Elvis Presley's "Blue Christmas," and Brenda Lee's "Rockin' Around The Christmas Tree." Eighth, comedy and humor are central features in a variety of Christmas recordings such as Elmo 'N' Patsy's "Grandma Got Run Over By A Reindeer" and The Singing Dogs barking rendition of "Jingle Bells." Finally, teachers and students alike will note that disagreements are inevitable in respect to categorizing songs like "Jingle Bell Rock," "Merry Christmas Darling," or "Please Come Home For Christmas" into either that traditional/secular or the non-traditional/secular categories. At this point the issues of social change and public perception can be discussed since "Frosty" and "Rudolph," today regarded as traditional Christmas figures, were strictly novelty characters of non-traditional invention during the 1950s.

In order to highlight the historical evolution of Christmas recordings, a broad survey of thematic images must accompany the previous sacred/secular design. Students should note that the fifty year period since 1940 has yielded many different types of recordings. More importantly, as observers of social change they need to recognize the impact of shifting thematic images. An initial point of interest might be the re-recording and revising of specific Christmas songs. Tradition is born out of popular longevity. Among the most noted Yuletide audio chestnuts are the following tunes.

A. Imitations Of Yuletide Success

If imitation is the most sincere form of flattery, then performers such as Bing Crosby, Gene Autry, and Charles Brown should feel extremely honored. Why have so many novice singers and established recording stars elected to release new versions of previously recorded Yuletide standards?

1. "White Christmas" (Decca 18429)
   by Bing Crosby (1942)
       a. Frank Sinatra—Columbia 36756 (1944)
       b. Jo Stafford—Capitol 319 (1946)
       c. Perry Como—RCA Victor 1970 (1947)
       d. The Ravens—National 9062 (1949)
       e. Mantovani—London 1280 (1952)
       f. Clyde McPhatter and The Drifters—Atlantic 1048 (1954)
2. "The Little Drummer Boy" (20th Century Fox 121)
   by The Harry Simeone Chorale (1958)
       a. Johnny Cash—Columbia 41481 (1959)
       b. The Jack Halloran Singers—Dot 16275 (1961)
       c. The Pipes and Drums of The Military Band of The Royal
          Scots Dragoon Guards—RCA 0709 (1972)
       d. Moonlion—P.I.P. 6513 (1976)
       e. Bob Seger and The Silver Bullet Band —A&M SP 3911 (1987)

B. Commercial Considerations

The commercial longevity of certain Christmas recordings produce continuing royalties for Bing Crosby, David Seville, Brenda Lee, Bobby Helms, and several others. Yet a few performers have elected to record new versions of their most famous, most popular holiday tunes. Why did this happen?

1. "The Christmas Song"
   by Nat "King" Cole
       a. Capitol 311 or 15201 (1946)
       b. Capitol 2955 (1954)
       c. Capitol 3561 (1960)
2. "Rudolph, The Red Nosed Reindeer"
   by Gene Autry
       a. Columbia 38610 (1949)
       b. Challenge 1010 (1957)

The final grouping of songs provided for student examination are structured strictly according to thematic variation. Historians can locate clue after clue about the nature of American culture through these popular recordings. Lines of evidence will not be singular or definitive, of course; the truth will be complex, contradictory, and obscured by various other concerns. But as students begin to recognize the blend of ideas, myths, values, and humor that undergird the nature of all human institutions, they will also begin to appreciate the difficulty of defining "culture" (especially their own) with clarity and ease. Ideally, some of their ethnocentric assumptions will totter and fall. The enjoyment of listening to known audio commodities—contemporary Christmas records—with enlightened, perceptive ears will stimulate students to become better, more critical thinkers in history and other disciplines as well.

The following topics offer an appropriate cross-section of themes that can be presented for classroom study.

C. Images Of Santa Claus

Father Christmas, St. Nicholas, Santa Claus or whatever else the Jolly Old Elf is called, this mythical character is central to the cultural definition of Christmas in the United States. How do the descriptions of St. Nick illustrate the goals of people who listen to popular lyrics?

1. "Boogie Woogie Santa Claus"
   (Exclusive 75x)
      by Mabel Schott (1948)
2. "C. B. Santa"
   (A & M 1887)
      by Homemade Theatre (1976)
3. "Donde Esta Santa Claus?"
   (Metro 20010)
      by Augie Rios (1958)
4. "Here Comes Santa Claus (Down Santa Claus Lane)"
   (Columbia 20377)
      by Gene Autry (1950)
5. "I Believe In Father Christmas"
   (Atlantic 3305)
      by Greg Lake (1975)
6. "I saw Mommy Kissing Santa Claus"
   (RCA Victor 5067)
      by Spike Jones (1952)
7. "Little Saint Nick"
   (Capitol 5096)
      by The Beach Boys (1963)
8. "The Man With All The Toys"
   (Capitol 5312)
      by The Beach Boys (1964)
9. "Mr. Santa Claus"
   (Fortune 550)
      by Nathaniel Mayer (1962)
10. "The Night Before Christmas Song"

(Columbia 39876)
  by Gene Autry and Rosemary Clooney (1952)
11. "Santa Baby"
 (RCA Victor 5502)
  by Eartha Kitt (1953)
12. "Santa Claus Is Comin' To Town"
 (Decca 23281)
  by Bing Crosby and The Andrews Sisters (1947)
13. "Santa Claus Is Watching You"
 (Mercury 72058)
  by Ray Stevens (1962)

D. Non-Christmas Holiday Songs

 The Yuletide season is notable for the diversity among Christmas tunes, with lyrical commentaries ranging from sacred images and secular materialism. How can the popularity of holiday recordings which refer to neither Jesus Christ nor Santa Claus be explained?

1. "Baby It's Cold Outside"
 (ABC—Paramount 10298)
  by Ray Charles and Betty Carter (1962)
2. "Frosty The Snowman"
 (Capitol 1203)
  by Nat "King" Cole, with The Pussy Cats (1951)
3. "Jingle Bells"
 (RCA EPA 9201)
  by Perry Como (1957)
4. "Let It Snow! Let It Snow! Let It Snow!"
 (Decca 18741)
  by Connie Boswell (1946)
5. "Sleigh Ride"
 (Decca 9-28463)
  by Bing Crosby (1953)

E. Unusual Yuletide Characters

 Christmas stories often highlight the roles of animals as symbols of innocence, kindness, and simplicity. The manger scene in Bethlehem emphasizes docile cattle and sheep, while the Santa Claus myth features sleeping mice and soaring reindeer. Why do contemporary recording artists often introduce unusual Yuletide characters in their Christmas tunes?

1. "The Chipmunk Song"
 (Liberty 55168)
  by The Chipmunks (1958)
2. "Frosty The Snowman"
 (Columbia 38907)
  by Gene Autry (1951)
3. "The Happy Reindeer"
 (Capitol 4300)
  by Dancer, Prancer, and Nervous (1958)

4. "Rudolph, The Red Nosed Reindeer"
    (Columbia 38610)
        by Gene Autry (1949)
5. "Snoopy's Christmas"
    (Laurie 3416)
        by The Royal Guardsmen (1968)

F. Social Commentary In Christmas Songs

It is not uncommon for contemporary performers such as Bruce Springsteen, Pink Floyd, Stevie Wonder, or Midnight Oil to express social commentaries in their lyrics. However, it is rare to encounter political cynicism or social criticism in holiday recordings. Why have some artists deliberately utilized Christmas songs to communicate their public policy concerns?

1. "Dear Mr. Jesus"
    (PowerVision 8607)
        by PowerSource (1987)
2. "Do They Know It's Christmas?"
    (Columbia 04749)
        by Band Aid (1984)
3. "Green Chritma"
    (Capitol 4097)
        by Stan Freberg (1958)
4. "Happy Xmas (War is Over)"
    (Apple 1842)
        by John and Yoko and The Plastic Ono Band (1971)
5. "Pretty Paper"
    (Monument 830)
        by Roy Orbison (1963)
6. "7 O'Clock News/Silent Night"
    (Columbia CL 2563)
        by Simon and Garfunkel (1966)

G. Children's Perspectives On Christmas

Whether focusing on a newborn babe in the manger as viewed by "The Little Drummer Boy" or bemoaning the fact that a youngster who is nothing but bad gets "Nuttin'For Christmas," Yuletide recordings often utilize children's perspectives to capsule the nature and meaning of the December holiday. What individual values and culture ideas emerge from children's images of Christmas?

1. "All I Want For Christmas (Is My Two Front Teeth)"
    (RCA Victor 3177)
        by Spike Jones (1948)
2. "I Saw Mommy Kissing Santa Claus"
    (Columbia 39871)
        by Jimmy Boyd (1952)
3. "I'm Gonna Lasso Santa Claus"
    (Decca 9-30107)
        by Brenda Lee (1956)
4. "Little Becky's Christmas Wish"

(Warner Brothers 7154)
    by Becky Lamb (1967)
5. "The Little Drummer Boy"
  (20th Century Fox 121)
    by The Harry Simeone Chorale (1958)
6. "(I'm Getting) Nuttin' For Christmas"
  (MGM 12092)
    by Barry Gordon (1955)
7. "Santa Claus Is Coming To Town"
  (Vee-Jay 478)
    by The Four Seasons (1962)

H. Yuletide Parody Tunes And Sequel Songs

Why have performers like Allan Sherman, Stan Freberg, and David Seville utilized traditional Christmas songs as sources of comic parody or as initial resources for sequel tunes?

1. "Rudolph, The Red Nosed Reindeer"
  (Columbia 38610)
    by Gene Autry (1949)
      a. "Run Rudolph Run"
        (Chess 1714)
          by Chuck Berry (1958)
      b. "Rudolph The Red Nosed Reindeer"
        (Liberty 55289)
          by The Chipmunks with David Seville (1960)
2. "Happy Happy Birthday Baby"
  (Checker 872)
    by The Tune Weavers (1957)
      a. "Merry Merry Christmas Baby"
        (Dot 16166)
          by Dodie Stevens (1960)
3. "Jingle Bells"
  (RCA EPA 920)
    by Perry Como (1957)
      a. "Yingle Bells"
        (Capitol 781)
          by Yogi Yorgesson (1949)
      b. "Twistin' Bells"
        (Canadian American 120)
          by Santo and Johnny (1960)
      c. "Jingle Bells"
        (RCA PB 10129)
          by The Singing Dogs (1975)
      d. "Jingle Bells (Laughing All The Way)"
        (Warner Brothers 49877)
          by St. Nick (1981)
4. "All I Want For Christmas (Is My Two Front Teeth)"
  (RCA Victor 2963)
    by Spike Jones (1949)

a. "All I Want For Christmas (Is My Upper Plate)"
   (RCA 47-5456)
   by Homer and Jethro (1953)
5. "The Twelve Days Of Christmas"
   (Decca 25585)
      by Burl Ives (1962)
         a. "The Twelve Gifts Of Christmas"
            (Warner Brothers 5406)
            by Allan Sherman (1963)
6. "Mr. Sandman"
   (Cadence 1247)
      by the Chordettes (1954)
         a. "Mr. Santa"
            (Coral 9-61539)
            by Dorothy Collins (1955)

I. Holiday Loneliness

Joyous memories of holiday vacations, of family get-togethers, and of special times with a loved one dominate traditional Christmas songs. However, sociologists and psychologists have frequently noted the emotional stress encountered by individuals who find themselves alone on December 25th. How do Yuletide lyrics depict the feelings of these isolated Americans?

1. "Blue Christmas"
   (RCA 447-0647)
      by Elvis Presley (1957)
2. "Christmas Will Be Just Another Day"
   (Decca 31688)
      by Brenda Lee (1964)
3. "(It's Gonna Be A) Lonely Christmas"
   (Jubilee 5001)
      by The Orioles (1948)
4. "Just A Lonely Christmas"
   (Chance 1150)
      by The Moonglows (1953)
5. "Lonesome Christmas"
   (Swing Time 242)
      by Lowell Fulson (1950)
6. "Please Come Home For Christmas"
   (Asylum 45555)
      by The Eagles (1978)
7. "What Do The Lonely Do At Christmas?"
   (Stax 3215)
      by The Emotions (1973)

J. Sexually Suggestive Yuletide Songs

Whether sacred or secular, Christmas songs are generally wholesome, family-oriented tales emphasizing manger scenes, babes in toyland, and a red-clad elf guiding eight flying reindeer. But there are a few sexually suggestive Christmas tunes which seem totally out of character with "Silent Night" and "The Christmas Song." Why would artists release such atypical recordings at Christmas?

1. "Baby It's Cold Outside"
   (ABC-Paramount 10298)
      by Ray Charles and Betty Carter (1962)
2. "Back Door Santa"
   (Atlantic 2576)
      by Clarence Carter (1968)
3. "I'll Be Your Santa, Baby"
   (Stax 187)
      by Rufus Thomas(1973)
4. "Let It Snow! Let It Snow! Let It Snow!"
   (Decca 18741)
      by Connie Boswell (1946)
5. "Merry Christmas Baby"
   (Chess 1711)
      by Chuck Berry (1958)
6. "Santa Claus Is Back In Town"
   (RCA 447-0647)
      by Elvis Presley (1957)
7. "Santa Claus Wants Some Lovin'"
   (Stax 234)
      by Albert King (1974)

K. Bizarre Humor In Christmas Songs

While the humorous childhood perspectives presented in "I Saw Mommy Kissing Santa Claus" and "All I Want For Christmas (Is My Two Front Teeth)" are lighthearted extensions of youthful holiday concerns, the Yuletide season is also punctuated by off-the-wall recordings about vampires, wookiees, and other creatures from outer space. How do such bizarre tales capture the attention and interest of a record-buying public in the midst of religious worship and holiday shopping?

1. "Christmas Dragnet (Parts 1 and 2)"
   (Capitol 2671)
      by Stan Freberg (1953)
2. "Grandma Got Run Over By A Reindeer"
   (Soundwaves 4658)
      by Elmo 'N' Patsy (1981)
3. "Merry Christmas In The N.F.L."
   (Handshake 5308)
      by Willis "The Guard" and Vigorish (1980)
4. "Monster's Holiday"
   (Garpax 44171)
      by Bobby "Boris" Pickett and The Crypt Kickers (1962)
5. "Santa And The Satellite (Parts 1 and 2)"
   (Luniverse 107)
      by Buchanan and Goodman (1957)
6. "Santa And The Touchables"

(Rori 701)
> by Dickie Goodman (1961)

7. "What Can You Get A Wookiee For Christmas
(When He Already Owns A Comb)?"
(RSO 1058)
> by The Star Wars Intergalactic Droid Choir and Chorale (1980)

Although teachers should be certain to invite classroom contributions of recorded resources from students to demonstrate the breadth of Christmas song content, an album discography is provided in Table 6-B below. Instructors may utilize songs from these recent Christmas anthologies to "fill in the gaps" which will inevitably result from random student contributions. Beyond these albums, the Sound Recordings Archive at Bowling Green State University is available to educators to secure taped illustrations of specific holiday songs. Hopefully, the carols and Yuletide tunes played in future Decembers will become vital teaching tools, as well as signals of the always welcome Christmas recess.

Table 6-B

A Selected Discography of Anthology Albums
Featuring Traditional Christmas Songs,
Holiday Novelty Tunes, and Other
Seasonal Favorites,
1940-1988

Album Title (Record Number)	Year Of Release	Recording Artists Appearing On The Album
Christmas Comedy Classics (Capitol SL 9306)	1985	Mel Blanc, Stan Freberg, The Chipmunks, Yogi Yorgesson, and others
Christmas Is... Memorable Songs Of Christmas By Great Artists Of Our Time (Columbia P11417)	1972	Frank Sinatra, The Carpenters, Bing Crosby, The Mills Brothers, Julie Andrews, Patti Page and others
Christmas Rap (Profile PR 1247)	1987	Run-D.M.C., Sweet Tee, Dana Dane, The Showboys, Disco 4, and others
Christmas Rock Album (Priority SL 9465)	1986	Billy Squier, Queen, The Kinks, Dave Edmunds, Elvin Bishop, Elton John, and others
Cool Yule: A Collection Of Rockin' Stocking Stuffers (Rhino RNLP 70073)	1986	Chuck Berry, The Drifters, Ike and Tina Turner, Clarence Carter, James Brown, Jack Scott, and others
Dr. Demento's The Greatest Novelty Records Of All Time: Volume VI— Christmas (Phino RNLP 825)	1985	Spike Jones, Allan Sherman Tom Lehrer, Elmo 'N' Patsy, Cheech and Chong, and others

It's Christmas Album (RCA Loc 1035)	1957	Elvis Presley
It's Christmas Time Again (Stax MPS 8519)	1982	Little Johnny Taylor, Rufus Thomas, Albert King, The Staple Singers, Isaac Hayes, and others
The Little Drummer Boy (Kapp 3450)	1966	The Harry Simeone Chorale
Merry Christmas (Decca LP 8128)	1945	Bing Crosby
Mr. Santa's Boogie (Savoy SJL 1157)	1985	The Ravens, Little Esther Phillips, Big Maybelle, Charlie Parker, and others
Phil Spector's Christmas Album (Apple SW 3400)	1972	Darlene Love, The Ronettes, The Crystals, and others
Rhythm 'N' Blues Christmas (United Artists UA/La 654-R)	1976	Baby Washington, The Five Keys, B.B. King, Amos Milburn, Lowell Fulson, and others
Rockin' Christmas— The 50s (Rhino RNLP 066)	1984	The Penguins, Bobby Helms, The Moonglows, Marvin and Johnny, Ron Holden, and others
Rockin' Christmas— The 60s (Rhino RNLP 067)	1984	Santo and Johnny, The Turtles, Aretha Franklin, The Wailers, Bobby "Boris" Pickett and The Crypt Kickers, and others
Rockin' Little Christmas (MCA 25084)	1986	Brenda Lee, Dodie Stevens, The Surfaris, Chuck Berry, and others
The Stash Christmas Album 16 Blues And Jazz Classics (Stash ST 125)	1985	Fats Waller, Louis Armstrong, Ella Fitzgerald, Benny Goodman, and others
A Very Special Christmas (A&M SP 3911)	1987	The Pointer Sisters, Eurythmics, Whitney Houston, John Cougar Mellencamp, Sting, U2, Madonna, Bon Jovi, Stevie Nicks, Bryan Adams, Bruce Springsteen, Bob Seger, and others

Works Cited

Books

James H. Barnett, *The American Christmas: A Study In National Culture*. New York: Macmillan Company, 1954.

J.M. Colby and A. W. Purdue, *The Making Of The Modern Christmas*. Athens, Georgia: University Of Georgia Press, 1986.

Nancy Langstaff and John Langstaff, *The Christmas Revel Songbook: Carols, Processionals, Rounds, Ritual, and Childrens's Songs*. Boston: Dr. R. Godine, 1985.

Craig W. Pattillo (comp.), *Christmas On Record: Best Selling Christmas Singles And Albums Of The Past 40 Years*. Portland, Oregon: Braemar Books, 1983.

Articles

Mike Bailey, "Collecting Christmas Albums," *Goldmine*, No. 193 (December 18, 1987), pp. 12-16.

Russell W. Belk, "A Child's Christmas In America: Santa Claus As Deity, Consumption As Religion," *Journal Of American Culture*, X (Spring 1987), pp. 87-100.

B. Lee Cooper, "Christmas Songs: Audio Barometers Of Religious Tradition And Social Change In America, 1950-1987," *The Social Studies*, LXXIX (November/December 1988), pp. 278-280.

———. "Do You Hear What I Hear? Christmas Recordings As Audio Symbols Of Religious Tradition And Social Change In Contemporary America," *International Journal Of Instruction Media*, XVI, No. 2 (1988-89), in press.

Dr. Demento, "Santa And The Hot 100: The History Of Holiday Hit-Making," *Waxpaper*, II (October 28, 1977), pp. 18-20, 36.

Peter Doggett, "Rockin' Around The Christmas Tree!" *Record Collector*, No. 28 (December 1981), pp. 44-51.

Dave Harker, "The Average Popular Song," in *One For The Money: Politics And Popular Song* (London: Hutchinson and Company, Ltd., 1980), pp. 38-50.

Mark Lewisohn, "The Beatles' Christmas Records," *Record Collector*, No. 112 (December 1988), pp. 11-15.

Jon McAuliffe, "Christmas Collectibles," *Music World*, No. 80 (December 1980), pp. 6-12.

George Moonoogian, "Merry Christmas Baby," *Record Exchanger*, V (1978),' pp. 12-19.

———. "Remember When?" *Goldmine*, No. 31 (December 1978), p. 12.

Bob Munn, "Popular Christmas Music: A Collector's Guide," *Goldmine*, No. 115 (December 21, 1984), pp. 60-62.

Jordon Scoppa, "Picture This," *Music World*, No. 80 (December 1980), pp. 28-35.

Lydia Sherwood, "The Chipmunks Chatter—A Talk With Ross Bagdasarian, Jr.," *Goldmine*, No. 79 (December 1982), pp. 16-18, 23.

Joel Whitburn (comp.), "Christmas," in *Top Pop Albums, 1955-1985* (Menomonee Falls, Wisconsin: Record Research, Inc. 1985), pp. 462-466.

Joel Whitburn (comp.), "Christmas Singles, 1955-1986," in *The Pop Singles Annual, 1955-1986* (Menomonee Falls, Wisconsin: Record Research, Inc., 1987), pp. 666-668.

Unpublished Materials

B. Lee Cooper, "Do You Hear What I Hear: Investigating Songs Of The Yuletide Season, 1940-1988" (mimeographed paper and audio tape presentation at the 11th National Convention Of The American Culture Association in April 1989).

David A. Milberg (comp.), "Radio/TV Dave's Rock 'N' Roll Christmas: The Ultimate Collection Of Christmas Hits and Novelty Tunes" (mimeographed list of audio cassette recordings featuring original versions of songs performed over the past 48 years—1988 compilation), 20 pp.

William L. Schurk, "Santa Looked A Lot Like Daddy, And Daddy Looked A Lot Like Him: A 50-Year Perspective On Christmas Record Album Packaging And Artwork" (mimeographed paper presented at the 11th National Convention Of The American Culture Association In April 1989).

Chapter Seven
Death

"The Late Great Johnny Ace" was an especially thought-provoking song on Paul Simon's 1983 *Hearts And Bones* album. This tune, reminiscent of the classic death songs "American Pie" and "Abraham, Martin, and John," offers an individual's reflections on the frailty of human life. These three songs are more than just historical eulogies. They assess the psychological impact of death on an entire generation. This sounds extremely serious—hardly common fare for popular lyrics. Yet Paul Simon, Don McLean, and Dion DiMucci, along with a variety of other contemporary singers and songwriters, have succeeded in delivering informed and informative visions of human mortality.

The death theme is omnipresent in contemporary lyrics. Several scholars who have investigated this topic have elected to focus on the relatively narrow topic of teenage coffin songs. These studies, which emphasize narrative ballads that explore youthful experiences with either suicide or accidental death, usually examine recordings such as Mark Dinning's "Teen Angel," Jody Reynolds' "Endless Sleep," Ray Peterson's "Tell Laura I Love Her," The Shangri-Las' "Leader Of The Pack," and Dickey Lee's "Patches." Sociologist R. Serge Denisoff, a particularly perceptive popular music analyst, noted in 1983 that the short-lived popularity of love-lost-through-death songs was due to rapid cultural and political change during the mid-sixties. Specifically, Denisoff observed:

Several death songs in the latter half of the 1960s—"Ode To Billy Joe" and "Honey"—sold quite well. Still, the Teenage Coffin Song did not return after 1965. The demise of the Coffin Song correlates with the introduction of overt statements of social dissent as found in Barry McGuire's "Eve Of Destruction" and Glen Campbell's version of "Universal Soldier." Conversely, the "He's A Rebel," "Tell Laura I Love Her," "Patches" oriented songs were *passe* with the advent of the counterculture and its disavowal of the social ethic of the 1950s. . . ." (p. 121)

The notion of courtly love diminished during the early '60s, to be replaced by direct commentaries about overt physical attraction, spoken sexual desires, and frequent tales of non-marital liasons in the '70s and '80s. Similarly, the death theme became more visible and more broadly explored in popular lyrics after 1965. But many songs of death and dying were *not* simply teenage laments. These tunes explored more than drownings or accidental auto tragedies; they examined premediated homicides, spur-of-the-moment killings, and suicides. Even the gentle Beatles produced the delightfully sinister "Maxwell's Silver Hammer," a tune that rivals any Alfred Hitchcock thriller for murderous psychotic impact. What is even more interesting, though, is the fact that the death theme appears in such a variety of visages over the past forty years. Among these different perspectives are (a) aging and dying as natural life cycle events; (b) tragic, unexpected airline disasters and automobile crashes; (c) death as an accepted religious or existential event, (d) physical debilitation and demise attributed to drug abuse; (e) the passing of heroes or villains, (f) acts of murder and the slaying of murderers, (g) deaths of soldiers and other war-time casualties, and (h) suicide. As noted earlier, there are also a few epic hero songs which use the assassinations or accidental deaths of prominent political or musical figures as backdrops for generation-defining commentaries.

There is considerable discussion about aging in contemporary songs. From the tender side of thirty, Pete Townshend and The Who proclaim that they hope they die before they grow old. But "My Generation" isn't typical of the reflective songs about reaching maturity. Frank Sinatra offers two different assessments of fulfilled lives in "It Was A Very Good Year" and "My Way." The former tune chronicles the amorous evolution of a highly successful womanizer. The latter song, authored by Paul Anka, is a classic paen to individualism, freedom, and independence. Anticipating old age and hoping to establish a meaningful lifelong relationship is the theme of The Beatles' 1967 classic "When I'm Sixty-Four." But for those who are much closer to retirement age, the image of unfulfilled expectations seems to be far more common. Roy Clark obviously longs for "Yesterday, When I Was Young," while Peggy Lee questions in a disillusioned fashion "Is That All There Is?" The most frightening image of the aged—shoddy clothes, greasy hands, and snot running down his nose—is presented in Jethro Tull's grisly "Aqualung."

Death resulting from spectacular accidents is the backbone of many heroic tales. Trainwreck sagas about the brave engineer Casey Jones are legion in folk music. Within the popular song arena, automobile accidents and airline crashes constitute events which entail the unexpected loss of life. The tragedy of losing a loved one to a flight disaster is reported by The Everly Brothers in "Ebony Eyes." James Taylor's "Fire And Rain" explores a reflective reaction to an airplane crash, too. In addition to the previously cited car death songs by Mark Dinning and Ray Peterson, the foremost examples of four-wheel disasters are J. Frank Wilson and The Cavaliers' "Last Kiss," The Shangri-Las' "Give Us Your Blessing," and Jan and Dean's "Dead Man's Curve."

Death interrupts anticipated continuity. It is usually a complete surprise, a bitter shock. Death fosters grief, reverie, and a reminder of each person's mortality. Individual responses to life's finality vary in popular songs—just as they do in poetry, in literature, and in other forms of popular media. David Clayton-Thomas of Blood, Sweat, and Tears expresses confidence that "There'll be one child born in this world to carry on..." after he passes away. The peace of mind found in "And When I Die" is totally absent in the short-term anguish over personal losses in Thomas Wayne's "Tragedy," Bobby Goldsboro's "Honey," and Kenny Rogers and The First Edition's "Reuben James."

Several songs explore the death theme in an obscure or peculiar fashion. The 1960 Elvis Presley hit "Are You Lonesome Tonight?" was re-issued after his untimely death in 1977 and became more of a personal eulogy than a simple hymn of lost love. David Geddes reiterates a son-performing-in-honor-of-his-deceased-dad tale in "The Game Of The Season (A Blind Man In The Bleachers)."

Paul McCartney and Wings salute the murderous inclinations of daring secret agents in "Live And Let Die," while Kenny Rogers secures wisdom from a dying "Gambler" as they travel on a train allegedly bound to nowhere. Joe South sardonically observes that it doesn't matter what "Games People Play" because everyone eventually winds up riding to the cemetery in the back of a black limousine. Other recordings which focus on impending death include Blue Oyster Cult's "(Don't Fear) The Reaper," The Beatles' "Eleanor Rigby," Pacific Gas and Electric's "Are You Ready?," The Byrd's "Turn! Turn! Turn!," and Norman Greenbaum's "Spirit In The Sky."

Beyond references to the natural life cycle, beyond misfortunes of accidental demise, and beyond all other observations about inevitable mortality there are series of extremely violent lyrical perceptions. Death is not serene. It sometimes comes in a chemical disguise provided by Steppenwolf's dreaded "Pusher" and consumed by a "Snow Blind Friend." But drug abuse is most often a lonely form of self-victimization. In sharp contrast to solitary, debilitating deaths, the passing of figures that are larger than life—whether heroes or villains—is *always* noteworthy. In 1956 Lonnie Donegan resurrected the classic tale of the powerful, independent spike-driver "John Henry." One year before "The Ballad Of Davy Crockett" eulogized an authentic American hero of historic and mythic import. Fess Parker's tale of heroism was echoed by Marty Robbins' "Ballad Of The Alamo." Death was also the focus of lyrical historical exploration concerning British soldiers in Johnny Horton's "The Battle Of New Orleans" and Joan Baez's "The Night They Drove Old Dixie Down." The police and National Guard are viewed as contemporary death merchants rather than protectors of local peace and justice in "Ohio" by Crosby, Stills, Nash, and Young, in "Mad Dog" by Lee Michaels, and in "The Ballad Of Bonnie and Clyde" by Georgie Fame. Heros die, too. A soft-spoken giant of a man who saved his fellow miners from a cold, dark grave by sacrificing his own life is lauded by Jimmy Dean in "Big Bad John." Gene Pitney praises the killer of a gunslinger who needed to be killed in "(The Man Who Shot) Liberty Valance." Jim Stafford even offers praise for the cruel, cunning, mysterious, and death-dealing "Swamp Witch" who, in a moment of uncharacteristic humanism, provided a saving potion to spare a nearby town from plague.

Murder and mayhem seem miles away from teenage coffin songs as popular music themes. Yet homicide is a common feature in hit tunes throughout the past forty years. Traditional vengeance songs such as "Frankie and Johnny" and "Stagger Lee" have been successfully revived by Sam Cooke and Lloyd Price. Yet even more cold-blooded characters have found vinyl immortality since 1950. The wicked, killer-for-hire exploits of Bobby Darin's "Mack The Knife" were exceeded by the ungrateful, unprovoked, venomous attack by Al Wilson's "The Snake"; and the bloody deeds of Marty Robbins' "Big Iron" and Loren Greene's "Ringo" don't begin to match the psychotic bloodlust illustrated by Carole King's shotgun-wielding "Smackwater Jack" and The Beatles' mallet-carrying youth in "Maxwell's Silver Hammer."

The country music tradition continues to feed lyrical images of two-gun justice, violence, and death into the popular song arena. Johnny Cash must be content to sing the "Folsom Prison Blues" because he shot a man in Reno, just to watch him die. Obviously, casual homicide doesn't pay. Despite a mother's warning—"Don't Take Your Guns To Town"—the "Streets Of Laredo" death scene is re-enacted in several Marty Robbins songs, in the Kingston Trio's "Tom Dooley," in Eric Clapton's "I Shot The Sheriff," and in dozens of other country ballads. Of course, there are other reasons for committing murder. Vicki Lawrence seeks personal vengeance in "The Night The Lights Went Out In Georgia"; Steve Miller describes a man killed during a robbery in "Take The Money And Run"; Bobby Marchan depicts a jealous suitor who shoots his lover when he finds her entertaining his friends in "There's Something On Your Mind"; and, in a frightening example of cannibalism, The Buoys' speculate on the unspeakable disappearance of "Timothy."

Death at an elderly age is regrettable; death by accident is shocking and unexpected, but also unpreventable; murder is a singular event of individual violence motivated by greed, vengeance, fear, envy, anger, or insanity. But American society has reserved the most deliberate death-dealing activity for its young men. War is organized homicide. It is murder by carefully calculated plans, annihilation orchestrated by politicians, diplomats, generals, black marketeers, and numerous other "Masters of War." While Peter, Paul and Mary chide "The Cruel War" and sadly ask, "How many times must a canon ball fly?" in "Blowing In The Wind," The Kingston Trio state an even harsher truth: "Where have all the soldiers gone? Gone to graveyards everyone." The refrain to "Where Have All The Flowers Gone" indicts the military fighters, the politicians and diplomats, and the entire human race by asking, "When will they learn? When will they ever learn?" Victims of war include not only soldiers—as in "Billy, Don't Be A Hero" by Bo Donaldson, in "Billy And Sue" by Billy J. Kramer, and in "2+2=?" by The Bob Seger System—but also their friends and loved ones who are left to mourn battlefield deaths. Although Terry Nelson and C. Company intend to defend trauma-motivated actions in Vietnam, "The Battle Hymn of Lt. Calley" is actually a grisly reminder of the brutality, the arbitrariness, and the universal pain and death inflicted by military madness. As Edwin Starr shouted in 1970, "War! What is it good for? Absolutely nothing!" His conclusion is that only the undertaker benefits from organized killing.

The ultimate act of cowardice or bravery, of defiance or lunacy, is suicide. An individual's decision to choose death over life is the ultimate existential act. Songs which recount self-inflicted death are numerous, but generally melancholy and somewhat mysterious. Most often, an act of suicide is described by a forlorn lover, by a remaining relative, or by a sad and confused friend. Don McLean eulogizes Van Gogh's misanthropic artistic genius in "Vincent"; unidentified lovers mourn the loss of mates in "Endless Sleep," "Emma," and "Moony River"; an Indian couple produce a watery Romeo and Juliet death scene in "Running Bear"; Bobby Gentry is haunted by the tale of a young man who jumped off the Tallahachie Bridge in "Ode To Billy Joe"; and The Kinks and Simon and Garfunkel describe some very strange victims of society in "Richard Cory," "A Well Respected Man," and "A Most Peculiar Man."

A postscript to the death theme in popular music is found in the coda of tributes to political and singing/songwriting heroes who have died since 1950. Although John Lennon and Elvis Presley have been praised on vinyl in every imaginable fashion, no single popular music artist has yet garnered a more well-crafted, skillfully performed, and positively received recorded eulogy than Buddy

Holly. Don McLean's "American Pie" was not only a remembrance of the passing of a brilliant 1950s tunesmith, but also a metaphorical exploration of changes in American music from 1955 until the early 1970s. A song of similar historic scope, though totally political in nature and import, was Dion Dimucci's lament to the assassinated leaders Abraham Lincoln, the Rev. Martin Luther King, Jr., John F. Kennedy, and Robert F. Kennedy. The folkish song "Abraham, Martin, and John" was also issued by Moms Mabley, Smokey Robinson and The Miracles, and Tom Clay to cover all record-purchasing publics with versions of the popular sentimental hymn. Of course, the most all-inclusive tributes to contemporary musical artists have been produced by Tex Ritter's "I Dream Of A Hill-Billy Heaven" and The Righteous Brothers' "Rock And Roll Heaven."

In "American Pie" Don McLean utilizes the death of an individual popular music figure to symbolize the end of American innocence. Since Buddy Holly was killed in 1959, the year that marked the termination of rock's "Golden Age," McLean's commentary actually focuses on the evolution of recorded music thru the sixties. As in most epic tales, there are references to a broad spectrum of historical characters. In this case, nearly all are musicians. The lyrical chronology includes references to The Monotones ("The Book Of Love"), Marty Robbins ("A White Sport Coat And A Pink Carnation"), Elvis Presley, Bob Dylan, John Lennon, The Byrds, The Beatles, Mick Jagger ("Jumpin' Jack Flash") and The Rolling Stones, and Janis Joplin. For McLean, the passing of Buddy Holly—along with J.P. "The Big Bopper" Richardson and Ritchie Valens—was the ignition point for adolescent consciousness. A decade later the last vestiges of innocence were shredded by the horror of The Hell's Angel murders during the 1969 Altamount Music Festival. The image of Mick Jagger as Satan, contrasted to Buddy Holly's angelic demeanor, is obvious. But mortality remains the central spectre as the statement "The day the music died" is sung again and again.

Paul Simon, master songsmith, perceptive social analyst, and self-proclaimed child of the rock generation, seized the same historic scope as Don McLean to comment on death as a shaper of the social psyche. His song "The Late Great Johnny Ace" covers the 1954 to 1980 period. This melancholy tune focuses on three deaths. The strange Russian roulette, accidental suicide of rhythm and blues performer Johnny Ace is depicted as an unexplainably significant event in an adolescent's life. Ten years later the same music enthusiast labels 1964 as "The year of The Beatles...the year of The Stones." Yet the underlying event in the storyteller's image of the British musical invasion of America occurred in November 1963. Simon refers to 1964 as "a year after J.F.K." He and his girlfriend, obviously far removed from the scene of the Dallas assassination, are "...staying up all night and giving the days away" in mock revelry. The concluding incident in this brief tune is a stranger's 1980 announcement that John Lennon has died. No details of the New York City murder are mentioned. The singer adjourns to a bar, pumps coins into a jukebox with the stranger, and dedicates each song played to the late great Johnny Ace. The cycle of death is universal. It is complete from Ace to Lennon. This song updates Don McLean's meaning—"The day the music died," too.

Table 7-A
A Chronological List of Selected
Commercial Recordings Which Feature
Lyrical Commentaries On Death, 1953-1988

Year	Song Title (Record Number)	Artist
1953	"The Death Of Hank Williams" (King 1172)	Jack Cardell
1955	"The Ballad Of Davy Crockett" (Cadence 1256)	Bill Hayes
	"Sixteen Tons" (Capitol 3262)	Tennessee Ernie Ford
1956	"John Henry" (London 1650)	Lonnie Donegan and His Skiffle Group
1957	"(There'll Be) Peace In The Valley (For Me)" (RCA EP 4054)	Elvis Presley
1958	"Endless Sleep" (Demon 1507)	Jody Reynolds
	"Stagger Lee" (ABC-Paramount 9972)	Lloyd Price
	"Tom Dooley" (Capitol 4049)	The Kingston Trio
1959	"The Battle Of New Orleans" (Columbia 41339)	Johnny Horton
	"Don't Take Your Guns To Town" (Columbia 41313)	Johnny Cash
	"El Paso" (Columbia 41511)	Marty Robbins
	"The Hanging Tree" (Columbia 41325)	Marty Robbins
	"Mack The Knife" (Atco 6147)	Bobby Darin
	"Running Bear" (Mercury 71474)	Johnny Preston
	"Three Stars" (Crest 1057)	Tommy Dee, with Carol Kay and the Teen-Aires
	"Tragedy" (Fernwood 109)	Thomas Wayne
1960	"The Ballad Of The Alamo" (Columbia 41809)	Marty Robbins
	"Big Iron" (Columbia 41589)	Marty Robbins
	"Teen Angel" (MGM 12845)	Mark Dinning
	"Tell Laura I Love Her" (RCA 7745)	Ray Peterson
	"There's Something On Your Mind" (Fire 1022)	Bobby Marchan
1961	"Big Bad John" (Columbia 42175)	Jimmy Dean
	"Ebony Eyes" (Warner Brothers 5199)	The Everly Brothers

	"Frankie And Johnny" (Mercury 71859)	Brook Benton
	"I Dreamed Of A Hill-Billy Heaven" (Capitol 4567)	Tex Ritter
	"Moody River" (Dot 16209)	Pat Boone
1962	"(The Man Who Shot) Liberty Valance" (Musicor 1020)	Gene Pitney
	"Patches" (Smash 1758)	Dickey Lee
	"Where Have All The Flowers Gone?"(Capitol 4671)	The Kingston Trio
1963	"In The Summer Of His Years" (MGM 13203)	Connie Francis
1964	"Dead Man's Curve" (Liberty 55672)	Jan and Dean
	"Last Kiss" (Josie 923)	J. Frank Wilson and The Cavaleirs
	"Leader Of The Pack" (Red Bird 14)	The Shangri-Las
	"Ringo" (RCA 8444)	Lorne Greene
1965	"Eve Of Destruction" (Dunhill 4009)	Barry McGuire
	"Give Us Your Blessing" (Red Bird 030)	The Shangri-Las
	"The Streets Of Laredo" (Columbia 43313)	Johnny Cash
	"Turn! Turn! Turn!" (Columbia 43424)	The Byrds
	"The Universal Soldier" (Capitol 5504)	Glen Campbell
	"A Well Respected Man (Reprise 0420)	The Kinks
1966	"The Ballad Of The Green Berets" (RCA 8739)	S/Sgt Barry Sadler
	"Billy And Sue" (Hickory 1395)	B. J. Thomas
	"The Cruel War" (Warner Brothers 5809)	Peter, Paul and Mary
	"Eleanor Rigby" (Capitol 5715)	The Beatles
	"Green, Green Grass Of Home" (Parrot 40009)	Tom Jones
	"It Was A Very Good Year" (Reprise 0429)	Frank Sinatra
	"My Generation" (Decca 31877)	The Who
	"That's Life" (Reprise 0531)	Frank Sinatra
1967	"Ode To Billy Joe" (Capitol 5950)	Bobbie Gentry

1968	"Abraham, Martin, And John" (Laurie 3464)	Dion
	"Autumn Of My Life" (United Artists 50318)	Bobby Goldsboro
	"The Ballad Of Bonnie And Clyde" (Epic 10283)	Georgie Fame
	"Ballad Of John Dillinger" (Mercury 72836)	Billy Grammer
	"Delilah" (Parrot 40025)	Tom Jones
	"Folsom Prison Blues" (Columbia 44513)	Johnny Cash
	"Honey" (United Artists 50283)	Bobby Goldsboro
	"The Snake" (Soul City 767)	Al Wilson
	"A Tribute To A King" (Stax 248)	William Bell
	"2 + 2 = ?" (Capitol 2143)	The Bob Seger System
	"The Unknown Soldier" (Elektra 45628)	The Doors
1969	"And When I Die" (Columbia 45008)	Blood, Sweat, and Tears
	"Don't Cry Daddy" (RCA 47-9768)	Elvis Presley
	"Games People Play" (Capitol 2248)	Joe South
	"In The Ghetto" (RCA 47-9741)	Elvis Presley
	"In The Year 2525 (Exordium and Terminus)" (RCA 0174)	Zager and Evans
	"Is That All There Is?" (Capitol 2248)	Peggy Lee
	"Maxwell's Silver Hammer" (Apple 383—Album)	The Beatles
	"My Way" (Reprise 0817)	Frank Sinatra
	"Ruben James" (Reprise 0854)	Kenny Rogers and The First Edition
	"Six White Horses" (Epic 10540)	Tommy Cash
	"Yesterday, When I Was Young" (Dot 17246)	Roy Clark
	"You Gave Me A Mountain" (ABC 11174)	Frankie Laine
1970	"Are You Ready?" (Columbia 45158)	Pacific Gas and Electric
	"Fire And Rain" (Warner Brothers 7423)	James Taylor
	"Indiana Wants Me" (Rare Earth 5013)	R. Dean Taylor
	"Ohio" (Atlantic 2740)	Crosby, Stills, Nash and Young
	"Patches"	Clarence Carter

	(Atlantic 2748)	
	"Spirit In The Sky"	Norman Greenbaum
	(Reprise 0885)	
	"War"	Edwin Starr
	(Gordy 7101)	
1971	"American Pie"	Don McLean
	(United Artists 50856)	
	"Battle Hymn Of Lt. Calley"	C Company,
	(Plantation 73)	featuring
		Terry Nelson
	"Done Too Soon"	Neil Young
	(Uni 55278)	
	"The Night They Drove Old	Joan Baez
	Dixie Down"	
	(Vanguard 35138)	
	"One Tin Soldier (The Legend	Coven
	Of Billy Jack)"	
	(Warner Brothers 7509)	
	"Smackwater Jack"	Carole King
	(Ode 66019)	
	"Timothy"	The Buoys
	(Scepter 12275)	
	"When I'm Dead And Gone"	Bob Summers
	(MGM 14206)	
1972	"Alone Again (Naturally)"	Gilbert O'Sullivan
	(MAM 3619)	
	"Conquistador"	Procol Harum
	(A&M 1347)	
	"Freddie's Dead"	Curtis Mayfield
	(Curtom 1975)	
	"Papa Was A Rollin' Stone"	The Temptations
	(Gordy 7121)	
	"Vincent"	Don McLean
	(United Artists 50887)	
1973	"Daisy A Day"	Jud Strunk
	(MGM 14463)	
	"The Night The Lights Went	Vicki Larence
	Out In Georgia"	
	(Bell 45303)	
	"Swamp Witch"	Jim Stafford
	(MGM 14496)	
1974	"Billy, Don't Be A Hero"	Bo Donaldson and
	(ABC 11435)	The Heywoods
	"I Shot The Sheriff"	Eric Clapton
	(RSO 409)	
	"The Night Chicago Died"	Paper Lace
	(Mercury 73492)	
	"Rock And Roll Heaven"	The Righteous
	(Haven 7002)	Brothers
	"Seasons In The Sun"	Terry Jacks
	(Bell 45432)	
1975	"Emma"	Hot Chocolate
	(Big Tree 16031)	
	"Golden Years"	David Bowie
	(RCA 10441)	

	"The Last Game Of The Season (Blind Man In The Bleachers)" (Big Tree 16052)	David Geddes
1976	"Bohemian Rapsody" (Elektra 45297)	Queen
	"Sixteen Tons" (Atlantic 3323)	The Don Harrison Band
	"Take The Money And Run" (Capitol 4260)	The Steve Miller Band
	"The Wreck Of The Edmund Fitzgerald" (Reprise 1369)	Gordon Lightfoot
1977	"From Graceland To The Promised Land" (MCA 40804)	Merle Haggard and The Strangers
	"The King Is Gone" (Scorpion 135)	Ronnie McDowell
	"My Way" (RCA PB-11165)	Elvis Presley
1978	"Copacabana (At The Copa)" (Arista 0339)	Barry Manilow
	"The Gambler" (United Artists 1250)	Kenny Rogers
	"Only The Good Die Young" (Columbia 10750)	Billy Joel
1980	"(Ghost) Riders In The Sky (Arista 0582)	The Outlaws
	"He Stopped Loving Her Today" (Epic 50867)	George Jones
1981	"Grandma's Song" (Warner Brothers 49790)	Gail Davies
1982	"Dirty Laundry" (Asylum 69894)	Don Henley
1983	"The Late, Great Johnny Ace" (Warner Brothers 23942-Album)	Paul Simon
	"The Ride" (Columbia 03778)	David Allan Coe
1984	"Born In The U.S.A." (Columbia 04680)	Bruce Springsteen
	"Do They Know It's Christmas" (Columbia 04749)	Band Aid
1985	"All She Wants To Do Is Dance" (Geffen 29065)	Don Henley
	"Leader Of The Pack" (Atlantic 89478)	Twisted Sister
	"Nightshift" (Motown 1773)	The Commodores
	"Smuggler's Blues" (MCA 52546)	Glenn Frey
1986	"Spirit In The Sky" (I.R.S. 53880)	Doctor and The Medics
	"That's Life" (Warner Brothers 28511)	David Lee Roth
	"War" (Columbia 06432)	Bruce Springsteen

1987	"Smoking Gun"	The Robert
	(Mercury 888343)	Cray Band
1988	"Candle In The Wind"	Elton John
	(MCA 53196)	

Works Cited

Books

Howard F. Banney (comp.), *Return To Sender: The First Complete Discography Of Elvis Tribute And Novelty Records, 1956-1986*. Ann Arbor, Michigan; Pierian Press, 1987.

Robert Duncan, *Only The Good Die Young: The Rock 'N' Roll Book Of The Dead*. New York: Harmony Books, 1986.

Robert Somma (ed.), *No One Waved Good-Bye: A Casualty Report On Rock And Roll*. New York: Outerbridge and Dienstfrey, 1971.

Articles

Robert A. Armour and J. Carol Williams, "Death," in *Consise Histories Of American Popular Culture*, edited by M. Thomas Inge (Westport, Connecticut: Greenwood Press, 1982), pp. 86-96.

Donald Allport Bird, Stephen C. Holder, and Diane Sears, "Walrus Is Greek For Corpse: Rumor And The Death Of Paul McCartney," *Journal Of Popular Culture*, X (Summer 1976), pp. 110-121.

B. Lee Cooper, "Death," in *A Resource Guide To Themes In Contemporary American Song Lyrics, 1950-1985* (Westport, Connecticut: Greenwood Press, 1986), pp. 49-63.

_____ "The Outsider In Popular Music," in *Images Of American Society In Popular Music: A Guide To Reflective Teaching* (Chicago: Nelson-Hall, Inc., 1982), pp. 77-87.

B. Lee Cooper and Larry S. Haverkos, "Roll Over Beethoven," *Garfield Lake Review*, (Spring 1987), pp. 77-81.

R. Serge Denisoff, "Death Songs And Teenage Roles," in *Sing A Song Of Social Significance* (Bowling Green, Ohio: Bowling Green State University Popular Press, 1972), pp. 171-176.

_____ " 'Teen Angel': Resistance, Rebellion, And Death—Revisited: *Journal Of Popular Culture*, XVI (Spring 1983), pp. 116-122.

Peter Grendysa, "Chuck Willis' Two-Sided Epitaph Still Haunts Studio Musicians Today," *Record Collector's Monthly*, No. 16 (January 1984), pp. 1, 5.

Bob Kinder, "Rock And Roll Epitaph," in *The Best Of The First: The Early Days Of Rock And Roll* (Chicago: Adams Press, 1986), pp. 24-40.

James R. McDonald, "Suicidal Rage: An Analysis Of Hardcore Punk Lyrics," *Popular Music And Society*, XI (Fall 1987), pp. 91-102.

Michael Roos, "Fixin' To Die: The Death Theme In The Music Of Bob Dylan," *Popular Music And Society*, VIII, Nos 3/4 (1982), pp. 103-116.

Cynthia Rose, "Raves From The Grave: The Eternal Appeal Of Rock's Death Songs," *History Of Rock*, No. 29 (1982), pp. 574-575.

John C. Thrush and George S. Paulus, "The Concept Of Death In Popular Music: A Social Psychological Perspective," *Popular Music And Society*, VI (1979), pp. 219-228.

Nick Tosches, "Death In Hi-Fi, Or First Taste Of Tombstone," *Waxpaper*, III (March 3, 1978), pp. 18-19, 39.

Unpublished Materials

Richard Aquila, "Why We Cried: John Lennon And American Culture" (mimeographed paper presented at the 11th National Convention of The Popular Culture Association in March 1981).

Bruce Redfern Buckley, "Frankie And Her Men: A Study Of The Interrelations Of Popular And Folk Traditions" (Ph.D.: Indiana University, 1962).

B. Lee Cooper, R. Serge Denisoff, and William L. Schurk, "Buddy Holly's Last Tour: Event And Reaction" (mimeographed paper, audio tape, and panel discussion presented at the 7th Annual Convention Of The Midwest Popular Culture Association in October 1979).

Howard A. Doughty, "Phil Ochs: The Death And Transfiguration Of A Songwriter" (mimeographed paper presented at the 6th National Convention of The American Culture Association in March 1984).

Christine Ferreira, "Marvin Gaye: The Life/Work And Death Of A Trouble Man (mimeographed paper presented at the 15th National Convention of The Popular Culture Association in April 1985).

Richard D. Ralston, "Bad Dude Or Common Criminal? The Interrelationship Of Contemporary And Folk Values In The Ballad Of Stagolee" (mimeographed paper presented at the 14th National Convention Of the Popular Culture Association in March 1984).

Chapter Eight
Food and Drink

(with William L. Schurk)

America's food industry has attracted the attention of authors for decades. Even the use of background muzak in dining establishments has been investigated by popular culture researchers. It seems somewhat strange, therefore, that lyrical commentaries about culinary activities have received so little scholarly attention. Why have the recorded observations about cooking, eating, and socializing been overlooked? This study explores the imagery of America's eating and drinking through the lyrics of popular songs.

Food and drink are central factors in modern lyrics. In many cases, though, it is difficult to perceive any rationale for references to saltwater taffy, shortnin' bread, pumpkin pie, coconuts, mashed potatoes, and cherry wine in popular songs. The necessity of eating, combined with the plethora of available foods and liquid refreshments, seems to make musical commentaries about culinary activities random and undirected. Yet after careful examination, several distinct patterns of food-related observations become apparent. Some identifications are strictly serendipitous in regard to individual food items; others are quite specific for either logical or symbolic reasons; and still others utilize the social setting of dining as a means of communicating varying personal feelings.

This study identifies more than 200 food-related recordings and places them in five distinct categories. Although some of the songs feature overlapping ideas, and a few of the titles are used in two or more categories, the following descriptive system seems reasonable, functional, and inclusive. The specific categories represented are: (a) focal point, (b) personal desire, (c) social setting, (d) symbol or image, and (e) nonsense use. The definition for each of these areas is provided below, along with tables of songs which illustrate each category.

A. Focal Point

Every song has a title. This word or phrase becomes the formal identification tag for a distinct melody. For most musical compositions, the title is drawn directly from the lyrical content of the song. However, many tunes are strictly instrumental. In these cases the composer, the arranger, the performer, or someone else involved in the recording session arbitrarily assigns a title to the composition. Not infrequently, food or drink names are selected for song titles. Without rational explanation, Booker T and The M.G.'s cooked up "Green Onions," Al Hirt served "Java," Ray Charles belted down "One Mint Julep," and Herb Alpert and The Tijuana Brass sweetened the music scene with "Whipped Cream." Other instrumental recordings with food-related titles are provided in Table 8-A.

Table 8-A

Recordings Illustrating The Focal Point Theme

Song Title and Record Number	Recording Artist	Date of Release
"Apples And Bananas" (Dot 16697)	Lawrence Welk	1965
"Apricot Brandy" (Elektra 45647)	Rhinoceros	1969
"Cotton Candy" (RCA 8346)	Al Hirt	1964
"Fried Onions" (London 1810)	Lord Rockingham's XI	1958
"Gravy Waltz" (Dot 16457)	Steve Allen	1963
"Green Onions" (Stax 127)	Booker T. and The M.G.'s	1962
"Hot Cakes! 1st Serving" (Chess 1850)	Dave "Baby" Cortez	1963
"Hot Pepper" (RCA 8051)	Floyd Cramer	1962
"Java" (RCA 8280)	Al Hirt	1964
"Jellybread" (Stax 131)	Booker T. and The M.G.'s	1963
"Mo-Onions" (Stax 142)	Booker T. and The M.G.'s	1964
"My Sweet Potato" (Stax 196)	Booker T. and The M.G.'s	1966
"One Mint Julep" (Impulse 200)	Ray Charles	1961
"Pass The Peas" (People 607)	JB's	1972
"Peas 'N' Rice" (Prestige 450)	Freddie McCoy	1967
"Saltwater Taffy" (Legend 124)	Morty Jay and The Surferin' Cats	1963
"Whipped Cream" (A & M 760)	Herb Alpert and The Tijuana Brass	1965

B. Personal Desire

Food themes often appear in song lyrics as expressions of personal desire. These feelings range from a child's hunger for "Shortnin' Bread" or "Peanut Butter" to adult craving for coffee or alcohol—"Another Cup of Coffee," "Java Jive," "Cigarettes and Coffee Blues," "Bottle of Wine," "Drinking Wine Spo-Dee-O-Dee," and "Scotch and Soda." In times of extreme physical stress, even non-alcoholic liquids seem desirable. Such situations are presented in the desert format of "Cool Water" and in the prison scene of "Jailer, Bring Me Water."

Personal slavery to excesses of food or drink is also lyrically documented, though usually from a tongue-in-cheek perspective. Jimmy Buffett describes the listless, unobligated life of an alcoholic in "Margaritaville"; and Larry Groce condemns his weakness for taco chips, Ho-Ho's, Ding-Dong's, and moon pies over more healthful natural foods in "Junk Food Junkie." Additional recordings illustrating this category of songs are provided in Table 8-B.

Table 8-B

Recordings Illustrating The Personal Desire Theme

Song Title and Record Number	Recording Artist	Date of Release
"Animal Crackers In My Soup" (Musicor 1235)	Gene Pitney	1967
"Another Cup Of Coffee" (Mercury 72266)	Brook Benton	1964
"Bottle Of Wine" (Atco 6491)	The Fireballs	1967
"Cigarettes And Coffee Blues" (Columbia 42701)	Marty Robbins	1963
"Cool Water" (Top Rank 2055)	Jack Scott	1960
"Drinking Wine Spo-Dee O'Dee" (Mercury 73374)	Jerry Lee Lewis	1973
"I'll Just Have A Cup Of Coffee (Then I'll Go)" (Mercury 71732)	Claude Gray	1961
"Jailer, Bring Me Water" (Reprise 0260)	Trini Lopez	1964
"Java Jive" (Decca 3432)	The Ink Spots	1941
"Junk Food Junkie" (Warner Brothers 8165)	Larry Groce	1976
"Little Ole Wine Drinker, Me" (Reprise 0608)	Dean Martin	1967
"Margaritaville" (ABC 12254)	Jimmy Buffett	1977
"Peanut Butter" (Arvee 5027)	The Marathons	1961
"Scotch And Soda" (Capitol 4740)	The Kingston Trio	1962
"Shortnin' Bread" (Madison 136)	The Bell Notes	1960
"Spill The Wine" (MGM 14118)	Eric Burdon and War	1970
"Tiny Bubbles" (Reprise 0507)	Don Ho	1966

C. Social Setting

It is impossible to assess food references in popular recordings without acknowledging the key influence of social settings in food-related songs. "Tea For Two" is not simply a lyrical commercial for non-alcoholic beverages, but an intimate description of a quiet interlude; "Champagne Jam" is a commentary about a wild party; and "Scotch and Soda" is not simply an invitation for a friendly drink, but a lightheaded (and similarly lighthearted) tale about being overwhelmed by the presence of an infatuating woman. Even The Clovers' comic tale of marital entrapment which was the result of imbibing more than "One Mint Julep" relies upon physical setting and the social environment rather than just the liquid refreshment mentioned to produce the desired meaning.

Public dining arenas of diverse reputations, peopled by an array of pickled patrons and spicy waitresses, are grandly depicted in contemporary lyrics. Food is always present—but usually only as a means of defining the social context in the dining environment. According to Arlo Guthrie, a customer can secure absolutely anything desired at "Alice's Rock and Roll Restaurant." Obviously, there is a menu beyond the mere menu. Although the "Copacabana (At The Copa)" features high class cuisine, fancy drinks, passionate dancing, and homocidal intrigue, most songs illustrate more plebian settings and much more humble entrees. Listeners are invited to go "(Down At) Papa Joe's," to "The House Of Blue Lights," to the "Sugar Shack," the "Rib Joint," the "Hotel California," and even to "Smokey Joe's Cafe." The latter establishment features a plate of chili beans and a jealous chef carrying a lengthy butcher knife. This feisty cook objects to customer flirtation with his table-attending girlfriend, too.

Songs depicting private parties also highlight special foods, beverages appropriate to the festivities, and ample physical surroundings for both culinary and sexual indulgence. Whether romping in the grass on "Blueberry Hill," accepting an invitation to consume a seemingly endless array of gourmet delights from an over-anxious matron in "Come On-A My House," eating a simple "Cheeseburger In Paradise," returning from overseas to the joy of grilled hamburgers "Back In the U.S.A.," "Having A Party" with coke, pretzels, and potato chips, feasting on Cajun cooking at a "Jambalaya (on the Bayou)," devouring a ghoulish "Dinner With Drac," enjoying a southern community picnic in "Jackson," or attempting to fry up an evening meal in a "Haunted House," the foodstuffs mentioned in the lyrics both give and gain meaning via the special social context.

Highly emotional eating environments are common in contemporary recordings. Joyous occasions of youth, punctuated with popcorn and cotton candy, are illustrated in "Saturday Night At The Movies" and "Palisades Park." But more chilling, emotion-draining moments occur during the "Ode To Billie Jo" when a recently-discovered suicide is discussed over a family dinner. Worse yet, cannibalism is even suggested in "Timothy," the haunting tale of a bizarre mining disaster in which the survivors express guilt over the mysterious loss of their friend. And Wilson Pickett cannot bear to watch, let alone recount, what is being eaten, drunk, or smoked in the pad where "Mama Told Me Not to Come." Finally, a southern plant of questionable nutritious value is the focal point of Tony Joe White's story about a family of thieves and murderers. "Polk Salad Annie" is not a lesson in truck patch gardening; it is a tale of economic depravation, malnutrition, and resulting violence. Other recordings illustrating the social setting theme are listed in Table 8-C.

Table 8-C

Recordings Illustrating The Social Setting Theme

Song Title and Record Number	Recording Artist	Date of Release
"Alice's Rock And Roll Restaurant" (Reprise 0877)	Arlo Guthrie	1969
"Back In The U.S.A." (Chess 1729)	Chuck Berry	1959
"Back In The U.S.A." (Asylum 45519)	Linda Ronstadt	1978
"Banana Boat (Day-O)" (RCA 6771)	Harry Belafonte	1957
"Banana Boat Song" (Glory 249)	The Tarriers	1957
"Blueberry Hill" (Imperial 5407)	Fats Domino	1956
"Breakfast For Two" (Fantasy 758)	Country Joe McDonald	1975
"Breakfast In Bed" (Atlantic 2606)	Dusty Springfield	1969
"Champagne Jam" (Polydor 14504)	The Atlanta Rhythm Section	1978
"Cheesburger In Paradise" (ABC 12358)	Jimmy Buffett	1978
"Chug-A-Lug" (Smash 1926)	Roger Miller	1964
"Come On-A My House" (Columbia 39467)	Rosemary Clooney	1951
"Copacabana (At The Copa)" (Arista 0339)	Barry Manilow	1978
"Dinner With Drac" (Cameo 130)	John "The Cool Ghoul" Zacherle	1958
"(Down At) Papa Joe's" (Sound Stage 2507)	The Dixiebelles, with Cornbread and Jerry	1963
"Greasy Spoon" (Federal 12508)	Hank Marr	1964
"Haunted House" (Hi 2076)	Jumpin' Gene Simmons	1964
"Having A Party" (RCA 8036)	Sam Cooke	1962
"Hotel California" (Asylum 45386)	The Eagles	1977
"The House Of Blue Lights" (Mercury 70627)	Chuck Miller	1955
"Jackson" (Reprise 0595)	Nancy Sinatra and Lee Hazlewood	1967
"Jambalaya (On The Bayou)" (Fantasy 689)	The Blue Ridge Rangers	1973

"Long Tall Glasses (I Can Dance)" (Warner Brothers 8043)	Leo Sayer	1975
"Mama Told Me (Not To Come)" (Dunhill 4239)	Three Dog Night	1970
"Mama Told Me Not To Come" (Atlantic 2909)	Wilson Pickett	1972
"Meet Me At Grandma's Joint" (Savoy 1123)	Georgie Stevenson	1954
"Ode To Billie Jo" (Capitol 5950)	Bobbie Gentry	1967
"One Mint Julep" (Atlantic 963)	The Clovers	1952
"Palisades Park" (Swan 4106)	Freddy Cannon	1962
"Polk Salad Annie" (Monument 1104)	Tony Joe White	1969
"Rib Joint" (Savoy 1505)	Sam Price	1957
"A Rose And A Baby Ruth" (ABC-Paramount 9765)	George Hamilton IV	1956
"Saturday Night At The Movies" (Atlantic 2260)	The Drifters	1964
"Scotch And Soda" (Capitol 4740)	The Kingston Trio	1962
"Scotch And Soda" (Viva 29543)	Ray Price	1983
"Smokey Joe's Cafe" (Atco 6059)	The Robins	1955
"Stella's Candy Store" (Yardbird 1326)	Sweet Marie	1973
"Sugar Shack" (Dot 16487)	Jimmy Gilmer and The Fireballs	1963
"Sunday Barbecue" (Capitol 3997)	Tennessee Ernie Ford	1958
"Tea For Two" (Atco 6286)	Nino Tempo and April Stevens	1964
"Timothy" (Scepter 12275)	The Bouys	1971
"Tip On In" (Excello 2285)	Slim Harpo	1967
"Wedding Cake" (MGM 14034)	Connie Francis	1969
"Whatch' Got Cookin' In Your Oven Tonight" (MCA 52297)	The Thrasher Brothers	1983
"Whiskey, Women, And Loaded Dice" (King 4628)	Stick McGhee	1954

D. Symbol or Image

Recordings which use food and drink in a symbolic style tend to emphasize the senses of sight and taste in order to communicate certain personal attitudes and feelings. For example, the desire for affection is often expressed in terms of hunger. Songs illustrating this type of unfulfilled longing are Paul Revere's "Hungry" and Bruce Springsteen's "Hungry Heart." The Coasters and Otis Blackwell present even more colorful language in expanding upon this hunger-oriented metaphor in "I'm A Hog For You" and "I'd Rather Kiss You Than Eat."

Images of the good life—wealth, security, health, and overall well-being—are often communicated through verbal pictures of feasts of unimaginable proportion. Such extremes of culinary luxury are portrayed in "Big Rock Candy Mountain" and "Long Tall Glasses (I Can Dance)." Matchless liquid satisfaction is displayed in "Drinkin' Wine Spo-Dee-O-Dee." Food is also employed to illustrate the natural order of a continuing personal relationship and the mutual affection felt by a loving couple. Little Milton declares that if his passion isn't genuine, then "Grits Ain't Groceries" and eggs ain't poultry. In similar fashion, O.C. Smith used the images of "Little Green Apples" to symbolize Divine support for his loving feelings.

Sweetness, communicated symbolically in the form of candy, honey, and sugar, is common referent not only to the Chicago Bears' Walter Payton, but also to many, many passionate men and women depicted in popular songs. Whether a "Candy Girl" or a "Candy Man," the object of audio affection is always instructed to "Save Your Sugar For Me." Not surprisingly, even interracial dating is couched in sweet symbolism by Neil Young in "Cinnamon Girl" and by The Rolling Stones in "Brown Sugar." More common references to loved ones include "Sugar Dumpling," "Sugar Plum," "Sugar Sugar," "Sweets For My Sweet," and "What A Sweet Thing That Was." Of course, not all loving relationships last forever. To insure continued affection, Dusk suggests "Treat Me Like A Good Piece Of Candy"; The Guess Who are more emphatic in declaring that there will be "No Sugar Tonight" if proper standards of behavior aren't followed.

Unsuccessful relationships are also exhibited in food-related imagery. The Osmonds argue that a poor dating experience with "One Bad Apple" shouldn't permanently spoil a young girl's perspective toward other men. William Bell warns that "You Don't Miss Your Water" until the well of new suitors has gone dry. Yet another recording emphasizes the ability of one person to see value in another even though that individual has been ignored and rejected by a previous lover. This attitude appears in "One Man's Leftovers (Is Another Man's Feast)." Finally, The Newbeats and Robert John described in kitchen-centered terms the break-up of a relationship because the girl preferred eating chicken and dumplings with a new boyfriend rather than preparing "Bread And Butter" and toast and jam for her former beau. Additional records depicting the use of food-related imagery are provided in Table 8-D.

Table 8-D

Recordings Illustrating The Symbol Or Image Theme

Song Title and Record Number	Recording Artist	Date of Release

Record Number	Artist	Release
"Apples, Peaches, Pumpkin Pie" (Smash 2086)	Jay and The Techniques	1967
"Big Rock Candy Mountain (Era 3019)	Dorsey Burnette	1960
"Bread And Butter" (Hickory 1269)	The Newbeats	1964
"Bread And Butter" (Motown 1664)	Robert John	1983
"Brown Sugar" (Rolling Stones 19100)	The Rolling Stones	1971
"Candy Girl" (Vee-Jay 539)	The Four Seasons	1963
"Candy Man" (MGM 14320)	Sammy Davis, Jr.	1972
"Candy Man" (Monument 447)	Roy Orbison	1961
"Cinnamon Girl" (Reprise 0911)	Neil Young	1970
"Coconut Woman" (RCA 6885)	Harry Belafonte	1957
"Don't Mess With My Man" (Ron 328)	Irma Thomas	1960
"Drinkin' Wine Spo-Dee-O-Dee" (Atlantic 873)	Stick McGhee	1949
"Girl With The Hungry Eyes" (Grunt 11921)	Jefferson Starship	1980
"Grits Ain't Groceries (All Around The World)" (Checker 1212)	Little Milton	1969
"How Blue Can You Get" (Decca 27648)	Louis Jordan	1951
"Hungry" (Columbia 43678)	Paul Revere and The Raiders	1966
"Hungry Heart" (Columbia 11391)	Bruce Springsteen	1980
"I Can't Help Myself" (Motown 1076)	The Four Tops	1965
"I'd Rather Kiss You Than Eat" (Cub 9092)	Otis Blackwell	19??
"I'm A Hog For You" (Atco 6146)	The Coasters	1959
"Let Me Go Home, Whiskey" (Aladdin 3164)	Amos Milburn	1953
"Little Green Apples" (Columbia 44616)	O.C. Smith	1968
"Long Tall Glasses (I Can Dance)" (Warner Brothers 8043)	Leo Sayer	1975
"Maneater" (RCA 13354)	Daryl Hall and John Oates	1982

"No Sugar Tonight" (RCA 0325)	Guess Who	1970
"One Bad Apple" (MGM 14193)	The Osmonds	1971
"One Man's Leftovers (Is Another Man's Feast)" (Hot Wax 7009)	100 Proof Aged In Soul	1971
"One Mint Julep" (Atlantic 963)	The Clovers	1952
"Save Your Sugar For Me" (Monument 1206)	Tony Joe White	1970
"Sugar Dumpling" (RCA 8631)	Sam Cooke	1965
"Sugar Plum" (Mercury 71975)	Ike Clanton	1962
"Sugar, Sugar" (Calendar 1008)	The Archies	1969
"Sugar, Sugar" (Atlantic 2722)	Wilson Pickett	1970
"Sweets For My Sweet" (Atlantic 2117)	The Drifters	1961
"Treat Me Like A Good Piece Of Candy" (Bell 45148)	Dusk	1971
"You Don't Miss Your Water" (Stax 116)	William Bell	1962

E. Nonsense Use

This final category of food-related songs may seem to be closely related to the arbitrary title system cited in the initial section of this chapter. It is. Various dance crazes, and tunes which provide the rhythms for dancing, have been assigned random food titles with no apparent rationale. This trend is readily noted in "Mashed Potatoes." A particularly bouncy, lyrically benign set of songs produced during the late 1960s became known as "Bubble Gum Music." The titles of recordings from this genre reflected hunger for affection in food-related titles such as "Chewy Chewy," "Goody Goody Gumdrops," "Jam Up Jelly Tight," and "Yummy Yummy Yummy."

There is also an off-the-wall group of recordings which utilize the names of specific foods as background elements to achieve a sense of comic absurdity. The Kingsmen's vocal interjections of artichokes, green beans, broccoli, cabbage, corn and so on in the tale of the "Jolly Green Giant" illustrates this approach. Other bizarre formats for food commentaries appear in "Eat It," "Does your Chewing Gum Lose Its Flavor (On The Bedpost Overnight)," "I Love Rocky Road," "On Top Of Spaghetti," and "Rubber Biscuit." Humorous tales are also concocted about potent elixurs, special medications, and missing meat delicacies. These recordings include "Love Potion No. 9," "Jeremiah Peabody's Poly Unsaturated Quick Dissolving Fast Acting Pleasant Tasting Green And Purple Pills," and "Who Stole The Keeshka?" Examples of other recordings which illustrate this category are listed in Table 8-E.

Recordings Illustrating The Nonsense Use Theme

Song Title and Record Number	Recording Artist	Date of Release
"Bacon Fat" (Epic 9196)	Andre Williams	1957
"Beans In My Ears" (Phillips 40198)	The Serendipity Singers	1964
"Bubble Gum Music" (Buddah 78)	Rock And Roll Dubble Bubble Trading Card Co. of of Philadelphia—19141	1969
"Chewy Chewy" (Buddah 70)	The Ohio Express	1968
"Coconut" (RCA 0718)	Nilsson	1972
"(Do The) Mashed Potatoes" (Dade 1804)	Nat Kendrick and The Swans	1960
"Does Your Chewing Gum Lose Its Flavor (On The Bedpost Over Night)" (Dot 15911)	Lonnie Donegan and His Skiffle Group	1961
"The Eggplant That Ate Chicago" (Go Go 100)	Dr. West's Medicine Show and Junk Band	1966
"The Fish" (Cameo 192)	Bobby Rydell	1961
"Goody Goody Gumdrops" (Buddah 71)	The 1910 Fruitgum Co.	1968
"Gravy (For My Mashed Potatoes)" (Cameo 219)	Dee Dee Sharp	1962
"Hot Pastrami" (Dot 16453)	The Dartells	1963
"Hot Pastrami And Mashed Potatoes" (Roulette 4488)	Joey Dee and The Starliters	1963
"I Love Rocky Road" (Rock 'N' Roll 03998)	Weird Al Yankovic	1983
"Jam Up Jelly Tight" (ABC 11247)	Tommy Roe	1970
"Jelly Jungle (Of Orange Marmalade)" (Buddah 41)	The Lemon Pipers	1968
"Jeremiah Peabody's Poly Unsaturated Quick Dissolving Fast Acting Pleasant Tasting Green And Purple Pills" (Mercury 71843)	Ray Stevens	1961
"Jolly Green Giant" (Wand 172)	The Kingsmen	1965
"Love Potion No. 9" (United Aritsts 180)	The Clovers	1959

"Mashed Potato Time" (Cameo 212)	Dee Dee Sharp	1962
"Mashed Potatoes" (Checker 1006)	Steve Alaimo	1962
"Mashed Potatoes U.S.A." (King 5672)	James Brown	1962
"On Top Of Spaghetti" (Kapp 526)	Tom Glazer and The Do-Re-Mi Children's Chorus	1963
"Peppermint Twist" (Roulette 4401)	Joey Dee And The Starliters	1962
"The Popcorn" (King 6240)	James Brown	1969
"Strawberry Shortcake" (Smash 2142)	Jay and The Techniques	1968
"Yummy Yummy Yummy" (Buddah 38)	The Ohio Express	1968
"Rubber Biscuit" (Josie 803)	The Chips	1956
"Rubber Biscuit" (Atlantic 3 64)	The Blues Brothers	1979
"Who Stole The Keeshka?" (Select 719)	The Matys Brothers	1963

There are few broad conclusions that can be drawn from this preliminary investigation of food-related recordings. It is amazing to note the frequency, variety, and breadth of meaning attributed to various foods in contemporary songs. The fact that pizza was seldom mentioned, despite its high profile in the teenage diet, is of singular interest. The distinctions that can be drawn between food as nutritional substance and food as either symbolic reference or social environment definer is also genuinely significant. Finally, it is relatively easy to understand why the most common elements of the social life are often the most easily overlooked and most often downplayed in social research. This is why popular culture studies can be helpful in attempting to understand human behavior. Hopefully, contemporary recordings about the emotional conflicts of a "Junk Food Junkie" and the superstitious belief in "Love Potion No. 9" can provide ample food for future scholarly thought.

Table 8-F

A Selected Discography of 78 R.P.M. Records and
Albums (LP) Containing References To Dining,
Food, and Related Culinary Activities*

Theme Category and Song Title	*Recording Artist*	*Record Number and Release Format*
Breakfast		
"Breakfast"	Alan Hull	Elektra EKS 75075 (LP)
"Breakfast Boo-ga-loo"	Gary Farr	Atco SD 7034 (LP)

*Created by William L. Schurk under the title " 'Yes, We Have No Bananas': The Image Of Food And Eating In Popular Song" for presentation at the 12th Annual Meeting of the Midwest Popular Culture Association in Bloomington, Indiana on October 4, 1984.

"Breakfast Food Song"	Don Bowman	RCA Victor LSP 2831 (LP)
"Breakfast In Bed"	Dusty Springfield	Atlantic SD 8214 (LP)
"Breakfast, My Dear"	Bob Peck	Jubilee JGM 1035 (LP)
"Breakfast On the Grass"	The Midniters	Whittier WS 5002 (LP)
"Cooking Breakfast For The One I Love"	Fanny Brice	RCA Victor LPV 538 (LP)
"Eat Your Cornflakes"	Laurie Styvers	Warner Brothers WS 1946 (LP)
"Ham And Eggs"	Leadbelly, Cisco Houston, and Woody Guthrie	Stinson SLP 48 (LP)

Lunch

"Lunch Time"	George Hamilton IV	RCA Victor LSP 4066 (LP)
"Lunch Toters"	Kingston Trio	Capitol ST 2081 (LP)
"Luncheon Ballad"	Suzanne Astor,	Warner Brothers BS 2551 (LP)
	Marilyn Child, Madiline Kahn, and Nancie Phillips	

Dinner Or Supper

"Supper"	Side Show	Atlantic SD 8261 (LP)
"Supper On The Table"	Dorothy Loudon	Coral CRL 757265 (LP)
"Supper Time"	Speer Family	RCA Victor LPM 1144 (LP)
"Supper Time"	Annette Sanders	Monmouth Evergreen MES 6811 (LP)
"Suppertime"	Snoopy (Bill Hinnant)	Atlantic SD 7252 (LP)

Desserts

"An Apple For The Teacher"	Bing Crosby and Connie Boswell	Decca DL 4254 (LP)
"Cut Yourself A Piece Of Cake And Make Yourself At Home"	Bill Murray	Victor 19114 (78)
"I Scream, You Scream, We All Scream For Ice Cream"	Radio Ed and Bobby Dixon	Banner 6166 (78)
"I've Never Seen A Straight Banana"	Billy Jones and Ernset Hare	Columbia 898-D (78)
"If I Knew You Were Comin' I'd've Baked A Cake"	Eileen Barton	National 9103 (78)
"Nigger Love A Watermelon, Ha! Ha! Ha!"	Harry C. Browne	Columbia A1999 (78)
"RC Cola And Moon Pie"	Big Bill Lester	Capitol 1488 (78)
"Watermelon On The Vine"	Harry and Jeannie West	Counterpoint CPST 545 (LP)
"When You Dunk A Donut Don't It Make It Nice"	Six Jumping Jacks	Brunswick 3254 (78)
"Why Aren't Yez Eatin' More Oranges (From Sunny Cal-i-for-Ni-ay)"	The Happiness Boys (Jones and Hare)	Victor 19865 (78)
"Yes, We Have No Bananas"	Billy Jones	Vocalion 14579 (78)

Meat Dishes

"Barbecued Hot Dog"	Happy Johnson and His International Jive Five	Columbia 38267 (78)
"Dunderbecke"	Oscar Brand	Tradition TLP 1014 (LP)
"Fido Is A Hot Dog Now"	Billy Murray	Victor 17260 (78)
"My Bologna"	Weird Al Yankovic	Rhino RNLP 010 (LP)
"One Meat Ball"	The Andrews Sisters	Decca 18636 (78)
"Pickle In The Middle (And The Mustard On Top)"	Artie Aurback	Mercury 3016 (78)
"Please Warm My Wiener"	Bo Carter	Yazoo L 1043 (LP)
"Spam"	The Cast of Monty Python's Flying Circus	Charism CAS 1049 (LP)

The Main Course And Side Dishes

"Animal Crackers In My Soup"	Shirley Temple	20th Century Fox TFM 3102 (LP)
"The Ballad Of Chicken Soup"	Carole King	Ode SP 77027 (LP)
"Bean, Bacon, And Gravy"	Pete Seeger	Folkways FH 5251 (LP)
"Beans Taste Fine"	Shel Silverstein	Atlantic SD 8257 (LP)
"Chicken Soup With Rice"	Carole King	Ode SP 77027 (LP)
"Eating Goober Peas"	Carl Sandburg	Columbia ML 5339 (LP)
"Horay For Spinach"	Skinny Ennis Orchestra	Victor 26212 (78)
"I'm Just Wild About Animal Crackers"	Irving Aaronson and His Commanders	RCA Victor LPV 557 (LP)
"Take An Old Cold Tater"	Little Jimmy Dickens	Columbia 20548 (78)

Coffee And Tea

"The Coffee (They've Got An Awful Lot Of Coffee In Brazil)"	Frank Sinatra	Columbia CL 2474 (LP)
"A Cup Of Coffee, A Sandwich, And You"	Gertrude Lawrence	Audio Fidelity AFLP 709 (LP)
"Hot Coffee"	Billy Jones and Ernest Hare	Columbia 534-D (78)
"Java Jive"	The Ink Spots	Decca DXSB 7182 (LP)
"Tea For Two"	Fred Waring's Pennsylvanians	RCA Victor LPV 554 (LP)

Ethnic Foods

"Bagel Call Rag"	Mickey Katz	Capitol 1284 (78)
"Boiled Crawfish (At Te Maurice)"	Tex Ritter	Capitol 1071 (78)
"Good Old Turnip Greens"	The Westerners	Melotone 6-10-59 (78)
"Hungarian Goulash, No. 5"	Allan Sherman	Warner Brothers WS 1501 (LP)
"Jambalaya"	Hank Williams	MGM E 3412 (LP)
"Niggah Loves His Possum"	Arthur Collins and Byron G. Harlan	Victor 17256 (78)
"On Top Of Spaghetti"	The Do-Re-Mi Children's Chorus	Kapp KS 3621 (LP)

"Poke Salad Green"	Leon Payne	Capitol 2055 (78)
"Red Beans And Rice"	Kokomo Arnold	Blues Classics BC 4 (LP)
"Tater Pie"	Hank Penny and His California Cowhands	RCA Victor 21-046 (78)

Fast Food and Junk Food

"Cheesburger In Paradise"	Jimmy Buffett	ABC AA 1046 (LP)
"Eat It"	Weird Al Yankovic	Rock 'N' Roll BFZ 39221 (LP)
"Junk Food Junkie"	Larry Groce	Warner Brothers BS 2933 (LP)
"McDonald's Hamburgers"	Biff Rose	United Artists UA-LA 009-F (LP)

Extra Stuff

"Get 'Em From The Peanut Man (Hot Nuts)"	Lil Johnson	Champion 50002 (78)
"Molasses, Molasses (It's Icky Sticky Goo)"	Spike Jones and His City Slickers	RCA Victor 20-3939 (78)

Eating In General

"Eats A Little More"	The Willis Brothers	Masterpiece MLP 204 (LP)
"Eat A Little Something"	Lillian Roth	Columbia KOS 2180 (LP)
"Eat, Eat, Eat"	Danny Kaye	Decca 27829 (78)
"Eating In Kansas City"	The Hoodoo Rhythm Devils	Blue Thumb BTS 42 (LP)
"Etiquette Blues"	The Happiness Boys	"X" LVA 1008 (LP)
"Feed Me"	Ellen Greene	Geffen GHSP 2020 (LP)
"Food"	The Turtles	White Whale WWS 7118 (LP)
"Food, Glorious Food"	The Chorus Of Olivet	RCA Victor LSOD 2004 (LP)
"Home Cookin' "	Bob Hope and Margaret Whiting	Capitol 1042 (78)
"Save The Bones For Henry (Cause He Don't Eat No Meat)"	The Greenwood Country Singers	Kapp KL 1422 (LP)
"Sing For Your Supper"	The Benny Goodman Orchestra, with Martha Tilton	RCA Victor LPT 6703 (LP)
"A Soldier's Day (Soupy, Soupy)"	Geoffrey O'Hara	Victor 18451 (78)

Table 8-G

A Selected discography of 45 R.P.M. Records
Containing References to Dining, Food, and Related
Culinary Activities*

*Created by B. Lee Cooper under the title "Illustrating Culinary Images in Contemporary Recordings, 1950-1985" for presentation at the 14th Annual Meeting of the Midwest Popular Culture Association in Kalamazoo, Michigan on October 25, 1986.

Theme Category and Song Title	Recording Artist	Record Number and Year of Release
Dining Establishments		
"Alice's Rock And Roll Restaurant"	Arlo Guthrie	Reprise 0877 (1969)
"Copacabana (At The Copa)"	Barry Manilow	Arista 0339 (1978)
"(Down At) Papa Joes's"	The Dixiebelles, with Cornbread and Jerry	Sound Stage 2507 (1963)
"Hotel California"	The Eagles	Asylum 45386 (1977)
"The House Of Blue Lights"	Chuck Miller	Mercury 70627 (1955)
"Meet Me At Grandma's Joint"	Georgie Stevenson	Savoy 1123 (1954)
"Rib Joint"	Sam Price	Savoy 1505 (1957)
"Smokey Joe's Cafe"	The Robins	Atco 6059 (1963)
"Sugar Shack"	Jimmy Gilmer and The Fireballs	Dot 16487 (1963)
From The Bar		
"Apricot Brandy"	Rhinoceros	Elektra 45647 (1969)
"Bad, Bad Whiskey"	Amos Milburn	Aladdin 3068 (1951)
"One Mint Julep"	Ray Charles	Impulse 200 (1961)
"One Scotch, One Bourbon, One Beer"	Amos Milburn	Aladdin 3197 (1953)
"Pink Champagne"	Joe Liggins	Specialty 355 (1950)
"Red Red Wine"	Neil Diamond	Bang 556 (1968)
"Scotch And Soda"	Ray Price	Viva 29543 (1983)
"Tennessee Whiskey"	George Jones	Epic 04082 (1983)
"Tequila"	Hot Butter	Musicor 1468 (1973)
"Whiskey And Gin"	Johnny Ray	Okeh 6809 (1951)
"Whiskey, Gin, And Wine"	Joe Liggins	Specialty 402 (1951)
"Whiskey Whiskey"	Rita Coolidge	A & M 1414 (1973)
Breads, Salads, And Vegetables		
"Beans And Cornbread"	Louis Jordan	Decca 24673 (1949)
"Bread And Butter"	Robert Jordan	Motown 1664 (1983)
"Cole Slaw (Sorghum Switch)"	Louis Jordan	Decca 24633 (1949)
"Corn Bread"	Erskine Hawkins	RCA Victor 20-3326 (1949)
"Fat Meat 'N' Greens"	Edgar Hayes	Exclusive 78X (1940)
"Fried Onions"	Lord Rockingham's XI	London 1810 (1958)
"Gravy (For My Mashed Potatoes)"	Dee Dee Sharp	Cameo 219 (1962)
"Green Onions"	Booker T. and The M. G.'s	Stax 127 (1962)
"Grits 'N' Corn Bread"	The Soul Runners	MoSoul 101 (1967)
"Homegrown Tomatoes"	Guy Clark	Warner Brothers 29595 (1983)
"Hot Biscuits"	Jay McShann	Down Beat 165 (1949)
"Hot Pepper"	Floyd Cramer	RCA 8051 (1962)
"Mangos"	Rosemary Clooney	Columbia 40835 (1957)
"Mashed Potatoes"	Steve Alaimo	Checker 1006 (1962)
"Peas 'N' Rice"	Freddie McCoy	Prestige 450 (1967)

Main Course

"Beef Stew"	Hal Singer	Savoy 686 (1949)
"Catfish"	The Four Tops	ABC 12214 (1976)
"Chicken In The Basket"	Billy Bland	Old Town 1016 (1956)
"Chicken Pot Pie"	Ken Jones	Almont 305 (1964)
"English Muffins And Irish Stew"	Sylvia Syms	Decca 29969 (1956)
"Frankfurter Sandwiches"	The Streamliners with Joanne	United Artists 880 (1965)
"Hot Pastrami"	The Dartells	Dot 16453 (1963)
"Hot Pastrami And Mashed Potatoes"	Joey Dee and The Starliters	Roulette 4488 (1963)

Dinner Beverages

"Cherry Berry Wine"	Charlie McCoy	Cadence 1390 (1961)
"Cherry Wine"	Little Esther	Federal 12142 (1953)
"Cool Water"	Jack Scott	Top Rank 2055 (1960)
"Country Wine"	Paul Revere and The Raiders	Columbia 45535
"Java"	Al Hirt	RCA 8280 (1964)
"Lemonade"	Louis Jordan	Decca 27324 (1951)
"Milk And Water"	Amos Milburn	Alladin 3240 (1954)

Desserts

"Apples, Peaches, Pumpkin Pie"	Jay and The Techniques	Smash 2086 (1967)
"Banana Split"	Kid King's Combo	Excello 2009 (1953)
"Cherry Pie"	Skip And Flip	Brent 7010 (1960)
"Ginger Bread"	Frankie Avalon	Chancellor 1021 (1958)
"Gooseberry Pie"	Grandpa Jones	RCA Victor 47-6006 (n.d.)
"Peaches 'N' Cream"	The Ikettes	Modern 1005 (1965)
"Raspberries, Strawberries"	The Kingston Trio	Capitol 4114 (1959)
"Strawberry Shortcake"	Jay and The Techniques	Smash 2142 (1968)

Snack Options

"Candy"	The Astors	Stax 170 (1965)
"Chocolate Sundae"	Kid King's Combo	Excello 2025 (1954)
"Cotton Candy"	Al Hirt	RCA 8346 (1964)
"I Love Rocky Road"	Weird Al Yankovic	Rock 'N' Roll 03998 (1983)
"Ice Cream Song"	The Dynamics	Cotillion 44021 (1969)
"Peanut Butter"	The Marathons	Arvee 5027 (1961)
"Peanuts"	Little Joe and The Thrillers	Okeh 7088 (1957)
"The Popcorn"	James Brown	King 6240 (1969)
"Soda Pop"	The Moonglows	Chess 1689 (1958)

Books

Margaret Cussler and Mary Louise de Give, *'Twixt The Cup And The Lip: Psychological And Socio-Cultural Factors Affecting Food Habits*. New York: Tayne Books, 1952.

Richard J. Hooker, *Food And Drink In America*. New York: Bobbs-Merrill Company, Inc., 1981.

Robin Le Mesurier and Peggy Sue Honeyman Scott, *Rock 'N' Roll Cuisine*. New York: Billboard Books, 1988.

Waverly Root and Richard de Rochemont, *Eating In America: A History*. New York: William Morrow and Company, 1976.

Articles

Padraic Burke, "Rolling Arts And Songs Of Plenty: The Urban Food Vendor," *Journal Of American Culture*, II (Fall 1979), pp. 480-487.

Charles Camp, "Food In American Culture: A Bibliographic Essay," *Journal Of American Culture*, II (Fall 1979, pp. 559-570.

Marge Colborn, "Tacky Or Tasteful? Fast-Food Joints Seen As Models Of Civilization," *Detroit News*, (December 30, 1986), pp. F3, F6.

"B. Lee Cooper and William L. Schurk, "Food For Thought: Investigating Culinary Images In Contempory American Recordings," *International Journal Of Instructional Media*, XIV, No. 3 (1987), pp. 251-262.

Laura Fissinger, "Joy Of Cooking: The Life Of Rock Caterers," *Rolling Stone*, No. 501 (June 4, 1987), pp. 32, 34.

Larry Groce, "Cogent Thoughts On The Junk Food Jones By One Who Knows... The Way To A Country's Heart," *Waxpaper*, I (July 22, 1976), p. 18-19.

Jerry King, "Fast Food," *Detroit News*, (November 17, 1986), pp. D1, D2.

Unpublished Materials

Charles Camp, "American Eats: Toward A Definition Of American Foodways" (Ph.D.: University of Pennsylvania, 1979).

B. Lee Cooper, "More Food For Thought: Images Of Culinary Activities In Contemporary Recordings, 1950-1985" (mimeographed paper and audio tape presentation at the 9th National Convention of The American Culture Association in March 1987).

William L. Schurk, "Did Skinny Minnie Dance The Too Fat Polka? To Eat Or Not to Eat In American Popular Song" (mimeographed paper presented at the 9th National Convention of the American Culture Association in March 1987).

———" 'Yes, We Have No Bananas': The Image of Food And Eating In Popular Song" (mimeographed paper presented at the 12th annual meeting of the Midwest Popular Culture Association in October 1984).

Chapter Nine
Telephones

"It's for you, Laura."

"Julie, your friend Terry wants to speak with you."

"Hey, Mike. The phone's for you. Don't stay on the line too long. Your mother is expecting an important call from Uncle Rich."

No American family can escape the ritual of telephone sharing. Although the jangling instrument may seem like a technological apple of discord tossed into an otherwise tranquil domestic scene, the telephone is actually a key human communication device. This is especially true for young persons. Due to their limited transportation options and because of weekday or weekend social curfews, youngsters are the most frequent phone users in American households. Just as teenagers dominate phone lines, many recording artists have utilized telephone conversation formats as settings for their comments about human relations. During recent years, for instance, youthful audiences have been attracted to the audio illustrations sung by The New Edition ("Mr. Telephone Man"), Stevie Wonder ("I Just Called To Say I Love You"), Midnight Star ("Operator"), Sheena Easton ("Telefone (Long Distance Love Affair)"), and Diana Ross ("Telephone"). It seems appropriate for teachers to adopt these twin elements of youth culture— telephones and popular music—to explore the complex nature of contemporary human relations.

It may seem peculiar to associate communication technology and rock recordings as educational resources. Yet the logic of this linkage is compelling. Over the centuries human beings have used song lyrics to transmit feelings of love, to praise events of public significance, to propagate ideas of personal value, and to provide reflective commentaries on themselves and their predecessors. As Marshall McLuhan notes, contemporary man lives at a time when different mediums of communication (radio, telephone, television, and motion pictures) dramatically affect the quality of intellectual messages. McLuhan asserts that human senses—of which contemporary audio and visual media are merely extensions—function to configure the awareness and the experiences of each of us. Thus, the products of modern electronic technology have become the content of learning and understanding in twentieth century America. In respect to the telephone itself, McLuhan provides the following perceptive thoughts in *Understanding Media: The Extensions Of Man.*

"The child and the teenager understand the telephone, embracing the cord and the ear-mike as if they were beloved pets." (p. 283)

"The phone is a participant form [of media] that demands a partner, with all the intensity of electric polarity. It simply will not act as a background instrument like radio." (p. 235)

"The telephone is an irresistible intruder in time or place... In its nature the telephone is an intensely personal form that ignores all the claims of visual privacy prized by literate man." (p. 238)

Beyond McLuhan's observations, it is fascinating to note how incessant telephone technology has become during the 1980s. Doctors carry beepers; lawyers utilize answering services, businessmen and career women own portable phones; and urban dwellers leave messages in individualized answering tapes. When assessing the human interactions which occur via the telephone, though, several general assumptions about "the instrument" and "the communication situation" become paramount. They are listed below in Table 9-A.

Table 9-A

Communication Assumptions about the Telephone

A. The telephone is...
  1. an intentional communication instrument
  2. highly available in both public and private settings
  3. stationary or mobile, depending upon the type of instrument being utilized
  4. an instrument which often allows a limited period of time for a verbal exchange
  5. a communication devise which requires a financial outlay, either immediate or delayed
B. Communication by telephone is...
  1. conducted with physical distance between the communicators
  2. subject to conflicting reactions between communicators due to varying personal attitudes, to mixed social settings, and even to different time zones
  3. limited to oral exchange with no facial expressions, no physical signs, and no written messages involved
  4. often unfulfilled due to receiving a busy signal, to dialing a wrong number, to gaining only a silent response, or to encountering an unexpected person when a connection is completed
  5. primarily one-to-one interaction, with the exception of office speaker systems, secret wiretaps, and electronic answering machines
  6. frequently utilized as a vehicle in dramatic performances, in comedy acts, or in popular song lyrics

Communication by telephone is immediate, intimate, and by choice; it is also oral and usually conducted at some distance. The telephone, even after the breakup of A.T.& T.'s monopoly, remains a timeless symbol of personal interaction. Since 1950 numerous song lyrics have contained references to telephone conversations, so it is particularly fitting that Ma Bell selected a popular song title—"Reach Out And Touch (Somebody's Hand)"—as an advertising motto.

The spectrum of messages delivered by phone is fascinating. Although Karla Bonoff claims that she's got something for her lover that must be delivered "Personally"—"I can't mail it, I can't phone it!"—most lyrics are more telephone sensitive. "Put your sweet lips a little closer to the phone," pleads Jim Reeves in "He'll Have To Go." "Let's pretend that we're together all alone," he continues.

Stevie Wonder, in "Do I Do," declares, "When I hear you on the phone, your sweet sexy voice turns my ear all the way on." For Cymarron, telephone "Rings" mean invitations to romantic relationships. But for Webb Pierce in "I Ain't Never," his calls lead only to continuing episodes of frustration caused by a fickle female. The Four Tops are unable to muster sufficient courage to telephone a loved one in "Just Seven Numbers (Can Straighten Out My Life)," while The Orlons plead with an angry lover "Don't Hang Up" or a romance will end. Steely Dan urges "Rikki Don't Lose That Number," while other singers simply make their home phone numbers available—The Marvelettes' "Beachwood 4-5789," Wilson Pickett's "634-5789 (Soulsville, U.S.A.)," The Carpenters' "Beachwood 4-5789," and Tommy Tuton's "867-5309/Jenny."

Love, expectation, exhilaration, and the mending of damaged relationships are not the only topics explored in lyrical telephone conversations. Sugarloaf describes their sweet, ironic revenge on a haughty talent agent who had mocked them with the standard "Don't Call Us, We'll Call You" putdown. Telephone operators function as surrogate marriage counselors for Chuck Berry, Johnny Rivers, and Fred Knoblock in "Memphis, Tennessee" (1959, 1964, 1983), as an amateur psychologist for Jim Croce in "Operator (That's Not The Way It Feels)," and as a religious go-between in The Manhattan Transfer's metaphorical song "Operator." Jealousy also thrives via long distance lines. Freddy Cannon is vexed when he encounters a continuing busy signal from his girlfriend's phone in "Buzz Buzz A-Diddle-It." He concludes that some endlessly yakking hounddog is sweet-talkin' his angel. Bobby Darin is even more direct in warning his girlfriend that "If A Man Answers" her phone when he calls, then their relationship is through. Finally, Dr. Hook faces the most frustrating dilemma of all. When his girlfriend's phone rings and he answers it, there is only silence from the caller. Dr. Hook's conclusion is that "When You're In Love With A Beautiful Woman" you shouldn't trust any of your male companions.

As a teacher examines the wide variety of telephone songs available for classroom use, several instructional formats emerge. The communication instruments themselves offer several options for investigation. Students readily note that telephones are *sound* machines (dialing, ringing, clicking, or rendering a busy signal) which enable two persons to communicate. Not unlike America's social security system, all people are identified as numbers ("Benchwood 4-5789," "867-5309/Jenny," "Lonesome 7-7203," "634-5789," or "777-9311"). Sometimes an "Answering Machine" or an "Operator" intervenes to postpone or to thwart a desired communication situation. Human emotions are often heightened in telephone call situations. The spectrum of personal feelings ranges from highly positive expectations ("Hot Line," "Chantilly Lace," and "I Just Called To Say I Love You") to extremely negative assumptions ("Mr. Telephone Man," "Buzz Buzz A-Diddle-It," and "Don't Hang Up"). Unexpected events frequently occur. "If A Man Answers," "Obscene Phone Caller," and "Memphis, Tennessee" illustrate situations which generate doubt, fear, and helplessness as a result of either making or receiving a telephone call. The occupational stall of "Don't Call Us, We'll Call You" is countered lyrically by the humorous "Ghostbusters" use of phone contacts to identify jobs. Finally, students should be challenged to examine telephone metaphors is popular recordings. As in the case of The Manhattan Transfer's "Operator," many songs focus on individuals who imagine the telephone functioning as something more exotic than an electronic communication device. The telephone operator may be envisioned as a long-distance dating service, a personal counselor, or a secret friend. Opportunities to explore the complexities of human relations through telephone songs abound.

The final section of this essay consists of an alphabetized discography of telephone-related recordings from the past forty years. These songs can be utilized to stimulate classroom discussions about human relations and communications technology.

Table 9-B

An Alphabetical List of 45 R.P.M.
Records Featuring Telephone-Related
Titles, Illustrations, or Themes,
1950-1988

Song Title (Record Number)	Performing Artist	Year of Release
"All Alone By The Telephone" (Polydor 14313)	The Checkmates, Ltd.	1976
"Answering Machine" (MCA 41235)	Rupert Holmes	1980
"Baby, Hang Up The Phone" (A & M 1620)	Carl Graves	1974
"Beachwood 4-5789" (Tamla 54065)	The Marvelettes	1962
"Beachwood 4-5789" (A & M 2405)	The Carpenters	1982
"Beep A Freak" (Total Experience 2405)	The Gap Band	1984
"Buzz Buzz A-Diddle-It" (Swan 4071)	Freddy Cannon	1961
"Call Me" (Chrysalis 2414)	Blondie	1980
"Call Me" (Atlantic 2706)	Aretha Franklin	1970
"Call Me" (Columbia 41253)	Johnny Mathis	1958
"Call Me" (A & M 780)	Chris Montez	1966
"Call Me" (Salsoul 2152)	Skyy	1982
"Call Me (Come Back Home)" (Hi 2235)	Al Green	1973
"Call Me Later" (Double Shot 145)	Foxy	1970
"Call Me Mr. 'Telephone' " (MCA 52576)	Cheyne	1985
"Call Me Up" (Columbia 07204)	Process And The Doo Rags	1987
"(Call Me) When The Spirit Moves You" (Atco 7222)	Touch	1980

"Call On Me"	Chicago	1974
(Columbia 46062)		
"Call Operator 210"	Floyd Dixon	1952
(Aladdin 3135)		
"Call Operator 210"	The Johnny Otis	1952
(Mercury 8289)	Orchestra	
"Calling Occupants Of	The Carpenters	1977
Interplanetary Craft"		
(A & M 1978)		
"Can't Hang Up The Phone"	Stonewall Jackson	1963
(Columbia 42628)		
"Chantilly Lace"	The Big Bopper	1958
(Mercury 71343)		
"Chantilly Lace"	Jerry Lee Lewis	1972
(Mercury 73273)		
"Death By Phone"	Scott Puffer	1979
(Yoyo 12249)		
"Dial My Number"	Pauli Carman	1986
(Columbia 05865)		
"Dial That Telephone"	Effie Smith	1965
(Duo Disc 107)		
"Do I Do"	Stevie Wonder	1982
(Tamla 1612)		
"Doctor's Orders"	Carol Douglas	1974
(Midland International 10113)		
"Don't Call Us, We'll Call You"	Sugarloaf	1974
(Claridge 402)		
"Don't Hang Up"	Elly Brown	1984
(Mirage 99687)		
"Don't Hang Up"	The Orlons	1962
(Cameo 231)		
"867-5309/Jenny"	Tommy Tutone	1982
(Columbia 02646)		
"Every Little Thing She	The Police	1981
Does Is Magic"		
(A & M 2371)		
"Get Off Of My Cloud"	The Rolling Stones	1965
(London 9792)		
"Ghostbusters"	Ray Parker, Jr.	1984
(Arista 9212)		
"Hang Up The Phone"	Annie Golden	1984
(MCA 52387)		
"Heart On The Line	Larry Willoughby	1983
(Operator, Operator)"		
(Atlantic Arts 99826)		
"He'll Have To Go"	Jim Reeves	1959
(RCA 7643)		
"Hot Line"	The Sylvers	1976
(Capitol 4336)		
"I Ain't Never"	Webb Pierce	1959
(Decca 30923)		
"I Just Called to Say	Stevie Wonder	1984
I Love You"		
(Motown 1745)		
"If A Man Answers"	Bobby Darin	1962

(Capitol 4837)

If A Man Answers (Hang Up the Phone)" (Mercury 71926)	Leroy Van Dyke	1962
"Just Seven Numbers (Can Straighten Out My Life)" (Motown 1175)	The Four Tops	1971
"Kissin' On The Phone" (ABC-Paramount 10239)	Paul Anka	1961
"Lonesome 7-7203" (Audiograph 474)	Darrell Clanton	1983
"Lonesome 7-7203" (King 5712)	Hawkshaw Hawkins	1963
"Lonesome 7-7203" (Decca 32078)	Burl Ives	1967
"Love On The Phone" (Casablanca 2242)	Suzanne Fellini	1980
"Ma Belle Amie" (Colossus 107)	Tee Set	1970
"Memorize Your Number" (Scotti Brothers 510)	Leif Garrett	1980
"Memphis" (Imperial 66032)	Johnny Rivers	1964
"Memphis, Tennessee" (Chess 1729)	Chuck Berry	1959
"Memphis, Tennissee" (Scotti Brothers 02434)	Fred Knoblick	1981
"Mr. Telephone Man" (MCA 52484)	New Edition	1984
"Miss You" (Rolling Stones 19307)	The Rolling Stones	1978
"Obscene Phone Caller" (Motown 1731)	Rockwell	1984
"Operator" (Tamla 54115)	Brenda Holloway	1965
"Operator (Fury 1064)	Gladys Knight and The Pips	1962
"Operator" (Atlantic 3292)	Manhattan Transfer	1975
"Operator" (Solar 69684)	Midnight Star	1984
"Operator" (RCA 13265)	The Tennessee Express	1982
"Operator, Long Distance Please" (MCA 52111)	Barbara Mandrell	1982
"Operator (That's Not The Way It Feels)" (ABC 11335)	Jim Croce	1972
"Personally" (Columbia 02805)	Karla Bonoff	1982
"Phones Been Jumping All Day (Casablanca 834)	Jeannie Reynolds	1975
"Please Come To Boston" (Epic 11115)	Dave Loggins	1974
"Private Number"	Judy Clay and	1968

(Stax 0005)	William Bell	
"Private Number"	The Jets	1986
(MCA 52846)		
"Rikki Don't Lost That Number"	Steely Dan	1974
(ABC 11439)		
"Ring My Phone"	Tommy Sands	1957
(Capitol 3723)		
"Rings"	Cymarron	1971
(Entrance 7500)		
"Ruby, Don't Take Your	Kenny Rogers	1969
Love To Town"		
(Reprise 0829)		
"777-9311"	The Time	1982
(Warner Brothers 29952)		
"634-5989 (Soulsville,	Wilson Pickett	1966
U.S.A.)" (Atlantic 2320)		
"634-5789"	Marlow Tackett	1982
(RCA 13347)		
"Telefone (Long Distance	Sheena Easton	1983
Love Affair)"		
(E.M.I. America 8172)		
"The Telephone"	Stand Borcson and	1957
(Kapp 198)	Doug Settenberg	
"Telephone"	Diana Ross	1985
(RCA 14032)		
"Telephone Baby"	Johnny Otis and	1959
(Capitol 4168)	Marci Lee	
"Telephone Bill"	Johnny "Guitar" Watson	1951
(DJM 1305)		
"Telephone Blues"	Floyd Dixon	1951
(Aladdin 3075)		
"Telephone Line"	The Electric Light	1977
(United Artists 1000)	Orchestra	
"Telephone Man"	Meri Wilson	1977
(GRT 127)		
"Telephone Me Some Lovin' "	Ernie Tucker and	n.d.
(Musicor 1005)	His Operators	
"Telephone Operator"	Pete Shelly	1983
(Arista 730)		
"The Telephone Song"	The Andrews Sisters	1951
(Decca 27310)		
"What's Your Name,	The Andrea True	1978
What's Your Number"	Connection	
(Buddah 582)		
"When You're In Love	Dr. Hook	1979
With A Beautiful Woman"		
(Capitol 4705)		
"Wichita Lineman"	Glen Campbell	1968
(Capitol 2302)		
"Wrong Number, Right Girl"	Verna William	n.d.
(Belinda 100)		

Works Cited

Books

Michael G. Corenthal, *Cohen On The Telephone: A History Of Jewish Recorded Humor And Popular Music, 1892-1942*. Milwaukee, Wisconsin: Yesterday's Memories Press, 1984.

Daniel J. Czitrom, *Media And The American Mind: From Morse To McLuhan*. Chapel Hill, North Carolina: The University of North Carolina Press, 1982.

Marshall McLuhan, *Understanding Media: The Extensions Of Man*. New York. New American Library, 1964.

Articles

Richard Barbieri, "Prime Time For the Telephone," *Channels*, V (May/June 1985), pp. 54-55.

Ken Barnes, "Heavy Phones: Calling Up The Telephone Songs,"*Radio And Records*, No. 568 (January 25, 1985), p. 46.

B. Lee Cooper, "Human Relations, Communications Technology, And Popular Music: Audio Images Of Telephone Use In The United States, 1950-1985," *International Journal Of Instructional Media*, XIII, No. 1 (1986), pp. 75-82.

Patterns

Chapter Ten
Answer Songs and Sequel Recordings

Answer songs* are tunes that respond to direct questions or continue to develop specific ideas and themes from earlier songs. They are as old as the multiple verse lyric poems performed by medieval troubadours. In the American oral entertainment tradition, they are rooted in the verbal one-upsmanship practiced by storytellers in barbershops, brothels, and bars along the coast of Mark Twain's fabled waterway. Answer songs are invariably linked to the mutual interests of performers and audiences in perpetuating and elaborating upon a humorous situation. Many songs were recorded during the first half of the twentieth century about the exploits of John Henry, Frankie and Johnny, and Stagger Lee. The heroics of the mythic steel-drivin' man echoed into the 1950s thanks to Lonnie Donegan and His Skiffle Group; the classic tale of alienated affection which prompted a homicide also transcended the Depression and World War II in recordings by Elvis Presley, Johnny Cash, and others; and the gambling and shooting incident involving the mysterious Stagger Lee and his ill-fated companion Billy found rebirth from its pre-1940 blues roots by Lloyd Price, Wilson Pickett, and Tommy Roe.

This chapter is not concerned with either traditional European or pre-Cold War American answer songs. The purpose of this investigation is to identify various American recordings from the 1950-1985 period which comprise the contemporary answer song system. Although the majority of songs which trigger recorded responses are themselves highly popular, the same can not be said of most offshoot tunes. For this reason answer discs are highly prized by most record collectors. Small pressings and limited sales of answer songs make them immediate rarities in the vinyl trade market. Beyond collecting, though, these recordings offer valuable illustrations of several American cultural traits. They are usually humorous, poking fun at a particular statement or a series of less-than-honorable activities; they invariably provide contrasting positions—both personal and political—to strongly stated viewpoints; they offer interesting,

*Throughout this study an "answer song" is broadly defined as a commercial recording that is directly related to a previously released record either by title, by lyrical content, or by melody. Although generally issued only weeks after an original tune has achieved popularity, response recordings occasionally appear months or even years later. The answer song, usually regarded as a novelty item by most singers, promoters, and record buyers, has provided initial public visibility for a few major artists (Smokey Robinson and The Miracles) and remains a continuing vehicle for the social satire of others (Ben Colder and Weird Al Yankovic).

sometimes unexpected, story expanding options; and they often translate common regional phrases, private domestic problems, and other personal concerns into a broad cultural context.

Can the total field of contemporary answer songs be segmented into identifiable patterns? Not very easily. Yet, upon closer scrutiny it becomes evident that even though the general form of most response recordings is constant, the functions of specific answer songs vary greatly. This latter fact permits the differentiation of the genre into six categories: (a) answers to direct questions; (b) responses to statements or commands; (c) challenges to stated positions or ideologies; (d) continuations of distinct storylines or themes; (e) follow-up statements to general ideas or themes; and (f) parodies of specific songs. The remainder of this chapter defines the meaning of each category listed above by exploring answer songs that fit each of the six formats. Numerous illustrations will be provided in tables throughout the text.

A. Answer To A Direct Question

In 1961 a *Time* journalist commented, "So far, there are only half a dozen versions of 'Are You Lonesome Tonight?', including the original by Elvis Presley which is now the nation's No. 1 hit. But if Elvis stays up there, there may well be a dozen variations of the theme. The 'Lonesome' craze is the most blatant example of pop music's latest fad: the answer song, which provides an answer to a question raised in an established hit." (p. 52)

The most easily explained justification for concocting, recording, and releasing an answer song is to respond to a direct question from a previous tune. The reactions to Elvis Presley's multiple pleas—"Are you lonesome tonight? Do you miss me tonight? Are you sorry we drifted apart?"—were consistently positive. Similar answer songs entitled "Yes, I'm Lonesome Tonight" were launched by Thelma Carpenter, Linda Lee, Jo Anne Perry, and Dodie Stevens. In addition, Jeanne Black wailed "Oh, How I Miss You Tonight." The same kind of reassuring responses had greeted The Shirelles a year earlier when their hit song "Will You Love Me Tomorrow" secured the following responses from three different artists—"Yes, I Will Love You Tomorrow," "You Know I'll Love You Tomorrow," and "Not Just Tomorrow, But Always."

In 1956 Frankie Lymon and The Teenagers produced the hit "Why Do Fools Fall In Love." The song's title appears at the end of a chain of questions ranging from "Why do birds sing so gay?" to "Why does my heart skip a crazy beat?" The answer songs to this record remained in the Lymon family. Frankie's brother Lewis produced a recording which asserted "I Found Out Why." Not to be outdone, Frankie countered with his own answer, couched in the form of yet another question—"Who Can Explain?" It is interesting to note that later in his career Frankie Lymon released yet another answer—"I Put The Bomp"—in response to Barry Mann's 1961 hit "Who Put The Bomp (In The Bomp, Bomp, Bomp)."

Perhaps the most negative response to a recorded query was delivered by Hook McCoy in 1980. His reaction to Gary Burbank's soap opera-inspired question "Who Shot J.R.?" was "I Don't Give A Diddly Damn Who Shot J.R." Of course, there are several recordings which have posed questions in their titles that never generated recorded responses. Lonnie Donegan's "Does Your Chewing Gum Lose Its Flavor On The Bedpost Overnight?" and Ed Ames' "Who Will Answer?" are examples of such songs. Other answered tunes are listed in Table 10-A below.

Table 10-A
Answer To A Direct Question

Song Title, Record Number, and Original Performer	*Response Title, Record Number, and Response Performer*
1. "Are You Lonesome Tonight?" (RCA 57-7810) by Elvis Presley (1960)	"Oh, How I Miss You Tonight" (Capitol 4492) by Jeanne Black "Yes, I'm Lonesome Tonight" (Coral 6224) by Thelma Carpenter "Yes, I'm Lonesome Tonight" (Shasta 146) by Linda Lee "Yes, I'm Lonesome Tonight" (Glad 1006) by Jo Anne Perry "Yes, I'm Lonesome Tonight" (Dot 16167) by Dodie Stevens
2. "Book of Love" (Argo 5290) by The Monotones (1958)	"Reading The Book Of Love" (Hull 735) by The Monotones
3. "Why Do Fools Fall In Love" (Gee 1002) by Frankie Lymon and The Teenagers (1956)	"I Found Out Why" (End 1000) by Lewis Lymon and The Teenchords "Who Can Explain?" (Gee 1018) by Frankie Lymon and The Teenagers
4. "Who Put The Bomp (In The Bomp, Bomp, Bomp)" (ABC-Paramount 10237) by Barry Mann (1961)	"We're The Guys" (Columbia 42162) by Bob and Jerry "I Put The Bomp" (Roulette 4391) by Frankie Lymon
5. "Who Shot J.R.?" (Ovation 1150) by Gary Burbank with Band McNally (1980)	"I Don't Give A Diddly Damn Who Shot J.R." (J-Ken 1015) by Hook McCoy
6. "Who Stole The Keeshka?" (Select 719) by The Matys Brothers (1963)	"Jashu Found The Keeshka" (Fayette 1627) by The Matys Brothers
7. "Will You Love Me Tomorrow" (Scepter 1211) by The Shirelles (1960)	"Not Just Tomorrow, But Always" (United Artists 290) by Bertell Dache "Yes, I Will Love You Tomorrow" (Atlantic 2091) by Jon E. Holiday

"You Know I'll Love You Tomorrow"
(Ry-An 501)
by Colly Williams

B. Response To A Statement Or Command

Among the most popular and frequently mentioned answer songs is Damita Jo's "I'll Save The Last Dance For You." This tune, released in response to The Drifters' 1960 statement "Save The Last Dance For Me," rose to No. 22 on the *Billboard* chart and remained a charted hit for twelve weeks. "You're Having The Last Dance With Me!" by The Townsmen was another reaction to The Drifters, but one that failed to achieve much popular support. These tunes illustrate that no question is necessary in a song title to spark a creative answer. A direct statement or observation is enough to provoke a lyrical comment. Thus, Jim Reeves' 1959 telephone call plea "He'll Have To Go" was countered by the statement "He'll Have To Stay"; The Silhouettes' occupational dilemma in "Get A Job" was answered positively by The Heartbeats' "I Found A Job" and by The Miracles' "Got A Job"; and in 1962 Sam Cooke's "Bring It On Home To Me" admonition was heeded by Carla Thomas' "I'll Bring It Home To You."

One of the most broadly answered recordings was Ruth Brown's 1953 release "Mama (He Treats Your Daughter Mean)." The answers to this song were varied. First, appeals were made to the man of the house by two artists—Benny Brown and Scat Man Crothers—in "Papa." The Five Keys claimed "Mama, Your Daughter Told A Lie On Me." Sax Kari echoed this answer with "Hush Your Lyin' Mouth." Finally, Gloria Irving took the hard line with the allegedly mistreated young woman by coldly observing "Daughter, That's Your Red Wagon." Additional examples of these types of answer songs are provided in Table 10-B.

Table 10-B
Response To A Statement Or Command

Song Title, Record Number, and Original Performer	*Response Title, Record Number, and Response Performer*
1. "Bring It On Home To Me" (RCA 8036) by Sam Cooke (1962)	"I'll Bring It Home To You" (Atlantic 2163) by Carla Thomas
2. "Dang Me" (Smash 1881) by Roger Miller (1964)	"Darn Ya" (Phillips 4027) by Teresa Brewer "Dern Ya" (Rik 126) by Ruby Wright
3. "Don't Let The Stars Get In Your Eyes" (RCA Victor 5064) by Perry Como (1952)	"I Let The Stars Get In My Eyes" (Decca 28473) by Goldie Hill
4. "Get A Job" (Ember 1029)	"I Found A Job" (Roulette 4054)

by The Silhouettes (1958)

by The Heartbeats
"Got A Job"
(End 1016)
by The Miracles

5. "He'll Have To Go"
   (RCA 7643)
   by Jim Reeves (1959)

"He'll Have To Stay"
(Capitol 4368)
by Jeanne Black
"He'll Have To Stay"
(ABC 10097)
by Corina Minette

6. "I'm Mad"
   (Chess 1538)
   by Willie Mabon (1953)

"I'm Glad"
(Checker 773)
by Mitze Mars

7. "In The Midnight Hour"
   (Atlantic 2289)
   by Wilson Pickett (1965)

"You Can't Love Me In The Midnight Hour"
(Atlantic 2309)
by Ann Mason

8. "Mama (He Treats Your Daughter Mean)"
   (Atlantic 986)
   by Ruth Brown (1953)

"Papa"
(Gotham 293)
by Benny Brown
"Papa"
(Recorded in Hollywood 142)
by Scat Man Crothers
"Mama, Your Daughter Told A Lie On Me"
(Aladdin 3175)
by The Five Keys
"Daughter, That's Your Red Wagon"
(States 115)
by Gloria Irving and Sax Kari
"Hush Your Lyin' Mouth"
(Great Lakes 1204)
by Sax Kari and His Band

9. "Save The Last Dance For Me"
   (Atlantic 2071)
   by The Drifters (1960)

"I'll Save The Last Dance For You"
(Mercury 71690)
by Damita Joe
"You're Having The Last Dance With Me!"
(Event 503)
by The Townsmen

10. "Shop Around"
    (Tamla 54034)
    by The Miracles (1960)

"Don'cha Shop Around"
(Guaranteed 219)
by Laurie David
"Don't Let Him Shop Around"
(Motown 1007)
by Debbie Dean
"Don't Have To Shop Around"
(Volt 127)
by The Mad Lads

11. "Wooden Heart"
    (Smash 1708)
    by Joe Dowell (1961)

"I Know Your Heart's Not Made Of Wood"
(Epic 9465)
by Marie Ann
"Your Heart's Not Made Of Wood"
(Madison 167)
by Terri Dean
"Your Heart's Not Made Of Wood"
(May 107)
by Joyce Heath

"You Don't Have A Wooden Heart"
(Coral 62285)
by Bobby Martin

C. Challenge To A Stated Position Or Ideology

Lyrics often contain strong personal sentiments or partisan political perspectives which performers wish to communicate to others. It is understandable that such recordings prompt answer songs which either support the original ideas, or offer contrasting opinions. The latter is the norm. Victor Lunberg's 1967 parental preaching in "An Open Letter To My Teenage Son" generated no fewer than six recorded responses. Although the 1960s were undoubtedly the golden age of politically-motivated recordings and answers—led by the "Eve Of Destruction" vs. "Dawn Of Correction" verbal battle between Barry McGuire and The Spokesmen—it would be an error to think that conflicting commentaries were limited to that decade. The naturalistic educational philosophy of Supertramp in the 1979 tune "The Logical Song" was challenged by The Barron Knights' "The Topical Song." On a more personalized level, "Big Mama" Thornton's condemnation of her lover as a lazy "Hound Dog" was refuted by Rufus Thomas in 1953. The tag "Bear Cat" was created to capsule numerous female shortcomings.

Table 10-C provides a profile of personally-biased, politically-motivated answer songs.

Table 10-C
Challenge To A Stated Position Or Ideology

Song Title, Record Number, and Original Performer	Response Title, Record Number and Response Performer
1. "Eve Of Destruction" (Dunhill 4009) by Barry McGuire (1965)	"Dawn Of Correction" (Decca 31844) by The Spokesmen
2. "Hound Dog" (Peacock 1612) by Willie Mae "Big Mama" Thornton (1953)	"Bear Cat" (Sun 181) by Rufus Thomas
3. "I'm In The Mood" (Modern 835) by John Lee Hooker (1951)	"I Ain't In The Mood" (Modern 851) by Helen Humes
4. "The Logical Song" (A & M 2128) by Supertramp (1979)	"The Topical Song" (Epic 50755) by The Barron Knights
5. "Okie From Muskogee" (Capitol 2626) by Merle Haggard and The Strangers (1969)	"The Only Hippie In Muskogee" (Curtaincall 35691) by C. Dean Draper
6. "An Open Letter To My Teenage Son" (Liberty 55996) by Victor Lunberg (1967)	"Hi Dad (An Open Letter)" (Imperial 66272) by Dick Clair "Letter To Dad" (Buddah 25) by Every Father's Teenage Son

"A Teenager's Answer"
(Tower 383)
by Keith Gordon
"An Open Letter To My Father"
(Dragonet 009)
by Bob Random
"A Teenage Son's Open Letter To
His Father"
(Date 1610)
by Robert Tamkin
"Letter From A Teenage Son"
(Philips 40503)
by Brand Wade

7. "This Diamond Ring" "Gary, Don't Sell My Diamond Ring"
   (Liberty 55756) (Liberty 55771)
   by Gary Lewis and The Playboys (1965) by Wendy Hill
8. "You Talk Too Much" "I Talked Too Much"
   (Roulette 4304) (Roulette 4314)
   by Joe Jones (1960) by Valerie Carr
   "I Don't Talk Too Much"
   (Ric 975)
   by Martha Nelson

D. Continuation Of A Distinct Storyline Or Theme

One type of answer song is quite different than the response to a direct question or the reaction to a statement or command. These tunes are actually extensions of previous hit recordings. They vary greatly. Sometimes they feature a new title with different lyrics, or the original title with supplementary lyrics; they may be produced by a new artist or by the performer of the original song; or they may employ a totally new melody, a slight variation on the original tune, or the same melody as the original recording. The key element to identifying these answer songs, though, is the fact that they continue to lyrically elaborate and expand upon a distinct storyline or theme which was launched in a previous recording.

Folklore is rich in extended storytelling. Popular recordings, which some scholars define as oral history resources, also present numerous examples of character and plot development through lyrical expansion. In the first half of the twentieth century the primary subjects of such vinyl soap operas were steel drivin' man John Henry, notorious badman and murderer Stagger Lee, and the ill-fated couple Frankie and Johnny. It was not unexpected that tales of these characters should continue to be heralded after 1950 as well. But the best illustration of a highly popular song which generated not only a series of cover versions, but also a number of answer recordings is the 1947 hit "Open The Door Richard!" In addition to the major releases of this song in 1947 by composer Jack McVea (Black and White 792), by stage performer Dusty Fletcher (National 4012), and by recording giant Louis Jordan (Decca 23841), fourteen other versions were issued. In the same year, six answer songs also appeared. They were: "I'm Going Back In There" (National 4014) by Dusty Fletcher; "I Ain't Gonna Open That Door" (Apollo 1042) by Stepin' Fletcher; "The Key's In The Mailbox" (Black and White 828) by Jack McVea and His Door Openers; "Richard Got

Hitched" (Black and White 828) by Jack McVea and His Door Openers; "My Name Ain't Richard" (Jewel 9000) by Reedum and Weep; and "I Ain't Gonna Open That Door" (International 219) by the Cedric Wallace Trio. Thus, "Open The Door Richard!" is an exemplary illustration of one of the most prolific answer song generators in record history.

Although answer songs are created for all kinds of lyrical situations, the storytelling mode seems to generate responses in three distinct categories: comic reactions to comic situations; varying observations to family relations; and multiple viewpoints about sexual prowess. The best humor-oriented responses to novelty recordings include the answers to Larry Vern's 1960 "Mr. Custer," to The Royal Guardsmen's 1966 "Snoopy vs. The Red Baron," to Napoleon XIV's 1966 "They're Coming To Take Me Away, Ha-Haaa!," to Joe Tex's 1967 "Skinny Legs And All," and to Randy Newman's 1977 "Short People." The domestic relations theme, which includes loved ones who are not yet married, is another rich source for answer songs. Classic illustrations include James Shepherd's travelling odyssey in "A Thousand Miles Away" and "Daddy's Home"; Ernie K-Doe's harangue against his "Mother-in-Law"; Johnny Cash's embarrassment at being "A Boy Name Sue"; Kenny Roger's barroom interlude with the fickle "Lucille" and her hardworking husband; The Vibrations determined faith in "My Girl Sloopy"; the fatherly protection described by Claude King in "Wolverton Mountain"; and the melancholy tale told by Herman's Hermits about Mrs. Brown's lovely daughter. Although most of the answers to these tunes are comic, they generally expand upon the original situation and reach different conclusions than the original artist.

The final examples within the continuation of a distinct storyline area are thematically oriented toward sexual prowess. The mildest incarnations of these lyrical brag-and-response activities are Gene Chandler's 1962 "Duke Of Earl" and Etta James' 1955 "Wallflower" (which emerged later that same year as "Dance With Me, Henry" by Georgia Gibbs). But while these songs utilized vague hints of romantic intent, three other tunes launched extended, outrageous, and unabashedly sexual tales of male and female indiscretions. In 1951 The Dominoes introduced the notorious Lovin' Dan. This "Sixty Minute Man" promised every young woman an hour-long scene of kissin', huggin', squeezing', and blowin' his top. Tales of Dan's antics multiplied. In 1954 Hank Ballard and The Midnighters chanted "Work With Me Annie" to an amused, titilated radio listening and record buying audience. The so-alled Annie Series of answer recordings exploded when The Midnighters reported that "Annie Had A Baby" and can't work anymore. This group of songs, which is directly related to the more sanitized "Wallflower"/"Dance With Me, Henry" records, constitute the best illustration of rampant answer tunes in the post-1950 period. Finally, one cannot overlook the classic macho images projected in 1955 by two Chicago-based performers. Muddy Waters' "Manish Boy" and Bo Diddley's "I'm A Man" sparked numerous immediate responses and have continued to fuel lyrical commentaries by groups over the following three decades. One need only to hear the opening bars of "Bad To The Bone," a tune composed by George Thorogood, to sense the continuing influence of the original 1955 recordings. Additionally, Thorogood's description of evil incarnate directly parallels the lyrical men of mayhem depicted by Muddy Waters and Bo Diddley.

Table 10-D
Continuation Of A Distinct Storyline Or Theme

Song Title, Record Number, and Original Performer	*Response Title, Record Number, and Response Performer*
1. "A Boy Named Sue" (Columbia 44944) by Johnny Cash (1969)	"A Girl Named Harry" (Happy Tiger Era 102) by Joni Credit "My Name Is Sue (But I'm A Girl)" (Contrast 604) by Johnny and Phil "A Girl Named Johnny Cash" (RCA 9839) by Jane Morgan "A Girl Named Sam" (Starday 877) by Lois Williams
2. "By The Time I Get To Phoenix" (Capitol 2015) by Glen Campbell (1967)	"By The Time You Get To Phoenix" (Capitol 2085) by Wanda Jackson "By The Time You Get To Phoenix" (Dunhill 4119) by Joanna Moore
3. "The Duke Of Earl" (Vee Jay 416) by Gene Chandler (1962)	"Duchess Of Earl" (Vee Jay 435) by The Pearlettes "Duchess Of Earl" (Big Top 3100) by Bobbie Smith "Walk On With The Duke" (Vee Jay 440) by Gene Chandler
4. "Hit The Road Jack" (ABC 10244) by Ray Charles (1961)	"I Changed My Mind, Jack" (ABC 10300) by Jo Anne Campbell "Well I Told You" (Carlton 564) by The Chantels
5. "Lucille" (United Artists 929) by Kenny Rogers (1977)	"A Woman's Reply" (Compass 003) by Charlotte Hurt "Thanks For Leaving, Lucille" (Gusto/Starday 164) by Sherri Jerrico "Lucille's Answer" (Epic 50444) by Julie Jones
6. "Manish Boy" (Chess 1602) by Muddy Waters (1955) "I'm A Man" (Checker 814) by Bo Diddley (1955)	"I'm Bad" (Checker 842) by Bo Diddley "I'm A Woman" (Dootone 378) by Mickey Champion and Roy Milton

"She's A Woman"
(Atco 6060)
by Beau Fairley and Jimmy Griffin
"W-O-M-A-N"
(Modern 972)
by Etta James
"I'm Grown"
(Excello 2106)
by Lightning Slim
"That's What They Want"
(Excello 2068)
by Jerry McCain and The Upstarts

7. "Mother-in-Law"
   (Minit 623)
   by Ernie K-Doe (1961)

"Son-in-Law"
(Challenge 9109)
by The Blossoms
"Son-in-Law"
(Witch 101)
Louise Brown
"My Mother-in-Law Is In
My Hair Again"
(Duke 378)
by Ernie K-Doe

8. "Mr. Custer"
   (Era 3024)
   by Larry Verne (1960)

"We're Depending On You Mr. Custer"
(Pip 100)
by The Characters
"Custer's Last Man"
(Motown 1002)
by Pop Corn and The Mohawks
"Ho Ho Mr. Custer"
(Personality 3501)
by Moe Nudenick
"Return Of Mr. Custer"
(Era 3139)
by Larry Verne

9. "Mrs. Brown You've Got
   A Lovely Daughter"
   (MGM 13331)
   by Herman's Hermits (1965)

"Mother Dear You've Got
A Silly Daughter"
(Philips 40290)
by Sharon Black
"Mrs. James, I'm Mrs. Brown's
Lovely Daughter"
(Capitol 5447)
by Connie Holiday
"Mrs. Schwarts You've Got An
Ugly Daughter"
(Associated Artists 3065)
by Marty
"A Frightful Situation"
(Challenge 59292)
by Mrs. Brown's Lovely Daughter Carol
"Mrs. Green's Ugly Daughter"
(Diamond 183)
by Kenneth Young and The English Muffins

10. "My Girl Sloopy"
    (Atlantic 2221)
    by The Vibrations (1964)

'(My Girl) Sloopy"
(Mala 512)
by Little Caesar and The Consuls

"Hang On Sloopy"
(Bang 506)
by The McCoys (1965)

11. "Ode To Billie Joe"
(Capitol 5950)
by Bobby Gentry (1967)

12. "Party Lights"
(Chancellor 1113)
by Claudine Clark (1962)

13. "Ruby, Don't Take Your Love
To Town" (Reprise 0829)
by Kenny Rogers and The First
Edition (1969)

14. "Say Man"
(Checker 931)
by Bo Diddley (1959)

15. "Short People"
(Warner Brothers 8492)
by Randy Newman (1977)

16. "Sixty Minute Man"
(Federal 12022)
by The Dominoes (1977)

"Sloopy's Gonna Hang On"
(Mercury 72494)
by The Debs

"The Return Of Billie Joe"
(Jack O'Diamonds 1006)
by Tommy Lee
"Mystery Of The Tallahatchie Bridge"
(Big A 103)
by Roger White

"I'm Sorry I Went"
(Valiant 6024)
by The Cannon Sisters
"Walk Me Home From The Party"
(Chancellor 1130)
by Claudine Clark

"Ruby's Answer"
(Little Darlin' 0029)
by Dori Helms
"Billy, I've Got To Go To Town"
(World Pacific 77927)
by Geraldine Stevens

"Say Man, Back Again"
(Checker 936)
by Bo Diddley

"Mr. Small"
(Vanguard 35200)
by The Mr. Men
"Tall People"
(Gusto 179)
by The Short People
"Tall People"
(Co-Star 101)
by Wee Willie Small

"Pedal Pushin' Papa"
(Federal 12114)
by The Dominoes (1952)
"Can't Do Sixty No More"
(Red Robin 108)
by The Du-Droppers (1952)
"Don't Stop Dan"
(King 4710)
by The Checkers (1954)
"Life Of Ease"
(Great Lakes 1201)
by The Imperials (1954)
"Can't Do Sixty No More"
(Federal 12209)
by Billy Ward and The Dominoes
(1955)
"The Hatchet Man"
(Spark 116)
by The Robins (1955)
"Dancin' Dan"
(Modern 1000)
by The Cadets (1956)

17. "Skinny Legs And All"
    (Dial 4063)
    by Joe Tex (1967)

by The Cadets (1956)
"I'll Take Those Skinny Legs"
(Twinight 106)
by Syl Johnson
"I'm Leroy—I'll Take Her"
(Jetstar 110)
by Bobby Patterson and The Mustangs

18. "Snoopy vs. The Red Baron"
    (Laurie 3366)
    by The Royal Guardsmen (1966)

"Red Baron's Revenge"
(GNP 385)
by The Delicatessen
"The Return Of The Red Baron"
(Laurie 3379)
by The Royal Guardsmen

19. "Stagger Lee"
    (ABC-Paramount 9972)
    by Lloyd Price (1958)
    "Stag-O-Lee"
    (Atlantic 2448)
    by Wilson Pickett (1967)

"Trail Of Stagger Lee"
(Concertone 250)
by Stella Johnson
"The Return Of Stagger Lee"
(United Artists 277)
by Don ReVels
"The Ballad Of Stagger Lee"
(Kent 320)
by The Senders
"Return Of Stagolee"
(King 5186)
by Titus Turner

20. "Taxi"
    (Elektra 45770)
    by Harry Chapin (1972)

"Sequel"
(Boardwalk 5700)
by Harry Chapin

21. "These Boots Are Made For Walkin' "
    (Reprise 0432)
    by Nancy Sinatra (1966)

"These Spurs Are Made For Ridin' "
(Black Beat 572)
by Gene Goza
"Put Your Boots Back On The Shelf"
(Rust 5105)
by Boots Walker

22. "They're Coming To Take Me
    Away, Ha-Haaa!"
    (Warner Brothers 5831)
    by Napoleon XIV (1966)

"I'm Normal"
(RPR 6404)
by The Emporer
"Don't Let Them Take Me Back, Oh No"
(Showcase 9810)
by Henry IX
"They Took You Away (I'm Glad,
I'm Glad)"
(Valiant 745)
by Josephine
"Down On The Funny Farm"
(Cameo 427)
by Josephine XIII

23. "A Thousand Miles Away"
    (Rama 216)
    by The Heartbeats (1956)

"500 Mile To Go"
(Gee 1047)
by The Heartbeats
"Daddy's Home"
(Hull 740)
by Shep and The Limelites (1961)
"What Did Daddy Do"
(Hull 751)

24. "The Wallflower"
    (Modern 947)
    by Etta James (1955)
    "Dance With Me Henry"
    (Mercury 70572)
    by Georgia Gibbs (1955)

25. "Wolverton Mountain"
    (Columbia 42352)
    by Claude King (1962)

26. "Work With Me Annie"
    (Federal 12169)
    by The Midnighters (1954)

by Shep and The Limelites
"Annie Met Henry"
(Modern 969)
by The Cadets
"Annie Met Henry"
(Chart 602)
by The Champions
"Hey, Henry!"
(Modern 957)
by Etta James
"Henry's Got Flat Feet"
(Federal 12224)
by The Midnighters
"Here Comes Henry"
(Modern 1010)
by Young Jesse
"Keep Off My Mountain"
(Dot 16385)
by Cliff Adams
"I'm The Girl From Wolverton
Mountain"
(Cameo 223)
by Jo-Ann Campbell
"I'm Going Down Wolverton
Mountain"
(Toppa 1066)
by Betty Luther
"My Name Ain't Annie"
(King 4752)
by Linda Hayes and The Platters
"Annie Don't Love Me No More"
(Symbol 215)
by The Hollywood Flames
"Eat Your Heart Out Annie"
(Capitol 3512)
by The Jordimars
"Annie Get Your Yo-Yo"
(Duke 345)
by Little Junior Parker (1962)
"Annie's Back"
(Specialty 692)
by Little Richard (1964)
"Annie's Answer"
(Vee Jay 118)
by Hazel McCallum and The El Doradoes
"Annie Had A Baby"
(Federal 12195)
by The Midnighters (1954)
"Annie's Aunt Fannie"
(Federal 12200)
by The Midnighters (1954)
"Annie Pulled A Humbug"
(Music City 746)
by The Midnights
"Annie Kicked The Bucket"

(Hollywood Star 789)
by The Nu-Tones
"Annie's Not An Orphan Anymore"
(Challenge 919)
by Rochell and The Candles
"I'm The Father Of Annie's Baby"
(Bruce 118)
by Danny Taylor

E. Follow-Up Statements To General
Ideas And Themes

As in other sections of this study, the functions of individual songs tend to blur across arbitrarily established categories. This is particularly evident in terms of separating the distinct storyline approach from a more general follow-up idea. Such inevitable overlapping is not a major problem, though. It merely acknowledges the richness of the answer song galaxy.

Follow-up themes are often related to either comedy tales or dance styles. David Seville's animal cronies Alvin, Theodore, and Simon were introduced in the 1958 hit "The Chipmunk Song." During the next four years, the same group produced varying tales of musical ("Alvin's Harmonica" and "Alvin's Orchestra"), political ("Alvin For President"), and dance ("The Alvin Twist") activities. These novelty tunes, particularly the latter one, provide the stylistic format for numerous other follow-up themes related to dancing. The 1960s twist craze led Hank Ballad and Chubby Checker to issue several thematically-connected tunes including "Twistin' U.S.A.," "Let's Twist Again," "Slow Twistin'," "La Paloma Twist," "Do You Know How To Twist,"and "Twist It Up." Even Danny and The Juniors urged their listeners to get "Back To The Hop." Rufus Thomas, trying to capitalize on a dance style he launched with his 1963 song "The Dog," produced three answer tunes to perpetuate the original movement.

Novelty tunes dominate the follow-up theme category. "My Ding-A-Ling," a humorous call-and-response song originally released in 1952 by Dave Bartholomew, generated three answer records by 1954; in 1972 Chuck Berry issued an audience-participation hit with the same song, and yet another answer song was produced. A less sexually suggestive type of humor may be found in recordings such as Jody Miller's "Queen Of The House" reaction to Roger Miller's "King Of The Road" and Sugar Pie De Santo's "Slip-In Mules" response to Tommy Tucker's "Hi-Heel Sneakers." It was probably predictable that Brian Hyland's 1960 story of a young woman clad in an overly-brief bathing suit would generate several different commentaries. During the following seven years three answer songs emerged—"1967 Itsy Bitsy Teenie Weenie Yellow Polka Dot Bikini," "Poor Begonia Caught Pneumonia," and "Four Shy Girls."

Table 10-E lists a variety of songs which fall within the follow-up theme category. It is particularly fascinating to note the lengthy periods of time that can elapse between the popularity of an original hit and the release of an answer tune. Ray Stevens' "Along Came Jones" was issued ten years after The Coasters' original; Danny and The Juniors' follow-up to their 1957 "At The Hop" was released in 1961; and Rodney Lay's "I Wish I Had A Job To Shove" reaction to Johnny Paycheck occurred five years after the original recording.

Table 10-E
Follow-Up Ideas And Themes

Song Title, Record Number and Original Performer	*Response Title, Record Number, and Response Performer*
1. "Along Came Jones" (Atco 6141) by The Coasters (1959)	"Along Came Jones" (Monument 1150) by Ray Stevens (1969)
2. "At The Hop" (ABC-Paramount 9871) by Danny and The Juniors (1957)	"Back To The Hop" (Swan 4082) by Danny and The Juniors (1961)
3. "The Chipmunk Song" (Liberty 55168) by The Chipmunks with David Seville (1958)	"Alvin's Harmonica" (Liberty 55179) by The Chipmunks with David Seville (1959) "Alvin's Orchestra" (Liberty 55233) by The Chipmunks with David Seville (1960) "Alvin For President" (Liberty 55277) by The Chipmunks with David Seville (1960) "The Alvin Twist" (Liberty 55424) by The Chipmunks with David Seville (1962)
4. "The Dog" (Stax 130) by Rufus Thomas (1963)	"Walking The Dog" (Stax 140) by Rufus Thomas (1963) "Can Your Monkey Do The Dog" (Stax 144) by Rufus Thomas (1964) "Somebody Stole My Dog" (Stax 149) by Rufus Thomas (1964)
5. "Hi-Heel Sneakers" (Checker 1067) by Tommy Tucker (1964)	"Slip-in Mules" (Checker 1075) by Sugar Pie DeSanto (1964)
6. "Itsy Bitsy Teenie Weenie Yellow Polka Dot Bikini" (Leader 805) by Brian Hyland (1960)	"1967 Itsy Bitsy Teenie Weenie Yellos Polka Dot Bikini" (Diamond 226) by Tommy Dae and High Tensions "Poor Begonia Caught Pneumonia" (Columbia 41790) by Jerri Lynne Fraser "Four Shy Girls" (Pioneer 71833) by The Girlfriends
7. "King Of The Road" (Capitol 5402) by Roger Miller (1965)	"Queen Of The House" (Capitol 5402) by Jody Miller
8. "Little Sister" (RCA 47-7908)	"Hey, Memphis" (Atlantic 2119)

by Elvis Presley (1961)

9. "My Ding-A-Ling"
   (King 4544)
   by Dave Bartholomew (1952)

by LaVern Baker
"Little Girl Sing Ting-A-Ling"
(Imperial 5210)
by Dave Bartholomew
"The Real Thing"
(Imperial 5305)
by The Spiders (1954)
"Toy Bell"
(Imperial 5314)
by The Bees (1954)
"My Ding-A-Ling"
(Chess 2131)
by Chuck Berry (1972)
"My Pussycat"
(Grassroots 1030)
by Miss Chuckle Cherry

10. "Oh, What A Night"
    (Vee Jay 204)
    by The Dells (1956)

"Oh, What A Day"
(Cadet 5663)
by The Dells (1970)
"December, 1963 (Oh, What A Night)"
(Warner Brothers 8168)
by The Four Seasons (1975)

11. "Papa's Got A Brand New Bag"
    (King 5999)
    by James Brown (1965)

"Mama's Got A Bag Of Her Own"
(End 1126)
by Anna King
"Mama's Got A Brand New Box"
(Normar 328)
by Vicky Lewis

12. "Take This Job And Shove It"
    (Epic 50469)
    by Johnny Paycheck (1977)

"I Wish I Had A Job To Shove"
(Churchill 94005)
by Rodney Lay (1982)

13. "The Twist"
    (King 5171)
    by Hank Ballard and
    The Midnighters (1960)
    "The Twist"
    (Parkway 811)
    by Chubby Checker (1960)

"Twistin' U.S.A."
(Parkway 811)
by Chubby Checker (1961)
"Let's Twist Again"
(Parkway 824)
by Chubby Checker (1961)
"Slow Twistin' "
(Parkway 835)
by Chubby Checker (1962)
"La Paloma Twist"
(Parkway 835)
by Chubby Checker (1962)
"Do You Know How To Twist"
(King 5593)
by Hank Ballard and
The Midnighters (1962)
"Twist It Up"
(Parkway 879)
by Chubby Checker (1963)

14. "Wimoweh"
    (Decca 27928)
    by The Weavers,
    with Gordon Jenkins (1952)
    "The Lion Sleeps Tonight"

"The Tiger's Wide Awake"
(Amy 840)
by The Romeos
"The Lion Is Awake"
(Lucky 41019)

(RCA 7954)   by Sammy and 5 Notes
by The Tokens (1961)

F. Parody Tunes

The answer song, by its nature a counterveiling statement, is often a parody of the recording to which it responds. Yet not all answers are designed to be humorous. Some recording stars have shaped their professional careers by drafting comic responses to hit tunes. Homer and Jethro, Ben Colder, Weird Al Yankovic, Allan Sherman, Stan Freberg and others strategically await opportunities to react to popular songs with their own creative parodies. Generally, parody song titles clearly establish linkage to original hits. Thus, there is no doubt as to the intent of Ben Colder's "Almost Persuaded No. 2," "Detroit City No. 2," and "Harper Valley P.T.A. (Later That Same Day)." Beyond the story continuation inherent in most parodies, singer/songwriters like Weird Al Yankovic often utilize the same melodies and rhythm patterns from hit tunes as background for zany themes such as "Eat It" and "I Love Rocky Road." This pattern is duplicated in Rotunda's "She's Got Colonel Sanders Thighs" parody of Kim Carnes' 1981 hit "Bette Davis Eyes."

Table 10-F lists illustrations of parody songs. Some of the most interesting tunes are politically inspired (Senator Bobby's laid back versions of "Mellow Yellow" and "Wild Thing"), while others portray less than heroic antics by such unlikely characters as "Cholley Oop," the "Uneasy Rider," and "The Leader Of The Laundromat."

Table 10-F
Parody Tunes

Song Title, Record Number, and Original Performer	Response Title, Record Number, and Response Performer
1. "Alley Oop" (Lute 5905) by The Hollywood Argyles (1960)	"Cholley Oop" (Trans—World 6904) by The Hong Kong White Sox
2. "Almost Persuaded" (Epic 10025) by David Houston (1966)	"Almost Persuaded No. 2" (MGM 13590) by Ben Colder "Almost Degraded" (Capitol 4047) by The Cornball Express
3. "The Ballad Of Easy Rider" (Columbia 44990) by The Byrds (1969)	"Uneasy Rider" (Kama Sutra 576) by The Charlie Daniels Band (1973)
4. "The Battle Of New Orleans" (Columbia 41339) by Johnny Horton (1959)	"The Battle Of Kookamonga" (RCA 7585) by Homer and Jethro
5. "Beat It" (Epic 03759) by Michael Jackson (1983)	"Eat It" (Rock 'N' Roll 04374) by Weird Al Yankovic
6. "Bette Davis Eyes" (EMI America 8077) by Kim Carnes (1981)	"She's Got Colonel Sanders Thighs" (Rude 101) by Rotunda
7. "Da Ya Think I'm Sexy?"	"Do You Think I'm Disco?"

(Warner Brothers 7520)
by Rod Stewart (1978)

8. "Desiderata"
   (Warner Brother 7520)
   by Les Crane (1971)
9. "Detroit City"
   (RCA 8183)
   by Bobby Bare (1963)
10. "Downtown"
    (Warner Brother 5494)
    by Petual Clark (1964)
11. "Harper Valley P.T.A."
    (Plantation 3)
    by Jeannie C. Riley (1968)

12. "I Love Rock 'N' Roll"
    (Broadwalk 135)
    by Joan Jett and The
    Blackhearts (1982)
13. "Leader Of The Pack"
    (Red Bird 014)
    by The Shangri-Las (1964)
14. "Mellow Yellow"
    (Epic 10098)
    by Donovan (1966)
15. "Mickey"
    (Chrysalis 2638)
    by Toni Basil (1982)
16. "Wild Thing"
    (Fontana 1548)
    by The Troggs (1966)

(Ovation 1132)
by Steve Dahl and
Teenage Radiation (1979)
"Deteriorata"
(Banana 218)
by National Lampoon (1972)
"Detroit City No. 2"
(MGM 13167)
by Ben Colder
"Crazy Downtown"
(Warner Brother 5614)
by Allan Sherman (1965)
"Harper Valley P.T.A.
(Later That Same Day)"
(MGM 13997)
by Ben Colder
"The Continuing Story Of Harper
Valley P.T.A."
(SSS 749)
by Der Mullins
"I Love Rocky Road"
(Rock 'N' Roll 03998)
by Weird Al Yankovic (1983)

"Leader Of The Laundromat"
(Roulette 4590)
by The Detergents
"Mellow Yellow"
(Parkway 137)
by Senator Bobby (1967)
"Ricky"
(Rock 'N' Roll 03849)
by Weird Al Yankovic
"Wild Thing"
(Parkway 127)
by Senator Bobby (1967)

This study constitutes only a preliminary investigation of the answer song phenomenon. The worlds of record collectors and sound recordings archivists must be merged in order to provide vinyl resources necessary for further scholarship. The answer song, in all its functional permutations, is a worthy subject for further popular culture research.

Works Cited

Books

B. Lee Cooper, *A Resource Guide To Themes In Contemporary American Song Lyrics, 1950-1985*. Westport, Connecticut: Greenwood Press, 1986.

Brett Williams, *John Henry: A Bio-Bibliography*. Westport, Connecticut: Greenwood Press, 1983.

Articles

Roy Adams "I Put The Bomp," *Record Exchanger*, No. 13 (1973), pp. 24, 26.

B. Lee Cooper, "Bear Cats, Chipmunks, And Slip-In Mules: The 'Answer Song' In Contemporary American Recordings, 1950-1985," *Popular Music And Society*, XII (Fall 1988), pp. 57-77.

_____ "Response Recordings As Creative Repetition: Answer Songs And Pop Parodies In Contemporary American Music," *OneTwoThreeFour: A Rock 'N' Roll Quarterly*, No. 4 (Winter 1987), pp. 79-87.

_____ "Sequel Songs And Response Recordings: The Answer Record In Modern American Music, 1950-1985," *International Journal Of Instructional Media*, XIII, No. 3 (1986), pp. 227-239.

Ren Grevatt, "Answer Songs Aren't New!" *Melody Maker*, XXXV (November 5, 1960), pp. 6-7.

George Moonoogian, "The Answer Record In R&B," *Record Exchanger*, No. 22 (1976), pp. 24-25, 28.

George Moonoogian and Chris Beachley, " 'Lovin' Dan: A Look Thirty Years Later— Does He Have 59 To Go?", *It Will Stand*, No. 20 (1980), pp. 4-7.

_____ "Oh, That Annie!" *Record Exchanger*, No. 23 (1977), pp.20-21.

John P. Morgan and Thomas C. Tulloss, "The Jake Walk Blues: A Toxicologic Tragedy Mirrored In American Popular Music," *Annals Of Internal Medicine*, LXXXV (December 1976), pp. 804-808.

"Same To You, Mac," *Time*, LXXVII (January 6, 1961), p. 52.

Doug Seroff, "Open The Door Richard!" *Record Exchanger*, No. 20 (1975), pp. 10-11.

Gordon Stevenson, "Race Records: Victims Of Benign Neglect In Libraries," *Wilson Library Bulletin*, L (November 1975), pp. 224-232.

Larry Stidom, "Larry's Corner," *Record Digest*, No. 19 (June 15, 1978), p. 38.

_____ "Larry's Corner," *Record Digest*, Nos. 22/23 (August 1, 1978), pp. 24-28ff.

_____ "Larry's Corner," *Music World And Record Digest*, No. 40 (May 9, 1979), p. 10.

_____ "Sheb Wooley a.k.a. Ben Colder: The Purple People Eater Revisited," *Goldmine*, No. 65 (October 1981), pp. 178-179.

Mark J. Zucker, " 'The Saga Of Lovin' Dan: A Study In The Iconography Of Rhythm And Blues Music Of The 1950s," *Journal Of Popular Culture*, XVI (Fall 1982), pp. 43-51.

Unpublished Materials

Bruce R. Buckley, "Frankie And Her Men: A Study Of The Interrelationship Of Popular And Folk Traditions" (Ph.D.: Indiana Univeristy, 1961).

B. Lee Cooper, "Yes, Bearcat, I'll Save The Last Dance For You: Answer Songs And Sequel Tunes In American Popular Music, 1950-1985" (mimeographed paper and audio tape presentation at the 8th National Convention of The American Culture Association in April 1985).

Richard D. Ralston, "Bad Dude Or Common Criminal: The Interrelationship Of Contemporary And Folk Values In The Ballad Of Stagolee" (mimeographed paper presented at the 14th National Convention of The Popular Culture Association in March 1984).

Chapter Eleven
Cover Records and Song Revivals

The development of contemporary American music is clearly reflected in the integration of black composers, performers, and their songs into mainstream popular records charts. Between 1953 and 1978 a fascinating role reversal occurred. During that quarter century black artists shifted from creators to revivalists. The same role reversal did not apply to white artists, who tended to evolve along a more conservative audience—acceptance continuum. How can this 25-year cycle of social change best be illustrated? What particular elements of black music dramatically entered the pop spectrum during the fifties, and later gained dominance by the end of the sixties? Why did black artists become more and more conservative during the late seventies? A careful examination of audio repetition—cover recordings and song revivals—offers a great deal of revealing information about changes in social, economic, and artistic life in America after 1953.

Financial Exploitation

The path to popular music success was extremely difficult for black performers during the early 1950s. Unless they were willing to adopt a white-oriented singing style such as that of Nat "King" Cole, black musicians invariably found themselves isolated from dominant recording companies—Decca, Columbia, RCA Victor, and Capitol—and thus separated from the majority of the record-buying public. Worse yet, when a black artist developed an original, potentially successful tune through a small, independent recording outfit—Savoy, King, Specialty, or Peacock—white artists, including Pat Boone, Gale Storm, and The Fontane Sisters, hurriedly supplied the white record purchasing audience with an acceptable "cover" version of the same tune. This cover phenomenon occurred frequently enough to confirm the suspicions that prejudice, plagiarism, and financial exploitation were central factors in American recording industry practices between 1953 and 1956.

Below are several examples of original recordings by black performers that were duplicated by white artists:

"At My Front Door"
  originally charted by The El Dorados
  (Vee Jay 147) on October 15, 1955
  cover recording charted by Pat Boone
  (Dot 15422) on October 29, 1955
"Church Bells May Ring"
  originally charted by The Willows

140

(Melba 102) on April 7, 1956
cover recording charted by The Diamonds
(Mercury 70835) on April 21, 1956

"Earth Angel (Will You Be Mine)"
originally charted by The Penguins
(Dootone 348) on December 25, 1954
cover recording charted by The Crew—Cuts
(Mercury 70529) on February 5, 1955
cover recording charted by Gloria Mann
(Sound 109) on February 12, 1955

"Eddie My Love"
originally charted by The Teen Queens
(RPM 453) on March 3, 1956
cover recording charted by The Fontane Sisters
(Dot 15450) on March 10, 1956
cover recording charted by The Chordettes
(Cadence 1284) on March 10, 1956

"Goodnight, Sweetheart, Goodnight"
originally charted by The Spaniels
(Vee Jay 107) on June 19, 1954
cover recording charted by The McGuire Sisters
(Coral 61187) on June 26, 1954
cover recording charted by Sunny Gale
(RCA Victor 5746) on July 17, 1954

"Hearts Of Stone"
originally charted by The Charms
(Deluxe 6062) on November 27, 1954
cover recording charted by The Fontane Sisters
(Dot 15265) on December 11, 1954

"I'm In Love Again"
originally charted by Fats Domino
(Imperial 5386) on April 28, 1956
cover recording charted by The Fontane Sisters
(Dot 15462) on May 26, 1956

"Ivory Tower"
originally charted by Otis Williams and His Charms
(Deluxe 6093) on March 31, 1956
cover recording charted by Gale Storm
(Dot 15458) on April 28, 1956

"(My Heart Goes) Ka—Ding Dong"
originally charted by The G—Clefs
(Pilgrim 715) on July 28, 1956
cover recording charted by The Diamonds
(Mercury 70934) on September 8, 1956

"Long Tall Sally"
    originally charted by Little Richard
    (Specialty 572) on April 7, 1956
    cover recording charted by Pat Boone
    (Dot 15457) on April 14, 1956

"Rip It Up"
    originally charted by Little Richard
    (Specialty 579) on July 7, 1956
    cover recording charted by Bill Haley and His Comets
    (Decca 30028) on August 11, 1956

"See Saw"
    originally charted by The Moonglows
    (Chess 1629) on September 1, 1956
    cover recording charted by Don Cornell
    (Coral 61721) on November 10, 1956

"Sh—Boom"
    originally charted by The Chords
    (Cat 104) on July 3, 1954
    cover recording charted by The Crew—Cuts
    (Mercury 70404) on July 10, 1954

"Silhouettes"
    originally charted by The Rays
    (Cameo 117) on October 14, 1957
    cover recording charted by The Diamonds
    (Mercury 71197) on November 4, 1957

"Tweedlee Dee"
    originally charted by LaVern Baker
    (Atlantic 1047) on January 15, 1955
    cover recording charted by Georgia Gibbs
    (Mercury 70517) on January 29, 1955

"Why Do Fools Fall In Love"
    originally charted by Frankie Lymon and The Teenagers
    (Gee 1002) on February 11, 1956
    cover recording charted by The Diamonds
    (Mercury 70790) on February 18, 1956
    cover recording charted by Gale Storm
    (Dot 15448) on March 3, 1956
    cover recording charted by Gloria Mann
    (Decca 29832) on March 10, 1956

The bulk of cover recordings and revivals of black songs by white artists were not intended to inflict terminal financial hardship on Afro-American artists. Rather, they served as indirect acknowledgments of the musical quality and sales attractiveness of original black material by white artists who were supported by more sophisticated record marketing approaches and public distribution resources. Several white performers, including Georgia Gibbs, Elvis Presley, The Crew-Cuts, and The Chordettes profited directly and often by producing songs originally released by blacks. For example, The Drifters' "Money Honey," Wynonie Harris' "Good Rockin' Tonight," Junior Parker's "Mystery Train," and Willie Mae Thornton's "Hound Dog" were easily adapted to the Presley repertoire. But beyond these Presley revival recordings are two points of greater significance. First, black music—although slightly altered rhythmically and occasionally lyrically castrated—began to reach beyond the segregated "Rhythm and Blues" charts into *Billboard's* "Top 100" lists during the 1955-59 period. Second, more and more white singers began to revive classic r & b tunes. During the '60s the careers of performers such as Dion DiMucci and Johnny Rivers were shaped significantly by their ability to adapt black material for contemporary audiences. Dion recorded The Drifters' "Ruby Baby," Chuck Berry's "Johnny B. Goode," and even Muddy Waters' blues classic "Hoochi Coochie Man." Meanwhile, Rivers revived several Chuck Berry hits, including "Brown-Eyed Handsome Man" and "Memphis, Tennessee," as well as tunes previously released by Smokey Robinson, Sam Cooke, Huey Smith and The Clowns, and Major Lance. Songs that had initially attracted attention from a limited audience— records played exclusively on black-oriented radio stations—were suddenly transformed into nationwide hits.

The following list of white remakes of songs originated by black artists further demonstrates this point:

"Baby I Need Your Lovin' "
   charted by The Four Tops
   (Motown 1062) on August 15, 1964
   charted by Johnny Rivers
   (Imperial 66227) on February 4, 1967

"Cupid"
   charted by Sam Cooke
   (RCA 7883) on June 5, 1961
   charted by Johnny Rivers
   (Imperial 66087) on February 20, 1965

"Drip Drip"
   charted by The Drifters
   (Atlantic 1187) on August 11, 1958
   charted by Dion DiMucci
   (Columbia 42971) on November 16, 1963

"Hound Dog"
   charted by Willie Mae "Big Mama" Thornton
   (Peacock 1612) on March 21, 1953

charted by Elvis Presley
(RCA 47-6604) on August 4, 1956

"Johnny B. Goode"
  charted by Chuck Berry
  (Chess 1691) on April 28, 1958
  charted by Dion DiMucci
  (Columbia 43096) on August 22, 1964

"Maybelline"
  charted by Chuck Berry
  (Chess 1604) on August 20, 1955
  charted by Johnny Rivers
  (Imperial 66056) on August 15, 1964

"Memphis, Tennessee"
  uncharted song by Chuck Berry
  (Chess 1729, the B-side of
  "Back in The U.S.A.")
  which charted on June 22, 1959
  charted by Johnny Rivers
  (Imperial 66032) on May 30, 1964

"Money Honey"
  charted by Clyde McPhatter and The Drifters
  (Atlantic 1006) on October 24, 1953
  charted by Elvis Presley
  (RCA EPA—821) on May 12, 1956

"Purple Haze"
  charted by The Jimi Hendrix Experience
  (Reprise 0597) on August 26, 1967
  charted by Dion
  (Laurie 3478) on January 25, 1969

"Rockin' Pneumonia And The Boogie Woogie Flu"
  charted by Huey "Piano" Smith and The Clowns
  (Ace 530) on August 12, 1957
  charted by Johnny Rivers
  (United Artists 50960) on October 7, 1972

"The Tracks Of My Tears"
  charted by The Miracles
  (Tamla 54118) on July 17, 1965
  charted by Johnny Rivers
  (Imperial 66244) on June 3, 1967

"Um, Um, Um, Um"
  charted by Major Lance
  (OKEH 7187) on January 4, 1964

charted by Johnny Rivers
(Big Tree 16106) on December 24, 1977

Social Commentary

Although the most blatant period of white-over-black cover recording activities ended after 1956, the practice of reviving or altering the lyrics of black songs in the hope of satisfying white audiences continued for several more years. One reason why many radio stations refused to play (and hence the white listening public failed to hear and purchase) some black songs released during the mid-1950s was that the lyrics frequently contained earthy, off-color comments or explicit sexual references.

In 1954 Hank Ballard and The Midnighters recorded several suggestive songs—including "Work With Me Annie" and "Annie Had A Baby"—describing the sexual exploits of a promiscuous young women. The explicit nature of her relationships with her male courtiers was too vivid for the public airwaves. However, the catchy rhythm of Ballard's "Annie" songs prompted a black female artist to produce a lyrically altered song entitled "The Wallflower." This new version eliminated much of the direct sexual commentary in the original "Annie" numbers, while providing a female response to Ballard's male-oriented tunes. The sales success of Etta James' "Wallflower" encouraged Mercury Recording Company staff writers to edit out *all* of the song's remaining suggestive lyrics in order to create a bouncy, wholesome song entitled "Dance With Me, Henry." Thus white pop singer Georgia Gibbs produced a truly kingsized pop hit in 1955, while Hank Ballard's tunes and Etta James' song continued to appeal only to a relatively small "race record" audience.

Another illustration of lyric alteration occurred in the case of one of the most famous early rock 'n' roll hits, "Shake, Rattle, And Roll." This song, as first performed by Joe Turner in 1954, describes in detail the sheerness of a sexy woman's nightgown ("...the sun comes shinin' through") and her enticing physical endowment ("...I can't believe that whole mess belongs to you") in the bedroom. With slight line changes, which included shifting the setting of the singer's commentary from the boudoir into the kitchen, Bill Haley and His Comets succeeded in transforming Turner's moderately successful Atlantic recording into a smash hit for Decca.

Other kinds of lyric alterations have been utilized to call attention to social injustices. In 1972, for instance, Roberta Flack interrupted her bluesy version of "Somewhere" with the startling cry—"This ain't no *West Side Story* !"—in order to emphasize the reality of racial inequality in New York City. Curtis Mayfield, in his 1972 "live" performance album, added several lines of rambling social commentary about disc jockey and radio station management censorship that was exercised against The Impressions' hit song "We're A Winner." And Solomon Burke cleverly converted Creedence Clearwater Revival's tale of youthful travel aboard the Mississippi sternwheeler "Proud Mary" into an attack against slavery and the post—Civil War caste system of black servitude.

"Work With Me Annie"
    charted by The Midnighters
    (Federal 12169) on April 14, 1954

"Annie Had A Baby"
    charted by The Midnighters
    (Federal 12195) on August 25, 1954
"The Wallflower"
    charted by Etta James
    (Moden 947) on February 9, 1955
"Dance With Me, Henry"
    charted by Georgia Gibbs
    (Mercury 70572) on March 26, 1955

* * *

"Shake, Rattle And Roll"
    charted by Joe Turner
    (Atlantic 1026) on April 28, 1954
    charted by Bill Haley and His Comets
    (Decca 29204) on August 21, 1954

* * *

"We're A Winner"
    charted by The Impressions
    (ABC 11022) on December 30, 1967
    uncharted release by Curtis Mayfield
    (Curtom 1966) in 1971

* * *

"Proud Mary"
    charted by Creedence Clearwater Revival
    (Fantasy 619) on January 25, 1969
    charted by Solomon Burke
    (Bell 783) on May 3, 1969

Musical Creativity and Artistic Tribute

Another interesting trend in song revival practice has been the desire of black performers to return to their musical roots by reproducing hit tunes originally performed by other Afro-American artists. This stylistic vitality has produced many significant propular hits. Aretha Franklin's 1967 success with the tune "Respect," originally authored by the talented but ill-fated soul singer Otis Redding, is typical of the black-over-black revival practice. The peculiar genius of Lady Soul also led her to revive two other previously released black hits—Don Covay's "See Saw" and Dionne Warwick's "I Say A Little Prayer." Before his death in 1967, Redding also offered new renditions of hits originally released by other noted black artists, including James Brown's "Papa's Got A Brand New Bag" and Sam Cooke's "Shake," which he dynamically performed in 1967 at The Monterey Pop Festival.

The following tunes were reintroduced by black artists, who brought innovative rhythm patterns and new vocal styling to established hit songs:

"C.C. Rider"
    charted by Chuck Willis
    (Atlantic 1130) on April 20, 1957
    charted by LaVern Baker
    (Atlantic 2167) on December 1, 1962
"Everybody Needs Somebody To Love"
    charted by Solomon Burke
    (Atlantic 2241) on July 18, 1964
    charted by Wilson Pickett
    (Atlantic 2381) on February 4, 1967

"For Your Precious Love"
    charted by Jerry Butler and The Impressions
    (Abner 1013) on June 16, 1958
    charted by Garnet Mimms and The Enchanters
    (United Artists 658) on November 23, 1963

"I Heard It Through The Grapevine"
    charted by Gladys Knight And The Pips
    (Soul 35039) on October 21, 1967
    charted by Marvin Gaye
    (Tamla 54-176) on November 23, 1968

"I Say A Little Prayer"
    charted by Dionne Warwick
    (Scepter 12203) on October 21, 1967
    charted by Aretha Franklin
    (Atlantic 2546) on August 17, 1968

"Lipstick Traces (On A Cigarette)"
    charted by Benny Spellman
    (Minit 644) on May 5, 1962
    charted by The O'Jays
    (Imperial 66102) on May 8, 1965

"Living For The City"
    charted by Stevie Wonder
    (Tamla 54242) on November 10, 1973
    charted by Ray Charles
    (Crossover 981) on September 13, 1975

"Never can Say Goodbye"
    charted by The Jackson 5
    (Motown 1179) on April 3, 1971
    charted by Isaac Hayes
    (Enterprise 9031) on May 15, 1971
    charted by Gloria Gaynor
    (MGM 14748) on November 2, 1974

"Papa's Got A Brand New Bag"
  charted by James Brown
  (King 5999) on July 17, 1965
  charted by Otis Redding
  (Atco 6636) on November 30, 1968

"Respect"
  charted by Otis Redding
  (Volt 128) on September 4, 1965
  charted by Aretha Franklin
  (Atlantic 2403) on April 29, 1967

"River Deep—Mountain High"
  charted by Ike and Tina Turner
  (Philles 131) on May 28, 1966
  charted by The Supremes and The Four Tops
  (Motown 1173) on November 28, 1970

"See Saw"
  charted by Don Covay and The Goodtimers
  (Atlantic 2301) on November 13, 1965
  charted by Aretha Franklin
  (Atlantic 2574) on November 23, 1968

"Shake"
  charted by Sam Cooke
  (RCA 8486) on January 9, 1965
  charted by Otis Redding
  (Vol 149) on May 20,1967

"Stagger Lee"
  charted by Lloyd Price
  (ABC-Paramount 9972) on December 8, 1958
  charted by Wilson Pickett
  (Atlantic 2448) on November 4, 1967

"The Tracks Of My Tears"
  charted by The Miracles
  (Tamla 54118) on July 17, 1965
  charted by Aretha Franklin
  (Atlantic 2603) on March 15, 1969

"The Twist"
  charted by Hank Ballard and The Midnighters
  (King 5171) on July 18, 1960
  charted by Chubby Checker
  (Parkway 811) on August 1, 1960

"You Send Me"
  charted by Sam Cooke
  (Keen 34013) on October 21, 1957
  charted by Aretha Franklin

Perhaps an even more interesting question concerning the relationship of black music to record revivals is: How did black performers respond to the "new music" from Great Britain during 1964 and after? The answer is obvious. While most white journalists sang the praises of The Beatles, The Rolling Stones, and other groups from the far side of the Atlantic, black artists recognized them as kindred musical spirits who shared deep respect for songs from the early rhythm 'n' blues tradition. While The Beatles sang the hits of Chuck Berry ("Roll Over Beethoven") and Larry Williams ("Slow Down") and The Stones lauded Slim Harpo ("I'm A King Bee") and Marvin Gaye ("Hitch Hike"), American blacks commenced their own restyling of a variety of British song hits. The Beatles provided ample material for Wilson Pickett ("Hey Jude") and Ike and Tina Turner ("Let It Be" and "Get Back"). The Rolling Stones' lyrics also proved appropriate for Muddy Waters ("Let's Spend The Night Together") and Otis Redding ("Satisfaction").

The use of white material by black musicians was not limited to British songwriting talent, either. As the list below indicates, black performers successfully transformed the record revival practice from a tactic of racial parasitism into a strategy for professional harmony and mutual musical exchange:

"Abraham, Martin And John"
  charted by Dion
  (Laurie 3464) on October 26, 1968
  charted by Moms Mobley
  (Mercury 72935) on June 28, 1969
  charted by Smokey Robinson and The Miracles
  (Tamla 54184) on July 5, 1969

"Bridge Over Troubled Waters"
  charted by Simon and Garfunkel
  (Columbia 45079) on February 7, 1970
  charted by Aretha Franklin
  (Atlantic 2796) on April 17, 1971
  charted by Linda Clifford
  (RSO 921) on March 24, 1979

"Eleanor Rigby"
  charted by The Beatles
  (Capitol 5715) on August 27, 1966
  charted by Ray Charles
  (ABC/TRC 11090) on June 8, 1968
  charted by Aretha Franklin
  (Atlantic 2683) on November 8, 1969

"For What It's Worth (Stop, Hey What's That Sound)"
  charted by The Buffalo Springfield
  (Atco 6459) on January 28, 1967
  charted by The Staple Singers
  (Epic 10220) on September 23, 1967

"Hey Jude"
 charted by The Beatles
 (Apple 2276) September 14, 1968
 charted by Wilson Pickett
 (Atlantic 2591) on December 21, 1968

"(I Can't Get No) Satisfaction"
 charted by The Rolling Stones
 (London 9766) on June 12, 1965
 charted by Otis Redding
 (Volt 132) on March 5, 1966

"Love The One You're With"
 charted by Stephen Stills
 (Atlantic 2778) on December 12, 1970
 charted by The Isley Brothers
 (T-Neck 930) on June 19, 1971

"We Can Work It Out"
 charted by The Beatles
 (Capitol 5555) on December 18, 1965
 charted by Stevie Wonder
 (Tamla 54202) on March 13, 1971

"Yesterday"
 charted by The Beatles
 (Capitol 5498) on September 25, 1965
 charted by Ray Charles
 (ABC/TRC 11009) on November 11, 1967

Conclusion

Cover recordings and revivals of previously successful songs ultimately broadened the base of the music revolution in the United States from 1953— 1978. Black artists, at first victimized, eventually joined their fellow white performers in financial prosperity through skillful use of the record revival system. The emergence of marvelously creative black rock 'n' rollers during the mid— 1950s—Little Richard, Fats Domino, Chuck Berry, Larry Williams, and Bo Diddley—provided a prophetic basis for what was to come during the mid-1960s— from Liverpool, Detroit, Memphis, New York City, and Chicago. The homogenization of rock, made possible through both covers and revivals, was accomplished to a great extent during the decade before The Beatles. Just as the U.S. Supreme Court struck down the "separate, but equal" theory of education, so too the American record buying public destroyed the old "race record" barrier in popular music after 1954.

As this study demonstrates, repetition in recordings proved to be an unexpected blessing for many black performers. The theft of potential sales by white artists who covered rhythm 'n' blues tunes during the mid-fifties undeniably cost some black singers access to both mainstream fame and popular chart dollars. The integrationist tendency of the rock 'n' roll revolution was not to be denied, though. The distinctive musical power of Chuck Berry, Sam Cooke, Lloyd Price, Clyde McPhatter, and dozens of others withstood the early cover challenge and ultimately fostered a vibrant period of black artistic independence. Ironically, as the British Invasion lionized many rhythm 'n' blues singers, the recordings of many youthful black stars shifted from creative to revivalist tendencies. This conservative approach, perhaps predictable, was yet another sign of commercial success. It should surprise no one that the late 1980s continue to feature revivalist tunes such as "The Twist" by The Fat Boys. In contemporary music, where songs with established track records offer high hit prospects, black artists *and* white artists continue to utilize revival tactics to insure *Billboard* and *Cash Box* recognition. Repetition is still alive and well!

Coda: Recent Revival Releases By
Black Recording Artists

"Earth Angel (Will You Be Mine)"
   charted by The Penguins (Dootone 348)
   on December 25, 1954
   charted by The New Edition
   (MGM 52905) on August 23, 1986

"Funny How Time Slips Away"
   charted by Joe Hinton
   (Back Beat 541) on August 15, 1964
   charted by The Spinners
   (Atlantic 89922) on December 11, 1982

"In The Midnight Hour"
   charted by Wilson Pickett
   (Atlantic 2289) on July 10, 1965
   released by Wilson Pickett
   (Motown 1916) in 1987

"Jumpin' Jack Flash"
   charted by The Rolling Stones
   (London 908) on June 8, 1968
   charted by Aretha Franklin
   (Arista 9528) on September 27, 1986

"Let's Stay Together"
   charted by Al Green
   (Hi 2202) on December 4, 1971
   charted by Tina Turner
   (Capitol 5322) on January 21, 1984

"Magic Carpet Ride"
   charted by Steppenwolf
   (Dunhill 4161) on October 5, 1968
   released by Grandmaster Flash and The Furious Five
   (Elektra 69380) in 1988

"My Guy"
   charted by Mary Wells
   (Motown 1056) on April 4, 1964
   charted by Sister Sledge
   (Cotillion 47000) on January 1, 1982

"My Toot Toot"
   charted by Jean Knight
   (Mirage 99643) on May 4, 1985
   released by Denise LaSalle
   (Malaco 2112) in 1985
   released by John Fogerty with Rockin' Sidney
   (Warner Brothers 28535) in 1986

"Pink Cadillac"
   uncharted song by Bruce Springsteen
   (Columbia 04463),
   the B-side of "Dancing in The Dark"
   which charted on May 26, 1984
   released by Natalie Cole
   (Manhattan 50117) in 1988

"Stand By Me"
   charted by Ben E. King
   (Atco 6194) on May 8, 1961
   charted by Maurice White
   (Columbia 05571) on August 31, 1985
   charted by Ben E. King
   (Atlantic 89361) on October 4, 1986

"Tears On My Pillow"
   charted by Little Anthony and The Imperials
   (End 1027) on August 11, 1958
   charted by The New Edition
   (MGM 53019) on January 31, 1987

"The Twist"
   charted by Chubby Checker
   (Parkway 811) on August 1, 1960
   released by The Fat Boys
   (Tin Pan Apple 887571) in 1988

"Walk This Way"
   charted by Aerosmith

(Columbia 10449) on November 20, 1976
charted by Run-D.M.C.
(Profile 5112) on July 26, 1986

"Why Do Fools Fall In Love"
charted by Frankie Lymon and The Teenagers
(Gee 1002) on February 11, 1956
charted by Diana Ross
(RCA 12349) on October 17, 1981

"You Send Me"
charted by Sam Cooke
(Keen 34013) on October 21, 1957
charted by The Manhattans
(Columbia 04754) on March 2, 1985

Works Cited

Books

George Albert and Frank Hoffman (comps.), *The Cashbox Black Contemporary Singles Charts, 1960-1984*. Metuchen, New Jersey: Scarecrow Press, Inc., 1986.

Michael Bane, *White Boy Singin' The Blues: The Black Roots Of White Rock*. New York: Penguin Books, 1982.

Nelson George, *The Death Of Rhythm and Blues*. New York: Pantheon Books, 1988.

Frank Hoffman (comp.), *The Literature Of Rock, 1954-1978*. Metuchen, New Jersey: Scarecrow Press, Inc., 1981.

Frank Hoffman and B. Lee Cooper (comps.), *The Literature Of Rock II, 1979-1983*, 2 Volumes. Metuchen, New Jersey: Scarecrow Press, Inc., 1986.

Jerry Osborne and Bruce Hamilton (comps.), *Original Record Collector's Price Guide To Blues, Rhythm & Blues, And Soul*. Phoenix, Arizona: O'Sullivan, Woodside and Company, 1980.

Big Al Pavlow (comp.). *The R&B Book: A Disc-History of Rhythm & Blues*. Providence, Rhode Island: Music House Publishing, 1983.

Joel Whitburn (comp.), *Top R&B Singles, 1942-1988*. Menomonee Falls, Wisconsin: Record Research Inc., 1988.

Articles

Paul Ackerman, "R&B Tunes' Boom Relegates Pop Field To Cover Activity," *Billboard* LXVII (March 26, 1955), pp. 18, 22.

Carl Belz, "Early Rock: Crossovers and Covers," in *The Story of Rock*, second edition (New York: Harper and Row, 1972), pp. 25-30

Steve Chapple and Reebee Garofalo, "Black Roots, White Fruits: Racism In The Music Industry," in *Rock 'N' Roll Is Here To Pay: The History And Politics Of The Music Industry* (Chicago: Nelson-Hall, Inc., 1977), pp. 231-267.

B. Lee Cooper and Verdan D. Traylor, "Establishing Rock Revivals In Contemporary Music, 1953-1977," *Goldmine*, No. 36 (May 1979), pp. 37-38.

B. Lee Cooper, "Record Revivals As Barometers Of Social Change: The Historical Use Of Contemporary Audio Resources," *JEMF Quarterly*, XIV (Spring 1978), pp. 38-44.

_____ "Response Recordings As Creative Repetition: Answer Songs And Pop Parodies In Contemporary American Music," *OneTwoThreeFour: A Rock 'N' Roll Quarterly*, No. 4 (Winter 1987), pp. 79-87.

_____ "Sequel Songs And Response Recordings: The Answer Song In Modern American Music, 1950-1985," *International Journal Of Instructional Media*, XIII (1986), pp. 227-239.

_____ "The Song Revival Revolution Of The Seventies: Tapping The Musical Roots Of Rock," *Goldmine*, No. 42 (November 1979), p. 126.

Joe Ferrandino, "Rock Culture And The Development Of Social Consciousness," in *Side-Saddle On The Golden Calf: Social Structure And Popular Culture In America*, edited by George H. Lewis (Pacific Palisades, California: Goodyear Publishing Company, Inc., 1972) pp. 263-290.

Phyl Garland, "Crossover: A Bridge Over Pop Waters," *Billboard*, (June 9, 1979), pp. B.M. 14, 24 ff.

Charles Gillett, "The Black Market Roots Of Rock," in *The Sounds Of Social Change: Studies In Popular Culture*, edited by R. Serge Denisoff and Richard A. Peterson (Chicago: Rand McNally and Company, 1972), pp. 274-281).

Douglas B. Green, "Country Music: An American Heritage Of Musical Interplay," *Billboard*, (June 9, 1979), pp. BM 22, 36.

Paul Grein, "Oldies Still Goodies The Second Time Around," *Billboard*, (June 7, 1980), pp. P16-18.

Mike Harris, "Rock Classics: When Old Is New," *Billboard*, (June 20, 1981), p. 34.

Jonathan Kamin, "Taking The Roll Out Of Rock 'N' Roll: Reverse Acculturation," *Popular Music And Society*, II (Fall 1972), pp. 1-17.

Rich Lonz, "50s Covers," *Record Exchanger*, IV (1975), pp. 18-22.

Jim McFarlin, "Recycled Gold," *Detroit News*, (November 2, 1986), pp. J1, J8.

Bill Millar, "Rockin' 'N' Drifting'," in *The Drifters: The Rise And Fall Of The Black Vocal Group* (New York: Collier Books, 1971), pp. 65-92.

George Moonoogian, "Elvis And The Originals," *Record Exchanger*, III (February 1973), p. 16.

Tony Neale, "A Musical Retrospective From The '50s To The Present," *Music World*, No. 91 (November 1981), pp. 9-14.

Bob Sarlin, "Rock-And-Roll!" in *Turn It Up (I Can't Hear The Words): The Best Of The New Singer/Song Writers* (New York: Simon and Schuster, 1973), pp. 29-37.

Arnold Shaw, "Sh-Boom," in *The Rockin' 50s: The Decade That Transformed The Pop Music Scene* (New York: Hawthorn Books, Inc., 1974), pp. 73-79.

Robert Snyder, "Cover Records: What? When? And Why?" *Record Digest*, I (July 1, 1978), pp. 3-18.

Gerry Wood, "Country-R&B Swap Songs," *Billboard*, (December 17, 1977), pp. 1, 62, 67.

Unpublished Materials

Jonathan Liff Kamin, "Rhythm And Blues In White America: Rock And Roll As Acculturation And Perceptual Learning" (Ph.D.: Princeton University, 1975).

Chapter Twelve
Nursery Rhymes and Fairy Tales

Some commentators on contemporary society have contrasted modernity with traditional cultures by calling attention to our relative impoverishment in the area of myths and rituals. Such analyses fail to take note of the fact that our society's consciousness is being shaped by a number of narratives—narratives that play the same role in this culture as mythologies play in other cultures.

Symbols and myths are also characterized by a certain kind of ambiguity which...allow cultures to adapt and reinterpret them in response to changing environmental and social conditions.... It could be argued that the mass media is contemporary society's "tribal storyteller." Unlike the mythology of traditional cultures, however, our society's mythology is contained in abstract plot structures which incarnate in many different guises.

James R. Lewis
"Adam And Eve On Madison
Avenue: Symbolic Inversion
In Popular Culture"
Studies In Popular Culture (1987)

Lyricists of popular songs derive their ideas from every imaginable source. They often adapt and reinterpret traditional characters and themes from established cultural artifacts. During the past four decades scores of *Billboard*-charted songs have utilized personalities and images drawn from children's literature to define or decorate lyrical passages. In some cases, the song titles clearly denote such literary borrowing. However, it is not uncommon for textual references to be drawn directly from nursery rhymes, fairy tales, or childhood chants even though such borrowing is not clearly related to song titles.

Most writers who examine the lyrical content of modern music tend to concentrate on social issues such as courtship, death, education, and women's roles. Other analysts investigate specific historical periods or significant individual events cited in particular recordings. It is rare to encounter studies searching lyrics for the sources of images, ideas, allegories, and metaphors from literary materials or from long-standing oral tradition. The information assembled in Table A illustrates this latter phenomena. It is important to note that classical sources such as The Holy Bible, William Shakespeare's plays, and books by Lewis Carroll and Charles Dickens are intermixed with popular culture references to television programs, comic books, motion pictures, and newspaper comic strips in the eclectic realm of song lyrics.

Table 12-A
Selected Illustrations Of Literary Resources And
Film Scripts Adapted For The Lyrics
Of Popular Songs, 1955-1985

Title of Popular Recording (Record Company and Number)	Year of Release	Resource for Images or Illustrations in Song Title or Lyric
1. "Adam And Eve" (ABC-Paramount 10082)	1960	Old Testament
2. "Alice In Wonderland" (RCA 8137)	1963	Lewis Carroll's *Alice's Adventures In Wonderland*
3. "Alley-Oop" (Lute 5905)	1960	Newspaper Comic Strip
4. "The Bible Tells Me So" (Coral 61467)	1955	New Testament
5. "Garden Of Eden" (Vik 0226)	1956	Old Testament
6. "Guitarzan" (Monument 1131)	1969	Edgar Rice Burroughs' *Tarzan Of The Apes*
7. "House At Pooh Corner" (United Artists 50769)	1971	A.A. Milne's *The House At Pooh Corner*
8. "The Jolly Green Giant" (Wand 172)	1965	Television Commercial
9. "(Just Like) Romeo And Juliet" (Golden World 9)	1964	William Shakespeare's *Romeo And Juliet*
10. "Lord's Prayer" (A&M 1491)	1974	New Testament
11. "Magic Carpet Ride" (Dunhill 4161)	1968	"Aladdin And The Wonderful Lamp: from *The 1,001 Arabian Nights*
12. "Oliver Twist" (Spiral 1407)	1962	Charles Dickens' *Oliver Twist*
13. "The Return Of The Red Baron" (Laurie 3379)	1967	Newspaper Comic Strip by Charles Schulz
14. "Rip Van Winkle" (Roulette 4541)	1964	Washington Irving's *Rip Van Winkle*
15. "Themes From The Wizard Of Oz" (Millennium 620)	1978	Frank L. Baum's *The Wizard Of Oz*
16. "Thou Shalt Not Steal" (RCA 7993)	1962	Old Testament
17. "Tom Sawyer" (Mercury 76109)	1981	Mark Twain's *The Adventures Of Tom Sawyer*
18. "Turn! Turn! Turn!" (Columbia 43424)	1965	Old Testament
19. "White Rabbit" (RCA 9248)	1967	Lewis Carroll's *Alice's Adventures In Wonderland*
20. "Wish I Could Fly Like Superman" (Arista 0409)	1979	Comic Book

Beyond the realms of traditional literature and popular film, contemporary song lyrics are also influenced by the broad variety of children's stories, games, toys, chants, fads, mythical heroes, and nonsense word play. That such ephemeral popular culture material informs lyrical content is hardly surprising. Nostalgia is not limited to midddle-aged men and women. Familiar lines from childhood experiences, linked to potent, powerful rhythm bases, are immensely attractive to teenage record buyers. This observation is not meant to imply that *every* childhood game or *every* personal experience can be translated into a pop hit. Still, the tendency to utilize youthful ideas and verbal play to create lyrical images is evident in Table 12-B.

Table 12-B

Selected Illustrations Of Childhood
Games And Verbal Terms Adapted To The
Titles And Lyrics Of Popular Songs,
1955-1985

Title of Popular Recording (Record Company and Number)	*Year of Release*	*Source of Images or Illustrations in Song Title or Lyric*
1. "ABC" (Motown 1163)	1970	Alphabet Game
2. "Ally Ally Oxen Free" (Capitol 5078)	1963	Children's Game
3. "Double Dutch Bus" (WMOT)	1981	Jump Rope Chant
4. "Finders Keepers, Losers Weepers" (Wand 171)	1965	Children's Chant
5. "Hide And Go Seek" (Mala 451)	1962	Children's Game
6. "Hoopa Hoola" (Atlantic 2002)	1958	Child's Toy
7. "Hop Scotch" (Canadian American 124)	1961	Children's Game
8. "The Hula Hoop Song" (Roulette 4106)	1958	Child's Toy
9. "Leap Frog" (MGM 12449)	1957	Children's Chant
10. "Liar, Liar" (Soma 1433)	1965	Children's Chant
11. "May I Take A Giant Step (Into Your Heart)" (Buddah 39)	1968	Children's Game
12. "Peanut Butter" (Arvee 5027)	1961	Children's Food
13. "Peek-A-Boo" (Josie 846)	1958	Children's Game
14. "Pin The Tail On The Donkey" (Columbia 43572)	1966	Children's Game
15. "Pop Goes The Weasel" (London 9501)	1961	Children's Game

16. "Rain Rain Go Away" (Epic 9532)	1962	Children's Chant
17. "Ready Or Not Here I Come (Can't Hide From Love)" (Philly Groove 154)	1968	Children's Game
18. "Right String But The Wrong Yo-Yo" (Okeh 7156)	1962	Child's Toy
19. "Rubber Ball" (Liverty 55287)	1960	Child's Toy
20. "Santa Claus Is Coming To Town" (Vee Jay 478)	1962	Children's Hero
21. "See Saw" (Chess 1629)	1956	Child's Toy
22. "Simon Says" (Buddah 24)	1968	Children's Game
23. "Skip A Rope" (Monument 1041)	1967	Children's Game
24. "Sticks And Stones" (ABC-Paramount 10118)	1960	Children's Tease

Tables 12-A and 12-B constitute a lengthy preamble for the remainder of this chapter. Although it is obvious that many song titles and lyric lines are directly linked to a variety of childhood experiences, no sources are more significant than nursery rhymes and fairy tales. Simple poetry from distant times continues to fuel our imaginations; brief and often humorous tales of rabbits and wolves, farmers and puppets, and Jacks, Jills, and kings are part of the longstanding oral tradition of American society. The adaptation of these tales to contemporary popular recordings occurs in varying ways. First, a melody and rhythm pattern are added. Second, the characters from the rhymes are translated into a story setting suitable for a two-and-a-half minute vocal recitation. Finally, the story is told not by a loving grandparent, a mother, a father, or a babysitter, but by a commercial recording artist.

Students of motion picture themes will readily acknowledge that numerous literary productions—texts, plot formats, human and superhuman characters, and even some talking animals—have found their way from printed pages into film scripts. Media sharing also carries over to television, where many new shows are drawn from the legitimate theatre and even from popular comic strips. The adaptations of Cinderella, Little Red Riding Hood, Little Jack Horner, and The Old Woman In The Shoe by contemporary composers seem quite logical in light of previous absorptions including Superman, The Wizard Of Oz, Snoopy, and Little Orphan Annie by both big screen and small screen producers.

Beyond overt title borrowing, though, popular music's use of nursery rhymes and other childhood tales is quite distinctive. First, the mere recitation of an imaginary character's name—Little Jack Horner, Tweedle Dee, The Piped Piper, or Old MacDonald—often symbolizes a particular attitude or specific set of behaviors. Very little explanation need be provided; no elaboration must be offered. The assumption is that everyone listening to the recorded lyric understands the implied meaning of the character's personality. Second, great latitude is usually taken in the lyrical re-telling of a fairy tale or a nursery rhyme. Such poetic license is not exercised merely to achieve better rhyme scheme patterns, either. Double entendre humor is often built into the updated lyrical children's stories. Wolves are actually two-legged women chasers; Little Red Riding Hood becomes a sleek, sexy, and fleeting object of libidinal desire. Third, the delivery style of performing artists such as The Big Bopper, Sam The Sham and The Pharoahs, and The Coasters was built upon vocal extremes and oral pyrotechnics that typify antics of the very best children's storytellers. No hoots, howls, huffs, puffs, snarls, wails, or giggles are spared. The audience is constantly reminded that rock 'n' rhymes are unabashedly non-conventional in vocal delivery styles. Fourth, singers and songwriters often interject absolutely singular phrases or names related to children's stories into songs which otherwise bear no situational relation to nursery rhymes or fairy tales. In a recording entitled "Nursery Rhymes," for instance, Bo Diddley mentions Little Jack Horner as lyrical decoration; similarly, Sleepy LaBeef steals the names of two nursery rhyme characters for the title of his instrumental tune "Jack And Jill Boogie." Finally, the listening audience is expected to make wholesale mental transfers between traditional nursery rhyme images and contemporary song characterization. Although not fully verifiable, one suspects that Leo Sayer extended the "Little Tommy Tucker sings for his supper" idea to create his humorous song "Long Tall Glasses (I Can Dance)." This same kind of interpolation might be applied to the recorded antics of characters spawned by Ray Stevens, David Seville, and Dickie Goodman as well. But proving such speculation is beyond the scope of this study.

The remainder of this chapter will outline the adaptations of twelve (12) children's tales to the lyrics of several popular recordings. A selected discography containing more than one hundred (100) recordings arranged alphabetically according to nursery rhyme or fairy tale title is also presented in Table 12-C.

1. Baa-Baa Black Sheep

Baa, Baa, Black Sheep, have you any
   wool?
Yes, sir, yes, sir, three bags full.
One for The Master, and one for
   The Dame,
And one for The Little Boy who lives
   down the lane.

Sam The Sham and The Pharoahs present a series of human characteristics in an anthropomorphic black sheep/white sheep dichotomy. The chorus for "Black Sheep" is drawn directly from the initial lines for the original nursery rhyme, with only the "Baa-baa" introduction absent. The first part of the song defines the black sheep as a lazy, drunken, irresponsible, neerdowell poet. This image is cast in sharp contrast to the more sober, conservative, wholesome independent white sheep. But as the lyrical tale proceeds, one discovers the good humor, the friendliness, and the good-natured fun of the black sheep, while his white-fleeced counterpart appears to be abysmally dull, selfish, greedy, and shallow. Even in death, the black sheep seems to be grinning from his open pine coffin at his raucous mourners. None of the original nursery rhyme

characters—The Master, The Dame, or The Little Boy who lives down the lane—
is included in this lyrical adaptation. The more puckish black-sheep-of-the-family
myth seems to be the thematic motivation for this lyrical composition.

> 2. Cinderella And The Glass Slipper
> There was once upon a time three sisters
> who lived in an old, high, stone house in
> a street not very far from the great
> square of the city where was the palace
> of the King. The two eldest of these
> sisters were old and ugly, which is bad
> enough. They were also sour and jealous,
> which is worse. And simply because the
> youngest (who was only their half-sister)
> was gentle and lovely, they hated her....

In "Cinderella" Paul Anka relates the humorous story of a young man's
frustration caused by missing a midnight curfew set by his date's parents. He
worries aloud that this indiscretion may mean that this is the last time he can
take his loved one away from her home. No Fairy Godmother, no Handsome
Prince, and no lost slippers are mentioned. It is actually a thematic parallel
to The Everly Brothers' "Wake Up, Little Susie"—without the sleeping at a
drive-in movie excuse, but with a sweet young thing named Cinderella serving
as the stroke-of-twelve attraction. On his "Cinderella" recording Jack Ross
performs an audience-assisted nightclub act. By skillfully reversing letters and
syllables throughout the tale—"The Pransome Hince," "her beet were too fig,"
and "two sisty uglers"—the fast-talking entertainer creates a drunken-sounding,
slapstick story. The fairy tale is presented in full, but admittedly telescoped form.
In "Cinderella Rockefella" Ester and Abi Ofarim yodel through a bizarre song
of mutual admiration which concludes with the unexplained linkage of Cinderella
and (you're the fella who rocks me) Rockefella. No logical connection is
conceivable. Paul Revere laments the day-time disappearance of a beautiful young
lady who infatuates him each evening. His pleas about her daylight wherabouts
remain unanswered throughout the song. No missing slipper clue is provided,
either. The frantic orchestration of the recording provides additional audio
evidence of the would-be lover's frustration. "Cinderella Sunshine" remains a
mystery lady.

> 3. Humpty Dumpty
> Humpty Dumpty sat on a wall,
> Humpty Dumpty had a great fall.
> All the King's horses and all the
>   King's men,
> Couldn't put Humpty together again.

Aretha Franklin begins by asserting that all the King's horses and all the
King's men couldn't put the broken hearts of two separated lovers together again.
She enlarges on the Humpty Dumpty metaphor by physical positioning. She
notes that the couple had been sitting on the wall of happiness, the wall of

love, the wall of security so high above—before their fatal fall. The ballad, apropriately entitled "All The King's Horses," defines an irreconcilable separation via the nursery rhyme parallel of a broken egg. In "(Ain't That) Just Like Me," The Coasters use the first four lines of the nursery rhyme to illustrate their helplessness toward their true love. The inevitability of "falling" for someone, unlike Aretha's sad conclusion, is the beginning rather than the end of a happy romantic relationship. Nevertheless, one senses that The Coasters thoroughly enjoy tumbling off of the wall, and look forward to many such happy interludes. Thus, the singularity of the Humpty Dumpty theme is corrupted by the love-seeking Coasters. LaVern Baker refers to her infatuation with a fickle lover as a "Humpty Dumpty Heart." The logic of her argument is difficult to follow since she describes herself as *still* sitting on the wall with a heart that has been mercilessly torn apart. Nevertheless, one immediately recognizes that the tale of the oval nursery rhyme character has informed much of this lyric. Whether broken, cracked, split, or otherwised damaged, it is clear that a loving relationship can readily be equated with an egg in many, many ways.

> 4. Jack And Jill
> Jack and Jill went up the hill,
> To fetch a pail of water.
> Jack fell down and broke
>   his crown,
> And Jill came tumbling after....

Tommy Roe ignores the traditional trip up and down the hill while producing a tune depicting dating practices. "Jack And Jill" are urged to "get right" in order to impress members of the opposite sex. Dancing, dress styles, and grooming are declared to be central social concerns. No pails, no water (except along the beach for surfing), and no broken crowns are in evidence. One doubts that the nursery rhyme story carries much weight in Roe's tune. This is not the case, however, in Ray Parker's song. His group Raydio recounts a lyrically hip version of Jack sitting on the hill waiting for a wandering Jill to come home (or at least to phone). The absence of female attention leads to infidelity, despite Jack's normal tendency to be as morally responsible as Little Red Riding Hood. The absence of Jill's attention is obviously regarded as a reasonable justification for philandering. Although this tale varies greatly from the nursery rhyme story, it does provide personal linkage between the two central characters. In addition, via reference to another nursery rhyme character, the singer further establishes the setting of the tune within a fairy tale system.

> 5. Jack The Giant Killer
> When good King Arthur reigned, there
> lived near the land's end of England
> in the county of Cornwall, a farmer who
> had only one son called Jack.... One day
> Jack happened to be at the townhall when
> the magistrates were sitting in council
> about the giant. He asked, "What reward
> will be given to the man who kills the

Cormoran?" "The giant's treasure," they
said, "will be the reward."

Except for the opening "Fe-Fe, Fi-Fi, Fo-Fo, Fum" chant, drawn directly
from the mythic giant who claimed that he could smell the blood of Englishmen,
The Coasters offer no other direct reference to this fairy tale. Nevertheless, the
humorous "Charlie Brown" is undoubtedly a salute to a contemporary anti-
establishment hero. Charlie Brown confronts the giant dimensions of public
school bureaucracy and lives to tell the tale. He breaks rules by smoking in
the auditorium, by gambling in the gymnasium, by throwing spit-balls in the
classroom, by writing on the wall, by goofing in the hallways, and so on. Charlie
Brown even has the audacity to refer to his English teacher as "Daddy-O." This
defiance of authority is emphasized by the main character's mocking refrain:
"Why is everybody always picking on me?" The giant authoritarism of the public
school environment is short-circuited by a wily, daffy, Jack-of-all-mischief.

6. Little Red Riding Hood
There was once upon a time a little
village girl, the prettiest ever seen
or known, of whom her mother was
dotingly fond. Her Grandmother was
even fonder of her still, and had a
little red hood made for the child,
which suited her so well that where-
ever she went she was known by the
name of Little Red Riding Hood....

Complete with introductory wolf-like howls, Sam The Sham greets a big-
eyed, full-lipped "Li'l Red Riding Hood" and escorts her through the spooky
old woods, comouflaged in his best sheep-suit. What a big heart he has! The
topic of physical attraction continues throughout the recording, which ends prior
to the couple's arrival at Grandma's house. In contrast to that woodsy scene,
The Big Bopper comes calling directly at Red's woodland home, claiming that
he heard about her good looks from the Three Little Pigs. Using a catchy bing-
bang-biddley-bang knock punctuated by threats to huff and puff and blow her
house down, The Bopper (admitting that he's really the notorious Big Bad Wolf
of the neighborhood) pleads with the young lady for some personal attention.
His stated desire is to shake the shack with rock 'n rollin' Red until Grandma
returns. But "Little Red Riding Hood" refuses his insistent pleas to go tick-
a-locka, tick-a-locka and let him in. Dee Clark also describes a wolf who wants
to rock 'n' roll. But this croonin' lobo follows the traditional fairy tale more
closely by putting Grandma out of her house, and then surprising Red with
his big eyes and his big arms. Although "Little Red Riding Hood" remains
an undescribed delicacy in the lyrical version, the conclusion of the story is
left to the listener's imagination. Meanwhile, The Coasters deliver an upbeat,
hepcat story about a red-caped chick that *every* wolf desires. In "Ridin' Hood"
the heroine is first seen proceeding to Grandma's house with a sack full of goodies.
Her groovy motivation attracts an ugly wolf who seeks to become her chaperon.
"Later dad," she responds. Although the wolf dashes ahead to Grandma's house,

Granny is prepared for an intruder and whomps him on the head ten times with her cane. The wounded wolf flees howlin' to the nearby wood. Finally, Stan Freberg, in a question-and-answer parody of Jack Webb's "Dragnet" series, investigates a gun-toting "Little Blue Riding Hood," ties Grandma up in order to get the facts on the sweet-talking, goodies ring participant, and then arrests the little female thief and her elderly relative.

With the exception of Stan Freberg's bizarre detective yarn, all lyrical references to Little Red Riding Hood are oriented toward potential sexual involvement. The carnivore in each story is attracted by the prey's shapely frame and desires a dance, a walk, or some other form of initial companionship as a prelude to further physical involvement. No notion of eating Grandma or stealing baked goodies is ever communicated. Thus the traditional nursery rhyme moral of "don't talk to strangers" evolves into a more updated, anti-chauvinist theme concerning male lasciviousness toward lonely, innocent young women.

> 7. Mary's Lamb
> Mary had a Little Lamb,
> Its fleece was white as snow;
> And everywhere that Mary went,
> The Lamb was sure to go....

The Coasters recite the first four lines of the original nursery rhyme, and then personalize their own situation by observing that the Little Lamb's behavior parallels a lover's subservient tendencies toward his loved one. Stevie Ray Vaughan is slightly more adaptive. His lyrical commentary reproduces the first four lines in tact, but then he deviates into a jive talkin' version of the Little Lamb sparkin' a wild time in the old schoolyard. No specifics of dancin', prancin', or romancin' are detailed. However, the playful guitar solo by Vaughan hints at a casual, joy-filled romp that—in Vaughan's own terms—broke *all* the teacher's rules.

> 8. *Old MacDonald*
> Old MacDonald had a farm.
> Ey-I, Ey-I, Oh.
> And on this farm he had a chick.
> Ey-I, Ey-I, Oh....

For The Chargers, The Five Keys, and Nolan Strong and The Diablos, the repetitive Old MacDonald chant offers an opportunity to explore rhythmic vocal blending in varying doo-wop styles. Whenever the word "chick" is used, however, one senses that the slang term for "woman" is being implied. The Five Keys create a center-frame story about domestic warfare between a hen-pecked farmer and his rolling-pin swinging wife. However, they soon return to the standard chant about chicks and ducks. The other vocal groups take less liberty with the words of the original rhyme, although Nolan Strong declares that the horrible aroma of the pigs pervades the entire farm. In sharp contrast, Frank Sinatra departs dramatically from the traditional tale to relate a totally new story about Old MacDonald's luscious daughter. She reportedly has a little curve here and a little curve there, a little wiggle here and a little wiggle there. After wowing the townspeople, the slick young chick from MacDonald's place traps the boy with the roving eye. The song, rather than recounting the pigs, chicks, and ducks of the children's tale, reiterates in distinctive Sinatraese the classic joke about the traveling salesman and the farmer's daughter.

> 9. The Three Little Pigs
> There was an old sow with three
> little pigs, and as she had not
> enough to keep them, she sent
> them out to seek their fortune.
> The first that went off and met a
> man with a bundle of straw, and
> said to him, "Please, man, give
> me that straw to build me a
> house." Which the man did, and
> the little pig built a house
> with it...

In "The Hair Of My Chinny Chin Chin" Sam The Sham and The Pharoahs transpose this fairy tale into the story of a young woman who has built a brick house around her previously-broken heart. Sam The Sham refers to the girl as "Red," which obviously relates to the little caped lady who traveled to Grandma's house. The Wolf, identified initially by a glorious introductory howl, threatens to huff and puff and blow down the dwelling which contains the three pigs and their sad-eyed female companion. Confusion arises concerning the relationship between the brick house around the girls's heart and the hiding place of the four folks being pursued by the Wolf. James Duncan provides a more direct, rockin' version of the traditional tale in his hully gully-driven "Three Little Pigs." Humorously, he gets only the house of clay and sticks built and destroyed by the huffing, puffing Big Bad Wolf before the brief recording terminates. The pigs are described as rompin' through the woods, just a-dancin' their jigs. Although the story is short-circuited, the singer's enthusiasm for the three porkers is clearly unabated. The Wolf loses out in both Sam The Sham's tune and in James Duncan's version as well. But the lengthy not-by-the-hair-of-my-chinny-chin-chin/then-I'll-huff-and-I'll-puff-and-I'll-blow-your-house-in exchange is ignored in both recordings.

> 10. There Was A Crooked Man
> There was a Crooked Man, and he
>   went a crooked mile;
> He found a crooked sixpence
>   against a crooked stile.
> He brought a crooked cat, which
>   caught a crooked mouse,
> And they all lived together
>   in a little crooked house.

The Serendipity Singers use an infectious, syncopated rhythm, sparse instrumentation, and lengthy vocal pauses to deliver a verbatim recitation of this nursery rhyme. No interpretation, adaptation, or alteration is required. Only the title of the recording—"Don't Let The Rain Come Down (Crooked Little Man)"—presents a reversed structure from the traditional text.

> 11. The Old Woman Who Lived In A Shoe
> There was an Old Woman who lived
> in a shoe,
> She had so many children she didn't
> know what to do.
> She gave them some broth
> without any bread,
> Then whipped them all soundly
> and sent them to bed.

After identifying the traditional nursery rhyme situation in the initial stanzas of "All Mama's Children," Carl Perkins shifts his lyric to a contemporary social mobility theme. Once the footwear-dwelling youngsters see urban life and the accompanying downtown party styles, they *all* want to bop. Dancing is symbolic of personal freedom and the remodeling of the old, battered shoe into a new blue suede mode (a none-too-subtle salute to Perkin's classic hit tune) illustrates the family's new-found materialistic success. The singer qualifies the shift from lower class life to a more wealthy existence by claiming that the kids don't want to live too fast, they just want to live in class. The lyric concludes with music echoing through the night from the blue suede mansion on the hill. Rock on, children.

> 12. The House That Jack Built
> This is the house that Jack built.
> This is the malt, that lay in
> the house that jack built
> This is the rat, that ate the
> malt, that lay in the house
> that Jack built.
> This is the cat, that killed the
> rat, that ate the malt,
> that lay in the house
> that Jack built....

In "The House That Jack Built," Aretha Franklin borrows the nursery rhyme's declaratory format to express her sadness at losing the love of a good man. This tune builds from brief comments about land, dreams, room, love, life, fences, gates, to the house itself. The singer laments that the loss of an upright man can't be replaced by the house, the car, or the rug remaining in Jack's house. All lyrical lines are clearly modeled after the stanza-adding structure of the traditional nursery chant.

Table 12-C
Selected Illustrations of Contemporary
Recordings Containing References To
Nursery Rhymes, Fairy Tales, And Other
Children's Stories

1. Baa-Baa Black Sheep, Have You Any Wool?
   a. "Black Sheep" (MGM 13747)
      by Sam The Sham and The Pharoahs (1967)
2. Can You Make Me A Cambric Shirt, Parsley,
   Sage, Rosemary, and Thyme
   a. "Scarborough Fair" (Columbia 44465)
      by Simon and Garfunkel (1968)
3. Cinderella And The Glass Slipper
   a. "Cinderella" (ABC-Paramount 10239)
      by Paul Anka (1961)
   b. "Cinderella" (Atlantic 3392)
      by Firefall (1977)
   c. "Cinderella" (Capitol 4078)
      by The Four Preps (1958)
   d. "Cinderella" (Dot 16333)
      by Jack Ross (1962)
   e. "Cinderella Rockefella" (Philips 40526)
      by Ester and Abi Ofarim (1968)
   f. "Cinderella Sunshine" (Columbia 44655)
      by Paul Revere and The Raiders (1968)
4. Georgie Porgie, Pudding And Pie
   a. "Georgie Porgie" (ERA 3142)
      by Jewel Akens (1965)
5. Hey Diddle Diddle, The Cat And The Fiddle
   a. "(Ain't That) Just Like Me" (Atco 6210)
      by The Coasters (1961)
   b. "Cat's In The Cradle" (Elektra 45203)
      by Harry Chapin (1974)
   c. "Hi Diddle Diddle" (Symbol 924)
      by Inez Foxx (1963)
   d. "Triangle Of Love (Hey Diddle Diddle)" (Sussex 212)
      by The Presidents (1971)
6. Hickory, Dickory, Dock, The Mouse Ran Up The Clock
   a. "Hickory, Dick, and Dock" (Liberty 55700)
      by Bobby Vee (1964)
7. Humpty Dumpty Sat On A Wall
   a. "(Ain't That) Just Like Me" (Atco 6210)
      by The Coasters (1961)
   b. "All The King's Horses" (Atlantic 2883)
      by Aretha Franklin (1972)
   c. "Humpty Dumpty" (CoCe 234)
      by The Vogues (1964)
   d. "Humpty Dumpty Heart" (Atlantic 1150)
      by LaVern Baker (1957)
8. Hush-A-Bye, Baby, On The Tree Top
   a. "Hushabye" (United Artists 50535)
      by Jay and The Americans (1969)
   b. "Hushabye" (Atlantic 2884)
      by Robert John (1972)
   c. "Hushabye" (Laurie 3028)
      by The Mystics (1959)
9. In Fir Tar Is, In Oak None Is
   a. "Mairzy Doats" (Kama Sutra 222)
      by Innocence (1967)

10. The Inky Dinky Spider
    a. "Inky Dinky Spider (The Spider Song)" (4 Corners 129)
       by The Kids Next Door (1956)
11. Jack And Jill Went Up The Hill
    a. "Jack and Jill" (Arista 0283)
       by Raydio (1978)
    b. "Jack and Jill" (ABC 11229)
       by Tommy Roe (1969)
    c. "Jack and Jill Boogie"
       by Sleepy LaBeef
12. Jack Be Nimble, Jack Be Quick
    a. "American Pie" (United Artists 50586)
       by Don McLean (1971)
13. Jack The Giant Killer
    a. "Charlie Brown" (Atco 6132)
       by The Coasters (1959)
14. Lavender's Blue, Diddle, Diddle
    a. "Lavender-Blue" (Big Top 3016)
       by Sammy Turner (1959)
15. Little Boy Blue, Come Bow Your Horn
    a. "Little Boy Blue" (Challenge 59014)
       by Huelyn Duvall (1959)
    b. "Little Boy Blue" (Dot 15444)
       by Billy Vaughn (1956)
16. Little Jack Horner Sat in The Corner
    a. "Ain't Misbehavin'" (Warner Brothers 28794)
       by Hank Williams, Jr. (1986)
    b. "Cherry Pie" (Brent 7010)
       by Skip and Flip (1960)
    c. "Nursery Rhyme"
       by Bo Diddley
17. Little Red Riding Hood
    a. "The Hair On My Chinny Chin Chin" (MGM 13581)
       by Sam The Sham and The Pharoahs (1966)
    b. "Li'l Red Riding Hood" (MGM 13506)
       by Sam The Sham and The Pharoahs (1966)
    c. "Little Blue Riding Hood" (Capitol 1697)
       by Stan Freberg (1951)
    d. "Little Red Riding Hood" (Mercury 713775)
       by The Big Bopper (1958)
    e. "Little Red Riding Hood"
       by Dee Clark
    f. "Ridin' Hood" (Atco 6219)
       by The Coasters (1961)
18. Mary Had A Little Lamb, Its Fleece Was White As Snow
    a. "(Ain't That) Just Like Me" (Atco 6210)
       by The Coasters (1961)
    b. "Mary Had A Little Lamb" (Apple 1851)
       by Paul McCartney (1972)
    c. "Mary Had A Little Lamb"
       by Stevie Ray Vaughan
    d. "Mary's Little lamb" (Colpix 644)
       by James Darren (1962)
19. Mary, Mary, Quite Contrary, How Does Your Garden Grow?
    a. "Pretty Maids All In A Row" (Asylum 45386)
       by The Eagles (1976)

20. Old King Cole Was A Merry Old Soul
   a. "Tweedlee Dee" (Atlantic 1047)
      by LaVern Baker (1955)
   b. "Tweedlee Dee" (Mercury 70517)
      by Georgia Gibbs (1955)
   c. "Tweedlee Dee" (MGM 14468)
      by Little Jimmy Osmond (1973)
21. Old MacDonald Had A Farm
   a. "Ol' MacDonald" (Capitol 4466)
      by Frank Sinatra (1960)
   b. "Old MacDonald" (RCA Victor 7301)
      by The Chargers 91958)
   c. "Old MacDonald" (Aladdin 3113)
      by The Five Keys (1951)
   d. "Old McDonald"
      by Nolan Strong and The Diablos
22. Peter Piper Picked A Peck Of Pickled Peppers
   a. "Peter Piper" (Polydor 2002)
      by Frank Mills (1979)
23. Pinocchio
   a. "Your Nose Is Gonna Grow" (Del-Fi 4181)
      by Johnny Crawford (1962)
24. Rock-A-Bye, Baby, Thy Cradle Is Green
   a. "And The Cradle Will Rock" (Warner Brothers 49501)
      by Van Halen (1980)
   b. "Bring Back Those Rockaby Baby Days" (Reprise 0760)
      by Tiny Tim (1968)
   c. "Rock-A-Bye Your Baby With A Dixie Melody" (Columbia 42157)
      by Aretha Franklin (1961)
   d. "Rock-A-Bye Your Baby With A Dixie Melody" (Decca 30124)
      by Jerry Lewis (1956)
   e. "Rock Your Little Baby To Sleep" (Roulette 4009)
      by Buddy Knox (1957)
25. The Rose Is Red, The Violet Is Blue
   a. "Roses Are Red (My Love)" (Epic 9509)
      by Bobby Vinton (1962)
26. The Sleeping Beauty
   a. "To A Sleeping Beauty" (Columbia 42282)
      by Jimmy Dean (1962)
27. The Tale Of Peter Rabbit
   a. "Peter Rabbit" (Smash 2034)
      by Dee Jay and The Runaways (1966)
28. Ten Little Injuns Standin' In A Line
   a. "Ten Little Indians" (Capitol 4880)
      by The Beach Boys (1962)
   b. "Ten Little Indians" (Epic 10248)
      by The Yardbirds (1967)
29. There Was A Crooked Man, And He Walked A Crooked Mile
   a. "Don't Let The Rain Come Down (Crooked Little Man)" (Philips 40175)
      by The Serendipity Singers (1964)
30. There Was An Old Woman Who Lived In A Shoe
   a. "All Mama's Children" (Sun 243)
      by Carl Perkins (1956)

31. This Is The House That Jack Built
   a. "The House That Jack Built" (Atlantic 2546)
      by Aretha Franklin (1968)
32. This Little Pig Went To Market
   a. "I'm A Hog For You" (Atco 6146)
      by The Coasters (1959)
33. This Old Man
   a. "This Old Man" (Private Stock 45052)
      by Purple Reign (1975)
34. Three Little Pigs
   a. "The Hair On My Chinny Chin Chin" (MGM 13581)
      by Sam The Sham and The Pharoahs (1966)
   b. "Three Little Pigs" (King 5966)
      by James Duncan (1964)
35. Twinkle, Twinkle Little Star, How I Wonder What You Are!
   a. "Little Star" (Apt 25005)
      by The Elegants (1958)
36. What Are Little Boys Made Of?
   a. "Sugar And Spice" (Destination 624)
      by The Cryan' Shames (1966)
   b. "Sugar and Spice" (Liberty 55689)
      by The Searchers (1964)
   c. "What Are Boys Made Of" (ABC-Paramount 10401)
      by The Percells (1963)
37. Wynken, Blynken, And Nod
   a. "Winkin', Blynken, And Nod" (Kapp 586)
      by The Simon Sisters (1964)
   b. "Wynken, Blynken, And Nod" (Sesame Street 49642)
      by The Doobie Brothers (1981)

What general conclusions may be drawn from surveying more than 100 songs containing either title or lyrical references to nursery rhymes and fairy tales? There are several. First, anthropomorphic imagery is alive and well in American popular recordings. The appearances of talking animals are a staple within novelty tune categories, although they are obviously used for effect in standard pop lyrics as well. Second, particular artists have adapted their broad vocal ranges to depicting nursery rhyme characters with great gusto. Dee Clark, Sam The Sham, and The Big Bopper proved to be particularly creative in vocalizing either initial hooks or in creating other attention-getting sounds. Better yet, the comedy routines and harmonic vocal interplay of The Coasters creates priceless dialogues among wolves, sheep, and pigs, as well as between distressed parents, hassled students, and frustrated school teachers. Third, while a few nursery rhymes are totally integrated with a rockin' rhythm pattern in unchanged verbal form—"This Old Man" and "Crooked Little Man"—most fairy tale characters are seized from their traditional settings and inserted into contemporary social problems (divorce, lost love, infidelity, drunkenness, greed, and poverty) and in modern physical settings (hotel or motel rooms, living rooms, bars, and drug stores). Simple wooded environs are apparently inappropriate for 32-bar urban tales of intrigue, conflict, or romance. Fourth, it is difficult to imagine a more diverse group of artists—white blues guitarist Stevie Ray Vaughan, black doo-wop singer Nolan Strong, classic pop crooner Frank Sinatra, sassy-brassy R&B vocalist LaVern Baker, and groups like The Searchers, The Five Keys, and

The Serendipity Singers—all utilizing nursery rhyme formats to produce pop hits. Finally, as a research afterthought, it should be noted how difficult it is to locate 1950s and 1960s recordings of nursery rhymes and fairy tales. The author wishes to express deep appreciation to William L. Schurk, The Sound Recordings Archivist at the William T. Jerome Library on the campus of Bowling Green State University. Without his concern and assistance in locating numerous 45 r.p.m. records released more than twenty years ago, this study could never have been completed.

Works Cited

Books

Humphrey Carpenter and Mari Prichard (comps.), *The Oxford Companion To Children's Literature*. New York: Oxford University Press, 1984.

Edna Johnson, Evelyn R. Sickels, and Frances Clarke Sayers (comps.), *Anthology Of Children's Literature* (third edition). Boston: Houghton Mifflin Company, 1959.

Iona Opie and Peter Opie (eds.), *The Oxford Dictionary Of Nursery Rhymes.*. London: Oxford University Press, 1951.

David R. Pichaske, *Beowulf To Beatles And Beyond: The Varieties Of Poetry*. New York: Macmillan Publishing Company, Inc., 1981.

Articles

B. Lee Cooper, "Beyond Flash Gordon and 'Star Wars': Science Fiction And History Instruction," *Social Ediucation*, XLII (May 1978), pp. 392-

———— "Images From Fairy Tales And Nursery Rhymes In The Lyrics Of Contemporary Recordings," *International Journal Of Instructional Media*, XV, No. 2 (1988), pp. 183-193.

———— "Popular Music, Science Fiction, And Controversial Issues: Sources For Reflective Thinking," *The History And Social Science Teacher*, XII (Fall 1976), pp. 31-45.

———— "Youth Culture," in *A Resource Guide Themes In Contemporary American Song Lyrics, 1950-1985* (Westport, Connecticut: Greenwood Press, 1986), pp. 265-337.

R. Gordon Kelly, "Children's Literature," in *Concise Histories Of American Popular Culture*, edited by M. Thomas Inge (Westport, Connecticut: Greenwood Press, 1982), pp. 56-63.

Bernard Mergen, "Games And Toys," in *Concise Histories Of American Popular Culture*, edited by M. Thomas Inge (Westport, Connecticut: Greenwood Press, 1982), pp. 147-156.

Roger B. Rollin, "The Lone Ranger And Lenny Skutnik: The Hero As Popular Culture," in *The Hero In Transition*, edited by Ray B. Browne and Marshall W. Fishwick (Bowling Green, Ohio: Bowling Green University Popular Press, 1983), pp. 14-45.

Unpublished Materials

B. Lee Cooper, "Little Red Riding Hood Meets Sam The Sham And The Pharoahs: A Selected Discography Of Popular Recordings Featuring Nursery Rhyme And Fairy Tale Themes, 1950-1985" (mimeographed paper and audio tape presentation at the Annual Conference of the Association of Recorded Sound Collections in May 1988).

_____ "Rock 'N' Rhymes: Three Decades Of Thematic Contributions From Fairy Tales, Nursery Rhymes, And Other Children's Literature To Contemporary Song Lyrics" (mimeographed paper and audio tape presentation at the 5th Annual Convention of the Midwest Popular Culture Association in October 1987).

_____ "Thematic Contributions To The Lyrics Of Contemporary Recordings From Children's Literature: A Preliminary Investigation" (mimeographed paper and audio tape presentation at the 93rd Annual Meeting of the Michigan Academy Of Science, Arts, And Letters in March 1989).

William Reynolds Ferris, "Black Folklore From The Mississippi Delta" (Ph.D.: University of Pennsylvania, 1969).

Kurt Robert Miller, "Heroes Found In Song Texts From Folk Music Of The United States" (D.M.A.: University of Southern California, 1963).

William L. Schurk, "Children's Songs On The Billboard Pop Charts, 1940-1980" (mimeographed discography and audio tape presentation at the 15th Annual Convention of the Midwest Popular Culture Association in October 1987).

Chapter Thirteen
Social Trends and Audio Chronology

Teachers are constantly searching for new ways to help students comprehend historical chronology. The examination of successive presidential administrations, long a staple of American history, focuses too narrowly on specific political events while ignoring more general social trends, long-range economic issues, and regional fads. Similarly, it is a continuing challenge to break away from the literary format of the traditional textbook and to encourage students to utilize various types of oral evidence. The following study is presented as a chronologically-structured bibliographic essay. However, rather than citing books and articles which describe, discuss, debate, and dissect particular historical topics, this study presents songs—mostly in the form of 45 r.p.m. recordings released over the past forty years—that confront and comment on a variety of social, political, and economic concerns. The period selected is admittedly arbitrary. That is, rather than beginning in the 50s or 60s, a genuinely comprehensive lyrical review of women's rights, race relations, governmental authority, unemployment, or military conflicts should include recordings dating back to 1900. For purposes of illustration, though, this essay examines only Rock Era images of political and social life in the United States.

With the exception of such familiar time-marking tunes as "Auld Lang Syne," "Happy Birthday," and "Pomp and Circumstance," few popular songs are viewed as historically relevant. Yet America's cultural experience belies this perception. From working on the Erie Canal to sauntering down the bloody streets of Laredo, from expressing the joys of four-wheeled travel in a merry Oldsmobile to chronicling the exploits of Jesse James, Billy The Kid, and other 19th century outlaws, oral tradition has served this country well. Popularity of a particular song has never meant historical accuracy, of course. But the events described in songs may be placed within a timeline context which, when supplemented by journals, novels, newspapers, and other literary sources, make audio reports become reasonable introductory resources.

During the first half of the twentieth century, for instance, it was commonplace to encounter statements of political discontent in folk songs. Elements of social criticism also frequently appeared in other forms of underground music from World War I until 1950. Over the past forty years, though, the lyrics of popular songs have emerged with strong ideological statements about a variety of subjects. Some of these songs are highly philosophical, stressing universal human concern over war, freedom, equality, brotherhood, love, and justice. But many popular songs relate directly to specific historical events (murders, trials, and wars) or continuing social and financial problems (economic instability, nuclear energy proliferation, and irresponsibility of political leadership) which motivate strong public feelings. The assassination of President John F. Kennedy in 1963, the burgeoning American military involvement in Southeast Asia after 1965, the struggle for black civil rights throughout the sixties and seventies, and the political cynicism generated by the Nixon presidency prompted increasing numbers of chart-topping anthems calling for more love, more peace, more brotherhood, and more rapid social and political change throughout the United States.

In 1983 three popular songs—"Undercover of the Night," "Synchronicity II," and "Crumblin' Down"—featured highly critical commentaries on the nature of contemporary American society. The Rolling Stones warned listeners to keep out of sight in order to avoid being victimized by South American death squads, by the race militia, by propaganda merchants, and by American militarists bent on stationing U.S. troops around the globe. "Undercover Of The Night" openly indicted the Reagan administration's foreign policy, while puzzling over the failure of American citizens to recognize, react to, and revolt against the inhumanity of U.S. government positions toward South Africa, Cuba, and El Salvador. The Police shifted their lyrical focus from the international scene to the domestic front. "Synchronicity II" described the suicidal fantasies of frustrated housewives, the permanently grey mornings created by industrial plants that belch polluting chemicals into the sky, and the rush-hour traffic maze where human beings driving automobiles resemble fast-moving lemmings encased in shiny metal boxes. Finally, in "Crumblin' Down," John Cougar Mellencamp abandoned both international and domestic issues to discuss intensely personal feelings. He questioned the possibility of achieving independence and self-fulfillment within a closed, materialistic social order. These three songs capsule the breadth and depth of political protest and social criticism contained in popular music between 1950 and 1990.

Lyrical commentaries on America's overseas imbroglios and foreign policies are invariably cast in extreme terms. That is, few tunes explore both sides of any particular activity or suspend judgment about the long-range implications of a specific decision. Barry McGuire challenged several decades of American diplomatic policies and practices in "Eve Of Destruction" (1965). But it was the expanding Southeast Asian conflict of the 60s and 70s that spawned the most hostile lyrical attacks. Anti-war songs included: "The Universal Soldier" (1965), "The Unknown Soldier" (1968), "Give Peace A Chance" (1969), "War" (1970), and "Military Madness" (1971). It would be incorrect to assume, however, that these anti-military melodies went unchallenged by patriotic tunesmiths. In fact, lyrical sentiments condemning such criticism of American military activities, supporting the honor and bravery of U.S. soldiers, and questioning the loyalty of those who would tarnish America's tradition of wartime unity were numerous. Nationalistic tunes included: "Ballad Of The Green Berets" (1966), "Gallant Men" (1967), and "Battle Hymn Of Lt. Calley" (1971).

Beyond the realm of international political commentary, American music is spiced with observations about and criticisms of a variety of domestic issues. Topics examined include such complex social concerns as racial discrimination, urban decay, governmental chicanery, and women's rights. Songs addressing these subjects range from "In The Ghetto" (1969), "Hey Big Brother" (1971), and "Immigration Man" (1972) to "Power" (1980), "Spirits in the Material World"

(1982), and "Dirty Laundry" (1982). The lyrics in these tunes throb with anger; they cry for social change. The sense of seeking a more humane social climate without identifying any political means to achieve this worthy goal is found in "A Change Is Gonna Come/People Gotta Be Free" (1970), "Woodstock" (1970), and "Imagine" (1971). Beyond these idealistic hymns there are also science fiction-like projections of current misdeeds presented lyrically in "Shape Of Things To Come" (1968), "In The Year 2525" (1969), and "Future Shock" (1973).

Finally, the frustrations of being a just man (or an honorable woman) living in an unjust society, of being denied the right to express opinions or to display artistic talents because of the crushing demands of social conformity, or of being alienated from work, from loved ones, or from personal possessions inevitably produces outcries of pain and anguish. Such feelings occur to young girls "At Seventeen" (1975) as well as to mature women like "Mrs. Robinson" (1968). Even close friends fail to realize that it's "Easy To Be Hard" (1969), that an individual can readily become an "Alien" (1981), that a person can be psychologically abused by the "Games People Play" (1969), that "People Are Strange" (1967) when they are denied fundamental human rights and social equality, and that "Smiling Faces Sometimes" (1971) lie and deceive. Demands for social conformity are illustrated in several songs, including "Little Boxes" (1964), "Pleasant Valley Sunday" (1967), "Society's Child (Baby, I've Been Thinking)" (1967), and "Harper Valley P.T.A." (1968). Worker frustration and fear of unemployment only serve to complicate feelings of personal alienation. Songs which feature particularly powerful attitudes about job-related difficulties are: "A Natural Man" (1971), "Take This Job And Shove It" (1977), "9 To 5" (1980), and "Allentown" (1982).

For history professors and social studies teachers the following audio chronologies present both an invitation and a challenge. Table 13-A features a year-by-year perspective of political events and social activities illustrated in selected popular recordings; Table 13-B presents a more general chronological profile of political protest and social criticism themes portrayed in hit songs. Although the time period of the latter Table (1960-1985) is more condensed than the former (1949-1988), the purpose of both illustrations is clear. They demonstrate that there is a wealth of lyrical material that can be introduced in college and high school classes to stimulate debates, to encourage essays, to produce time line concepts, and to promote investigation of contemporary social issues. Students themselves can often provide supplementary vinyl teaching resources, as well as additional ideas about specific topics to be examined. But the key person in the learning process is still the teacher. Without willingness to move beyond the traditional textbook, oral resources and audio chronology will remain an untested educational approach. Hopefully, teachers will respond favorably to these significant ideas—even if they are delivered by such a diverse crew as Midnight Oil, Chuck Berry, Helen Reddy, The Police, Creedence Clearwater Revival, Stevie Wonder, Bruce Springsteen, Madonna, Tina Turner, Billy Joel, Prince, and John Cougar Mellencamp. By thoughtfully examining relevant concerns about human relations, political responsibilities, and social ethics, educators of the 1990s can hush the harsh comment made by Paul Simon in "Kodachrome" (1973). "When I think back on all the crap I learned in high school," lamented the popular singer/songwriter, "it's a wonder I can think at all."

Table 13-A

A Year-By-Year Listing Of Selected Political
Events And Social Activities Illustrated In
Popular American Records, 1949-1988

Year	Political Events And Social Trends	Personalities Related To Events	Song Titles (Record Number)	Performing Artists (Year Of Release)
1949	Major league baseball becomes racially integrated with the appearance of Jackie Robinson as a member of the 1947 Brooklyn Dodgers; Robinson leads the National League with a .342 batting average in 1949	Jackie Robinson Branch Rickey Roy Campanella Larry Doby Satchel Paige Monte Irvin Luke Easter	"Did You See Jackie Robinson Hit That Ball?" (Decca 24675)	Buddy Johnson and His Orchestra (1949)
1950	Yuletide novelty tunes and comedy songs are particularly appealing to both children and the young parents of the post-war baby boom generation	Spike Jones Yogi Yorgesson Gene Autry Homer and Jethro Louis Jordan	"Yingle Bells" (Capitol 781)	Yogi Yorgesson (1949)
			"Rudolph, The Red-Nosed Reindeer" (Columbia 38610)	Gene Autry (1949)
			"Rudolph, The Red-Nosed Reindeer" (RCA Victor 3934)	Spike Jones and His City Slickers (1949)
1951	General Douglas MacArthur delivers his "Farewell Speech" to the U.S. Congress after being relieved of command in the Far East by President Harry S. Truman	Douglas MacArthur Harry S. Truman	"Old Soldiers Never Die" (RCA Victor 4146)	Vaughn Monroe and His Orchestra (1951)
1952	Jack Webb stars as Sgt. Joe Friday in the popular television detective series "Dragnet"	Jack Webb	"Dragnet Blues" (Capitol 2562)	Ray Anthony (1953)
			"St. George and The Dragonet" (Capitol 2596)	Stan Freberg (1953)
			"Little Blue Riding Hood" (Capitol 2596)	Stan Freberg (1953)
			"Dragnet Blues" (Modern 910)	Johnny Moore's Three Blazers (1953)
1953	The legendary country music singer and composer Hank Williams dies on January 1, 1953	Hank Williams	"The Death Of Hank Williams"	Jack Cardwell (1953)
			"I Dreamed Of A Hill-Billy Heaven" (Capitol 4567)	Tex Ritter (1961)
			"The Conversation" (RCA 13631)	Waylon Jennings, with Hank Williams, Jr. (1983)
1954	As black-and-white television viewing becomes more and more prominent in American	Milton Berle Jackie Gleason Ed Sullivan Jack Benny	"TV Is The Thing (This Year)" (Mercury 70214)	Dinah Washington (1953)

	homes, the Radio Corporation of America (RCA) begins to market the first color TV sets for $1,000	Howdy Doody Lucille Ball Desi Arnez Walt Disney Art Linkletter Robert Young Steve Allen Jack Paar	"TV Mama" (Atlantic 1016)	Joe Turner (1954)
1955	Walt Disney's television program "Davy Crockett" sparks a national craze for coonskin caps and stimulates patriotic feelings about Texas and The Battle of The Alamo	Fess Parker Walt Disney Bill Hayes	"Ballad Of Davy Crockett" (Columbia 40449)	Fess Parker (1955)
			"The Ballad Of Davy Crockett" (Cadence 1256)	Bill Hayes (1955)
			"Ballad Of Davy Crockett" (Capitol 3058)	Tennessee Ernie Ford (1955)
			"The Ballad Of Davy Crockett" (RCA 6041)	The Voices of Walter Schumann (1955)
			"The Yellow Rose Of Texas" (Columbia 40540)	Mitch Miller (1955)
1955	Rock 'N' Roll music emerges as a teenage fad with performing idol Elvis Presley, the motion picture "Blackboard Jungle", and a small group of disc jockeys gaining national attention	Fats Domino Chuck Berry Carl Perkins Elvis Presley Alan Freed	"Rock Around The Clock" (Decca 29124)	Bill Haley and His Comets (1955)
			"Ain't That A Shame" (Imperial 5348)	Fats Domino (1955)
			"Maybellene" (Chess 1604)	Chuck Berry (1955)
			"Blue Suede Shoes" (Sun 234)	Carl Perkins (1956)
			"Heartbreak Hotel" (RCA 47-6420)	Elvis Presley (1956)
1956	The traditional popular music establishment, represented by major recording companies and and their stables of white pop singers, fail to halt the integration of young black performers into the "Top 100" record charts	Pat Boone Crew Cuts Diamonds Fontane Sisters Georgia Gibbs Gale Storm	"Tutti Frutti" (Specialty 561)	Little Richard (1956)
			"Tutti Frutti" (Dot 15443)	Pat Boone (1956)
			"Why Do Fools Fall In In Love" (Gee 1002)	Frankie Lymon and The Teenagers (1956)
			"Why Do Fools Fall In Love" (Mercury 7079)	The Diamonds (1956)
			"Ivory Tower" (Deluxe 6093)	Otis Williams and His Charms (1956)
			"Ivory Tower" (Dot 15458)	Gale Storm (1956)
1957	The New York Yankees, following Don Larsen's perfect game victory in the 1956 World Series, continue to be baseball's dominant team	Mickey Mantle Whitey Ford Yogi Berra Casey Stengel	"Whatever Lola Wants" (Mercury 70595)	Sara Vaughan (1955)
			"I Love Mickey" (Coral 61700)	Teresa Brewer (1957)
1958	Rock 'N' Roll idol Elvis Presley is drafted into the U.S. Army and is stationed in West Germany	Elvis Presley Col. Tom Parker	"The All-American Boy" (Fraternity 835)	Bill Parsons (1958)
1958	The Hoola Hoop Craze is at its peak, becoming one of the most prominent fads of the fifties	Millions of Americans swiveling hollow plastic rings around their waists	"Hoopa Hoola" (Atlantic 2002)	Betty Johnson (1958)
			"The Hula Hoop Song" (Roulette 4106)	Georgia Gibbs (1958)
			"The Hula Hoop Song" (Coral 62033)	Teresa Brewer (1958)
1959	Three young singers— Buddy Holly, Ritchie	Buddy Holly Ritchie Valens	"Three Stars" (Crest 1057)	Tommy Dee (1959)

	Valens, and The Big Bopper—are killed in a plane crash near Mason City, Iowa on February 3, 1959	J.P. Richardson	"American Pie (Parts I & II)" (United Artists 50856)	Don McLean (1971)
1960	Congressional investigations are launched into bribes and illegal payments allegedly being made to station managers and disc jockeys to secure radio air time for specific records	Alan Freed Dick Clark	"The Old Payola Roll Blues" (Capitol 4329)	Stan Freberg (1960)
1960	U-2 Spy Plane pilot Francis Gary Powers is shot down over the Soviet Union on May 1, 1960	Dwight D. Eisenhower Francis Powers	"There's A Star Spangled Banner Waving #2 (The Ballad of Francis Powers)" (Savoy 3020)	Red River Dave (a.k.a. Dave McEnery) (1960)
1960	A dance craze called "The Twist" emerges, spawning motion pictures and launching night clubs such as The Peppermint Lounge	Hank Ballard Chubby Checker Joey Dee Dick Clark	"The Twist" (Parkway 811) "Peppermint Twist— (Roulette 4401) "Let's Twist Again" (Parkway 824) "Twist And Shout" (Wand 124) "Twistin' Matilda" (S.P.Q.R. 3300)	Chubby Checker (a.k.a. Ernest Evans) (1960) Joey Dee and The Starliters (1961) Chubby Checker (1961) The Isley Brothers (1962) Jimmy Soul (a.k.a. James McCleese) (1962)
1961	Soviet Cosmonaut Yuri A. Gagarin becomes the first human to orbit the earth; after brief flights by Alan Shephard and Virgil Grissom, John Glenn becomes the first American Astronaut to accomplish the same feat in 1962	Yuri Gagarin John Glenn John F. Kennedy Virgil Grissom Alan Shephard	"The Astronaut (Parts 1 & 2)" (Kapp 409)	Jose Jimenez (a.k.a. Bill Dana) (1961)
1961	A permanent barrier is erected between the Allied Occupation Zone and the Soviet controlled area in Berlin to halt the flow of East German refugees to the West	Nikita Khrushchev John F. Kennedy	"West Of The Wall" (Big Top 3097)	Toni Fisher (1962)
1962	The Civil Rights Movement moves forward by pushing for school integration, equal employment opportunities, and voting rights for black Americans	James Meredith George Wallace Robert F. Kennedy Martin Luther King, Jr. John F. Kennedy	"If I Had A Hammer" (Warner Brothers 5296) "Blowin' In The Wind" (Warner Brothers 5368) "We Shall Overcome" (Vanguard 35023) "I Have A Dream" (Gordy 7023)	Peter, Paul, and Mary (1962) Peter, Paul, and Mary (1963) Joan Baez (1963) Rev. Martin Luther King (1968)
1962	The U.S. launches the Telstar Satellite which allows international transmission of audio and video signals	National Aeronautics and Space Administration (NASA) officials	"Telstar" (London 9561)	The Tornadoes (1962)
1963	The assassination President John F. Kennedy by Lee Harvey Oswald in	John F. Kennedy Jackie Kennedy Lee Harvey	"In The Summer Of His Years" (MGM 13203)	Connie Francis (1963)

Year	Event		Song	Artist
	Dallas, Texas on November 22, 1963 stuns the entire nation	Oswald Lyndon B. Johnson Jack Ruby	"Abraham, Martin, and John (Laurie 3464)	Dion (9168)
1964	The triumph of Beatlemania in the United States and throughout the world signals the beginning of British influence in American rock music	John Lennon Paul McCartney George Harrison Ringo Starr	"We Love You Beatles" (London International 10614)	The Carefrees (1964)
1965	Following The Gulf of Tonkin Incident in 1964, U.S. ground troops are committed to active military participation in the Vietnamese Civil War	Lyndon B. Johnson Robert McNamara Dean Rusk	"Eve Of Destruction" (Dunhill 4009) "The Ballad Of The Green Berets" (RCA 8739) "Gallant Men" (Capitol 5805) "The Unknown Soldier" (Elektra 45628) "Fortunate Son" (Fantasy 634)	Barry McGuire (1965) SSgt. Barry Sadler (1966) Senator Everett McKinley Dirksen (1967) The Doors (1968) Creedence Clearwater Revival (1969)
1966	The Psychedelic Era begins marked by the dominance of California bands, distinct social commentary in song lyrics, and drug-related images and themes in movies, on concert posters, and in popular recordings	Timothy Leary Jimi Hendrix Jefferson Airplane The Byrds The Beatles	"Eight Miles High" (Columbia 43578) "Along Comes Mary" (Valiant 741) "White Rabbit" (RCA 9248) "Purple Haze" (Reprise 0597)	The Byrds (1966) The Association (1966) Jefferson Airplane (1967) The Jimi Hendrix Experience (1967)
1967	The Monterey Pop Festival features the first major gathering of the California "Love Generation"; it illustrates the power of combining top musical performers, a psychedelic atmosphere and a variety of counter culture issues	Janis Joplin Jimi Hendrix Otis Redding	"San Franciscan Nights" (MGM 13769) "San Francisco (Be Sure To Wear Flowers In Your Hair)" "For What It's Worth (Stop, Hey What's That Sound)" (Atco 6459) "Monterey" (MGM 13868)	Eric Burdon and The Animals (1967) Scott McKenzie (1967) The Buffalo Springfield (1967) Eric Burdon and The Animals (1967)
1968	The assassinations of civil rights champion Rev. Martin Luther King Jr. and liberal Democratic Senator Robert F. Kennedy shocks the nation; increased domestic unrest and growing protests against U.S. involvement in the Southeast Asian Conflict are evident	Lyndon B. Johnson Robert F. Kennedy Rev. Martin Luther King, Jr. Eugene McCarthy Hubert H. Humphrey Richard M. Nixon	"Abraham, Martin, and John" (Tamla 54184) "Outside Of A Small Circle Of Friends" (A&M 891) "Chicago" (Atlantic 2804)	Smokey Robinson and The Miracles (1968) Phil Ochs (1968) Graham Nash (1971)
1969	The outdoor concert at Max Yasgur's farm in upstate New York draws more than 400,000 fans and Woodstock becomes the non-violent symbol of the '60s generation —world peace, anti-war, slogans, and love beads	Joan Baez Jimi Hendrix Jefferson Airplane The Who Canned Heat	"Going Up The Country" (Liberty 56077) "Woodstock" (Atlantic 2723)	Canned Heat (1968) Crosby, Stills, Nash, and Young (1970)

1970	Four Kent State University students are killed by members of an Ohio National Guard Unit during anti-war demonstrations on the campus	Governor James Rhodes Richard M. Nixon Spiro Agnew	"Ohio" (Atlantic 2740) "War" (Gordy 7101) "America, Communicate With Me" (Barnaby 2016) "Ball Of Confusion (That's What The World Is Today)" (Gordy 7099)	Crosby, Stills, Nash, and Young (1970) Edwin Starr (1970) Ray Stevens (1970) The Temptations (1970)
1971	U.S. Army Lt. William Calley is court-marshalled for participating in the massacre of civilians in the Vietnamese village of My Lai	William Calley William Westmoreland Richard M. Nixon Henry Kissinger	"The Universal Soldier" (Hickory 1338) "Battle Hymn of Lt. Calley" (Plantation 73) "Military Madness" (Atlantic 2827)	Donovan (1965) C Company, featuring Terry Nelson (1971) Graham Nash (1971)
1972	The National Organization for Women (NOW) heads strides toward Congressional approval of the Equal Rights Amendment (the E.R.A. never gained sufficient support among the states to become a constitutional amendment)	Betty Friedan Gloria Steinam Shirley Chisholm	"I Am Woman" (Capitol 3350) "Your're So Vain" (Elektra 45824) "I'm A Woman" (Reprise 1319)	Helen Reddy (1972) Carly Simon (1972) Maria Muldaur (1974)
1973	The Watergate conspiracy, stemming from the unsuccessful attempt of members of the Nixon Administration to cover-up a 1972 break-in at Democratic National Headquarters in Washington, D.C., leads to the 1974 resignation of the President	Richard M. Nixon John Dean Sam Ervin H.R. Haldeman John Ehrlichman Archibald Cox John Mitchell	"Elected" (Warner Brothers 7631) "Watergrate" (Rainy Wednesday 202) "Sweet Home Alabama" (MCA 40258) "You Haven't Done Nothin' " (Tamla 54252)	Alice Cooper (1972) Dickie Goodman (1973) Lynyrd Skynyrd (1974) Stevie Wonder (1974)
1974	The nadir of public confidence in the honesty of American governmental leaders and anger over major economic difficulties caused by continuing oil shortages greets President Gerald R. Ford	Richard M. Nixon Gerald R. Ford	"Masterpiece" (Gordy 7126) "The Americans (A Canadian's Opinion)" "Energy Crisis '74" (Rainy Wednesday 206) "For The Love Of Money" (Philadelphia International 3544) "Living For The City" (Crossover 981) "You Haven't Done No-thin' " (Tamla 54252)	The Temptations (1973) Gordon Sinclair (1974) Dickie Goodman (1974) The O'Jays (1974) Ray Charles (1975) Stevie Wonder (1974)
1975	The Great Lakes ore vessel *Edmund Fitzgerald* sinks during a fierce storm on Lake Superior on November 11, 1975	The crew of the *Edmund Fitzgerald* and their bereaved relatives	"The Wreck Of The Edmund Fitzgerald" (Reprise 1369)	Gordon Lightfoot (1976)

1975	After generating a decade of public controversy, the man who is Cassius Clay, the "Louisville Lip", and Muhammad Ali wins the most dramatic fight of his boxing career in Manila against Joe Frazier	Muhammad Ali Joe Frazier Howard Cosell	"Black Superman-'Muhammad Ali' "(Pye 71012)	Johnny Wakelin and The Kinshasa Band (1975)
1976	The use of citizen band (C.B.) radio frequencies expands dramatically from truck drivers to the general automobile public	C.W. McCall Dave Dudley Red Sovine	"Convoy" (MGM 14839) "C.B. Savage" (Plantation 144) "Teddy Bear" (Starday 142)	C.W. McCall (1976) Rod Hart (1976) Red Sovine (1976)
1977	The drug-related death of Rock 'N' Roll idol Elvis Presley at his Graceland mansion in Memphis, Tennessee on August 16, 1977 shocks his fans	Elvis Presley Tom Parker	"The King Is Gone" (Scorpion 135) "From Graceland To The Promised Land" (MCA 40804) "Are You Lonesome To-Night?" (RCA 47-7810) "My Way" (RCA PB-11165) "The Elvis Medley" (RCA PB-13351)	Ronnie McDowell (1977) Merle Haggard (1977) Elvis Presley (1960) Elvis Presley (1977) Elvis Presley (1982)
1978	The Disco Craze, which swept urban dance centers, the popular music industry, and motion picture screens as well, is illustrated in the in the film "Saturday Night Fever."	John Travolta Barry Gibb Robin Gibb Maurice Gibb Donna Summer	"You Should Be Dancing" (RSO 853) "Stayin' Alive" (RSO 885) "Disco Inferno" (Atlantic 3389) "Last Dance" (Casablanca 926) "Night Fever" (RSO 889)	The Bee Gees (1976) The Bee Gees (1977) The Tramps (1977) Donna Summer (1978) The Bee Gees (1978)
1979	After the nuclear plant accident at Three Mile Island (T.M.I.) in Pennsylvania, the members of Musicians United For Safe Energy (M.U.S.E.) present a concert at Madison Square Garden to publicly challenge the continued use of atomic energy even for peaceful means	Jackson Browne Graham Nash John Hall Bonnie Raitt	"Plutonium Is Forever" (M.U.S.E. Album) "Power" (M.U.S.E. Album) "We Almost Lost Detroit" (M.U.S.E. Album)	Joan Hall (1979) The Doobie Brothers, with John Hall and James Taylor (1979) Gill Scott-Heron (1979)
1980	The evening television soap opera "Dallas" sustains high popularity by using a suspenseful ending in its final spring episode—villain J.R. Ewing is shot by an unidentified assailant	Larry Hagman Joan Collins Linda Gray Patrick Duffy	"Who Shot J.R.?" (Ovation 1150) "This Ain't Dallas" (Warner Brothers 28912)	Gary Burbank, with Band McNally (1980) Hank Williams, Jr. (1985)
1980	John Lennon, a founding member of The Beatles, is shot to death by Mark David Chapman in New York City on December 8, 1980	John Lennon Yoko Ono Mark David Chapman Paul McCartney	"Give Peace A Chance" (Apple 1809) "Imagine" (Apple 1840) "The Late, Great Johnny Ace" (Album)	John Lennon and The Plastic Ono Band (1969) Plastic Ono Band Paul Simon (1983)

Year	Social Trend	People	Song	Artist
1981	The physical fitness craze and health food concerns become major public pursuits, while video aerobics and fad dietary plans gain more and more popularity	Richard Simmons Jane Fonda Sylvestor Stallone	"Physical" (MCA 51182) "Muscles" (RCA 13348) "Eye of the Tiger" (Scotti Brothers 02912)	Oliva Newton-John (1981) Diana Ross (1982) Survivor (1982)
1982	Economic problems and unemployment hit sections of the industrial North-east and the farm belt in the Midwest; the gap between the rich and the poor in U.S. society widens under the Reagan Administration	Ronald Reagan George Bush David Stockman	"9 To 5" (RCA 12133) "Allentown" (Columbia 03413) "Pink Houses" (Riva 215) "Industrial Disease" (Warner Brothers 29880) "Mr. Roboto" (A&M 2525) "Rain On The Scarecrow" (Riva 884635)	Dolly Parton (1980) Billy Joel (1982) John Cougar Mellencamp (1983) Dire Straits (1983) Styx (1983) John Cougar Mellencamp (1986)
1983	There is increasing public skepticism about the quality of public schooling, the objectivity of television news broadcasts, and the fairness of the U.S. legal system	Mike Wallace Dan Rather Tom Brokaw Bob Woodward Carl Bernstein William Bennett Edwin Meese	"Another Brick In The Wall (Part II)" (Columbia 11187) "Dirty Laundry" (Asylum 69894) "Johnny Can't Read" (Asylum 69971) "Synchronicity II" (A&M 2571) "Born In The U.S.A." (Columbia 04680)	Pink Floyd (1980) Don Henley (1982) Don Henley (1982) Police (1983) Bruce Springsteen (1984)
1984	Two premiere black singers, Jackie Wilson and Marvin Gaye, die in 1984; Wilson had been in a coma since suffering a paralyzing stroke in 1975; while Gaye was murdered by his father	Jackie Wilson Marvin Gaye	"Nightshift" (Motown 1773)	The Commodores (1985)
1985	A national campaign is launched to halt the illegal importation of narcotics and to encourage young people to "Just Say No" to experimentation with marijuana and cocaine	Nancy Reagan Ronald Reagan Edwin Meese	"Cocaine" (RSO 1039) "I Want A New Drug" (Chrysalis 42766) "Smuggler's Blues" (MCA 52546) "Hip To Be Square" (Chrysalis 43065)	Eric Clapton (1980) Huey Lewis and The News (1984) Glenn Frey (1985) Huey Lewis and The News (1986)
1985	Famine conditions sweep North Africa, with particular difficulties for the starving people of Ethiopia, sparking relief efforts throughout Europe and North America	Bob Geldof Quincy Jones Michael Jackson Lionel Richie	"Do They Know It's Christmas?" (Columbia 04749) "We Are The World" (Columbia 04839)	Band Aid ——— Paul Young Boy George George Michael Phil Collins Duran Duran and others (1985) United Support of Artists (U.S.A.) for Africa ——— Stevie Wonder

Years	Political Events And Social Trends	Song Titles (Record Number)	Performing Artists (Year Of Release)
			Paul Simon Kenny Rogers Tina Turner Billy Joel Diana Ross and others (1985)
1986	The Chicago Bears succeed in winning the N.F.L. divisional championship and in conquering the New England Patriots in football's Super Bowl XX during January 1986	Jim McMahon Walter Payton Mike Ditka Laura Cooper Willie Gault Mike Singletary Richard Dent William "The Refrigerator" Perry	"Superbowl Shuffle" (Red Label 71012)	The Chicago Bears Shufflin' Crew (1986)
1987	Congressional hearings are convened to investigate numerous improprieties arising from the covert Iran-Contra arms for hostages deal which was directed by high-ranking members of the Reagan Administration	Oliver North John Poindexter William Casey Ronald Reagan Edwin Meese George Bush	"Undercover Of The Night" (Rolling Stone 99813) "All She Wants To Do Is Dance" (Geffen 29065) "The Gipper Gate Blues" (Live Performance)	The Rolling Stones (1983) Don Henley (1985) Barbara Dane (1987)
1988	Lyrical commentaries on issues such as child abuse, world hunger, civil rights, and economic inequality continue to emerge despite the failure of 1988 political candidates or other government officials to acknowledge that such major social problems exist	Michael Dukakis George Bush Jesse Jackson Ted Kennedy Mario Cuomo Ronald Reagan	"The Way It Is" (RCA 5023) "Luka" (A&M 2937) "Dear Mr. Jesus" (PowerVision 8603) "Beds Are Burning" (Columbia 07433)	Bruce Hornsby and The Range (1986) Suzanne Vega (1987) Power Source (1988) Midnight Oil (1988)

Table 13-B

A Chronological Profile Of Selected Political
Protest And Social Criticism Themes Illustrated
In Popular American Records, 1960-1985

Years	Political Events And Social Trends	Song Titles (Record Number)	Performing Artists (Year Of Release)
1960-1969	Demands for individual conformity in respect to race relations, sexual behavior, religious belief, and oral expression	"Town Without Pity" (Musicor 1009) "Little Boxes" (Columbia 42940) "A Well Respected Man" (Reprise 0420) "Dedicated Follower Of Fashion" (Reprise 0471) "Pleasant Valley Sunday" (Colgems 1007) "Society's Child (Baby, I've Been Thinking)" (Verve 5027)	Gene Pitney (1961) Pete Seeger (1964) The Kinks (1965) The Kinks (1966) The Monkees (1967) Janis Ian (1967)

		"Harper Valley P.T.A." (Plantation 3)	Jeannie C. Riley (1968)
		"The Son Of Hickory Holler's Tramp" (Columbia 44425)	O.C. Smith (1968)
1960-1969	Cynicism toward persons in positions of social or political authority	"Eve Of Destruction" (Dunhill 4009)	Barry McGuire (1965)
		"Subterranean Homesick Blues" (Columbia 43242)	Bob Dylan (1965)
		"For What It's Worth (Stop, Hey What's That Sound)" (Atco 6459)	The Buffalo Springfield (1967)
		"Mr. Businessman" (Monument 1083)	Ray Stevens (1968)
		"Outside Of A Small Circle Of Friends" (A&M 891)	Phil Ochs (1968)
		"Revolution" (Apple 2276)	The Beatles (1968)
		"Games People Play" (Capitol 2248)	Joe South (1969)
		"Monster" (Dunhill 4221)	Steppenwolf (1969)
1960-1985	Concern for the civil rights of women, minorities, and the poor	"If I Had A Hammer" (Warner Brothers 5368)	Peter, Paul and Mary (1962)
		"Blowin' In The Wind" (Warner Brothers 5368)	Peter, Paul and Mary (1963)
		"We Shall Overcome" (Vanguard 35023)	Joan Baez (1963)
		"Help The Poor" (ABC-Paramount 10552)	B.B. King (1964)
		"Keep On Pushing" (ABC-Paramount 10554)	The Impressions (1964)
		"Ninety-Nine And A Half (Won't Do)" (Atlantic 2334)	Wilson Pickett (1966)
		"Dead End Street" (Capitol 5869)	Lou Rawls (1967)
		"We're A Winner" (ABC 11022)	The Impressions (1967)
		"Give A Damn" (Mercury 72831)	Spanky and Our Gang (1968)
		"We're Rolling On (Part 1)" (ABC 11071)	The Impressions (1968)
		"Choice of Colors" (Custom 1943)	The Impresssions (1969)
		"Everyday People" (Epic 10407)	Sly and The Family Stone (1969)
		"Get Together" (RCA 9752)	The Youngbloods (1969)
		"In The Ghetto" (RCA 47-9741)	Elvis Presley (1969)
		"Why I Sing The Blues" (Bluesway 61024)	B.B. King (1969)
		"Indian Reservation (The Lament Of The Cherokee Reservation Indian)" (Columbia 45332)	The Raiders (1971)
		"Inner City Blues (Make Me Wanna Holler)" (Tamla 54209)	Marvin Gaye (1971)

		"I Am Woman" (Capitol 3350)	Helen Reddy (1972)
		"Immigration Man" (Atlantic 2873)	David Crosby and Graham Nash (1972)
		"Why Can't We Live Together" (Glades 1703)	Timmy Thomas (1972)
		"Woman Is The Nigger Of The World" (Apple 1848)	John Lennon (1972)
		"Half-Breed" (MCA 40102)	Cher (1973)
		"Masterpiece" (Gordy 7126)	The Temptations (1973)
		"For The Love Of Money" (Philadelphia International 3544)	The O'Jays (1974)
		"Living For The City" (Crossover 981)	Ray Charles (1975)
		"Takin' It To The Streets" (Warner Brothers 8196)	The Doobie Brothers (1976)
		"Ebony And Ivory" (Columbia 02860)	Paul McCartney and Stevie Wonder (1982)
1965- 1974	Criticism of American military involvement in Southeast Asia	"Home Of The Brave" (Capitol 5483)	Jody Miller (1965)
		"The Universal Soldier" (Hickory 1338)	Donovan (1965)
		"The Cruel War" (Warner Brothers 5809)	Peter, Paul and Mary (1966)
		"The Unknown Soldier" (Elektra 45628)	The Doors (1968)
		"Fortunate Son" (Fantasy 634)	Creedence Clearwater Revival (1969)
		"Give Peace A Chance" (Apple 1809)	John Lennon (1969)
		"Stop The War Now" (Gordy 7104)	Edwin Starr (1970)
		"War" (Gordy 7101)	Edwin Starr (1970)
		"Bring The Boys Home" (Invictus 9092)	Freda Payne (1971)
		"Military Madness" (Atlantic 2827)	Graham Nash (1971)
		"War Song" (Reprise 1099)	Neil Young and Graham Nash (1972)
		"Billy, Don't Be A Hero" (Mercury 73479)	Paper Lace (1974)
		"There Will Never Be Peace (Until God Is Seated At The Conference Table)" (Brunswick 55512)	The Chi-Lites (1974)
1965- 1974	Support for American military participation in the Southeast Asian conflict	"Ballad of The Green Berets" (RCA 8739)	S/Sgt. Barry Sadler (1966)
		"Gallant Men" (Capitol 5805)	Senator Everett Dirksen (1967)
		"Battle Hymn of Lt. Calley" (Plantation 73)	C Company, featuring Terry Nelson (1971)
1965- 1980	Reactions against political protest and social	"Dawn Of Correction" (Decca 31844)	The Spokesmen (1965)
		"Open Letter To My	Victor Lundberg

	criticism in the United States by persons supporting nationalism and patriotism	"Teenage Son" (Liberty 55996)	(1967)
		"Okie From Muskogee" (Capitol 2626)	Merle Haggard (1969)
		"The Fightin' Side Of Me" (Capitol 2719)	Merle Haggard (1970)
		"The American (A Canadian's Opinion)" (Avco 4628)	Gordon Sinclair (1974)
		"Sweet Home Alabama" (MCA 40258)	Lynyrd Skynyrd (1974)
		"In America" (Epic 50888)	The Charlie Daniels Band (1980)
1967-1970	Protests on American college campuses against the Vietnam conflict	"On Campus" (Cotique 158)	Dickie Goodman (1969)
		"Ohio" (Atlantic 2740)	Crosby, Stills, Nash and Young (1970)
1968	Assassinations of President John F. Kennedy (1963), The Rev. Martin Luther King, Jr., and Senator Robert F. Kennedy	"Abraham, Martin and John" (Laurie 3464)	Dion (1968)
		"I Have A Dream" (Gordy 7023)	Rev. Martin Luther King, Jr. (1968)
1968-1971	Trial of the "Chicago Seven" for alleged political subversion during the 1968 Democratic National Convention	"Chicago" (Atlantic 2804)	Graham Nash (1971)
1970-1979	Cynicism toward persons in positions of social or political authority	"American, Communicate With Me" (Barnaby 2016)	Ray Stevens (1970) (RCA 0325)
		"American Woman"	The Guess Who 1970
		"Ball Of Confusion (That's What The World Is Today)" (Gordy 7099)	The Temptations (1970)
		"A Change Is Gonna Come/People Gotta Be Free" (Bell 860)	The Fifth Dimension (1970)
		"Heaven Help Us All" (Tamla 54200)	Stevie Wonder (1970)
		"Teach Your Children" (Atlantic 2735)	Crosby, Stills, Nash and Young (1970)
		"Walk A Mile In My Shoes" (Capitol 2704)	Joe South (1970)
		"Woodstock" (Atlantic 2723)	Crosby, Stills, Nash and Young (1970)
		"(For God's Sake) Give More Power To The People (Brunswick 55450)	The Chi-Lites (1971)
		"George Jackson" (Columbia 45516)	Bob Dylan (1971)
		"Hey Big Brother" (Rare Earth 5038)	Rare Earth (1971)
		"Imagine" (Apple 1840)	John Lennon (1971)
		"Power To The People" (Apple 1830)	John Lennon (1971)
		"Smiling Faces Sometimes" (Gordy 7108)	Undisputed Truth (1971)

		"What's Going On" (Tamla 54201)	Marvin Gaye (1971)
		"Won't Get Fooled Again" (Decca 32846)	The Who (1971)
		"Dialogue (Part I and II)" (Columbia 45717)	Chicago (1972)
		"Elected" (Warner Brothers 7631)	Alice Cooper (1972)
		"You're The Man" (Tamla 54221)	Marvin Gaye (1972)
		"Watergrate" (Rainy Wednesday 202)	Dickie Goodman (1973)
		"You Haven't Done Nothin' " (Tamla 54252)	Stevie Wonder (1974)
		"At Seventeen" (Columbia 10154)	Janis Ian (1975)
		"Hurricane" (Columbia 10245)	Bob Dylan (1975)
		"My Little Town" (Columbia 10230)	Simon and Garfunkel (1975)
		"The Logical Song" (A&M 2128)	Supertramp (1979)
1970-1985	Concern about maintaining ecological balance, controlling pollution, and halting nuclear proliferation	"Big Yellow Taxi" (Reprise 0906)	Joni Mitchell (1970)
		"Mercy Mercy Me (The Ecology)" (Tamla 54207)	Marvin Gaye (1971)
		"Signs" (Lionel 3213)	The Five Man Electrical Band (1971)
		"The Family Of Man" (Dunhill 4306)	Three Dog Night (1972)
		"Power" (Gordy 7183)	The Temptations (1980)
1970-1985	Reaction to economic instability, unemployment, and automation in workplaces	"A Natural Man" (MGM 14262)	Lou Rawls (1971)
		"Living For The City" (Tamla 54242)	Stevie Wonder (1973)
		"Take This Job And Shove It" (Epic 50469)	Johnny Paycheck (1977)
		"9 To 5" (RCA 12133)	Dolly Parton (1980)
		"Allentown" (Columbia 03413)	Billy Joel(1982)
		"Industrial Disease" (Warner Brothers 29880)	Dire Straits (1983)
		"Mr. Roboto" (A&M 2525)	Styx (1983)
1980-1985	Cynicism toward persons in positions of social and political authority	"Another Brick In The Wall (Part II)" (Columbia 11187)	Pink Floyd (1980)
		"Controversy" (Warner Brothers 49808)	Prince (1981)
		"The American Dream" (Elektra 69960)	Hank Williams, Jr. (1982)
		"Dirty Laundry" (Asylum 69894)	Don Henley (1982)
		"Johnny Can't Read" (Asylum 69971)	Don Henley (1982)
		"Spirits In The Material World" (A&M 2390)	The Police (1982)
		"Still In Saigon" (Epic 02828)	The Charlie Daniels Band (1982)

"Used To Be" (Motown 1650)	Charlene and Stevie Wonder (1982)
"Crumblin' Down" (Riva 214)	John Cougar (1983)
"Pink Houses" (Riva 215)	John Cougar Mellencamp (1983)
"Synchronicity II" (A&M 2571)	The Police (1983)
"Undercover Of The Night" (Rolling Stones 99813)	The Rolling Stones (1983)
"War Games" (Atlantic 89812)	Crosby, Stills and Nash (1983)
"The Authority Song" (Riva 216)	John Cougar Mellencamp (1984)
"Do They Know It's Christmas?" (Columbia 04749)	Band Aid (1984)
"We Are The World" (Columbia 04839)	USA For Africa (1985)

Works Cited

Books

Sean Brickell and Rich Rothschild (comps.), *The Pages Of Rock History: A Day-By-Day Calendar Of The Births, Deaths, And Major Events Of Rock History.* Norfolk, Virginia: Donning Company, 1983.

R. Serge Denisoff, *Sing A Song Of Social Significance* (third edition). Bowling Green, Ohio: Bowling Green University Popular Press, 1983.

R. Serge Denisoff and Richard A. Peterson (eds.), *The Sounds Of Social Change: Studies In Popular Culture* Chicago: Rand McNally and Company, 1972.

Dan Formento, *Rock Chronicle: A 365 Day-By-Day Journal Of Significant Events In Rock History.* New York: Delilah Books, 1982.

Lois Gordon and Alan Gordon, *American Chronicle: Six Decades Of American Life, 1920-1980.* New York: Atheneum Books, 1987.

Bernard Grun, *The Timetables Of History: A Horizontal Linkage Of People And Events*, new, updated edition (New York: Touchstone Books, 1982), pp. 531-591.

Wayne Hampton, *Guerrilla Minstrels: John Lennon, Joe Hill, Woody Guthrie, and Bob Dylan*, Knoxville, Tennessee: University of Tennessee Press, 1986.

Herb Hendler, *Year By Year In The Rock Era: Events And Conditions Shaping The Rock Generations That Reshaped America.* Westport, Connecticut: Greenwood Press, 1983.

Christopher Lasch, *The Culture Of Narcissism: American Life In An Age Of Diminishing Expectations.* New York: Warner Books, 1979.

George Lipsitz, *Class Culture In Cold War America: A Rainbow At Midnight.* Brooklyn, New York: J.F. Bergin Publishers, Inc., 1981.

Herbert I. London, *Closing The Circle: A Cultural History Of The Rock Revolution.* Chicago: Nelson-Hall, Inc., 1984.

Dave Marsh, *Sun City: The Making Of The Record* New York: Penguin Books, 1985.

John Naisbitt, *Megatrends: The New Directions Transforming Out Lives.* New York: Warner Books, 1984.

John A. Neuenschwander, *Oral History As A Teaching Approach.* Washington. D.C.: National Education Association, 1976.

Lynda Rosen Obst (ed.), *The Sixties: The Decade Remembered Now, By The People Who Lived It Then.* New York: Random House/ Rolling Stone Press Book, 1977.

William L. O'Neill, *Coming Apart.* Chicago: Quadrangle Books, 1971.

John Orman, *The Politics Of Rock Music.* Chicago: Nelson-Hall, Inc., 1984.

John Paxton and Sheila Fairfield (comps.), *Chronology Of Culture: A Chronology Of Literature, Dramatic Arts, Music, Architecture, Three-Dimensional Art, And Visual Arts From 3,000 B.C. To The Present.* New York: Van Norstrand Reinhold Company, 1984.

Marianne Philbin (ed.), *Give Peace A Chance: Music And The Struggle For Peace.* Chicago: Chicago Review Press, 1983.

David Pichaske, *A Generation In Motion: Popular Music And Culture In The Sixties,* New York: Schirmer Books, 1979.

_____ *The Poetry Of Rock: The Golden Years.* Peoria, Illinois: Ellis Press, 1981.

Robert G. Pielke, *You Say You Want A Revolution: Rock Music In American Culture.* Chicago: Nelson-Hall, Inc., 1986.

Bruce Pollock, *When The Music Mattered: Rock In The 1960s.* New York: Holt, Rinehart and Winston, 1983.

David M. Potter, *People Of Plenty: Economic Abundance And The American Character.* Chicago: University of Chicago Press, 1954.

Charles A. Reich, *The Greening Of America.* New York: Random House, 1970.

Jerome L. Rodnitzky, *Minstrels Of The Dawn: The Folk-Protest Singer As A Cultural Hero.* Chicago: Nelson-Hall, Inc., 1976.

Patricia Romanowski (ed.) *Rolling Stone Rock Almanac: The Chronicles Of Rock And Roll.* New York: Collier Books, 1983.

Theodore Roszak, *The Making Of A Counter Culture: Reflections On The Technocratic Society And Its Youthful Opposition.* Garden City, New York: Doubleday Anchor Books, 1969.

Sohnya Sayres, Anders Stephanson, Stanley Aronowitz, and Fredric Jameson (eds.), *The '60s Without Apology.* Minneapolis, Minnesota: University of Minnesota Press, 1985.

Pete Seeger and Bob Reiser, *Carry It On: A History In Song And Pictures Of The Working Men And Women Of America.* New York: Simon and Schuster, 1985.

Irwin Silber (ed.), *Songs America Voted By.* Harrisburg, Pennsylvania: Stackpole Books, 1971.

Thad Sitton, George L. Mehaffy, and O.L. Davis, Jr., *Oral History: A Guide For Teachers (And Others).* Austin, Texas: University of Texas press, 1983.

John Street, *Rebel Rock: The Politics Of Popular Music.* New York: Basil Blackwell, 1986.

David P. Szatmary, *Rockin' In Time: A Social History Of Rock And Roll.* Englewood Cliffs, New Jersey: Prentice-Hall, Inc. 1987.

Laurence Urdang (ed.), *The Timetables Of American History.* (New York: Touchstone Books, 1981), pp. 352-417.

Ed Ward, Geoffrey Stokes, and Ken Tucker, *Rock Of Ages: The Rolling Stone History Of Rock And Roll.* New York: Rolling Stone Press/Sumit Books, 1986.

Rex Weiner and Deanne Stillman, *Woodstock Census: The Nationwide Survey Of The Sixties Generation.* New York: Viking Press, 1979.

Ian Whitcomb, *Whole Lotta Shakin': A Rock 'N' Roll Scrapbook,* London: Arrow Books/ E.M.I. Music Publishing, 1982.

Articles

H. Ben Auslander, " 'If Ya Wanna End War And Stuff, You Gotta Sing Loud': A Survey Of Vietnam-Related Protest Music," *Journal Of American Culture*, IV (Summer 1981), pp. 108-113.

Glenn A. Baker, "Recording The Right," *Goldmine*, No. 66 (November 1981), pp. 176-178.

_____ "Rock's Angry Voice," *Goldmine*, No. 74 (July 1982), pp. 10-11.

Gary Burns, "Trends In Lyrics In The Annual Top Twenty Songs In The United States, 1963-1972," *Popular Music And Society*, IX (1983), pp. 25-39.

George W. Chilcoat, "The Images Of Vietnam: A Popular Music Approach," *Social Education*, XLIX (October 1985), pp. 601-603.

Richard Cole, "Top Songs In The Sixties: A Content Analysis Of Popular Lyrics, *American Behavioral Scientist*, XIV (January/February 1971), pp. 389-400.

B. Lee Cooper, "Controversial Issues In Popular Lyrics, 1960-1985: Teaching Resources For The English Classroom," *Arizona English Bulletin*, XXIX (Fall 1986), pp. 174-187.

_____ "Examining Social Change Through Contemporary History: An Audio Media Proposal," *The History Teacher*, VI (August 1973), pp. 523-534.

_____ "Folk History, Alternative History, And Future History," *Teaching History: A Journal Of Methods*, II (Spring 1977), pp. 58-62.

_____ "Information Services, Popular Culture, And The Librarian: Promoting A Contemporary Learning Perspective," *Drexel Library Quarterly*, XVI (July 1980), pp. 24-42.

_____ "Mick Jagger As Herodotus And Billy Joel As Thucydides? A Rock Music Perspective, 1950-1985," *Social Education*, XLIX (October 1985), pp. 596-600.

_____ "Political Protest Movements And Social Trends Depicted In American Popular Music, 1960-1985: A Chronological Guide To Recorded Resources," *International Journal Of Instructional Media*, XIV, No. 2 (1987), pp. 147-160.

_____ "Popular Music: An Untapped Resource For Teaching Contemporary Black History," *Journal Of Negro Education*, XLVIII (Winter 1979), pp. 20-36.

_____ "Race Relations," in *A Resource Guide To Themes In Contemporary American Song Lyrics, 1950-1985* Westport, Connecticut: Greenwood Press, 1986), pp. 213-222.

_____ "Social Change, Popular Music, And The Teacher," in *Ideas For Teaching Gifted Students: Social Studies (Secondary)*, edited by Jackie Mallis (Austin, Texas: Multi Media Arts, 1979), pp. 9-19.

_____ "Social Concerns, Political Protest, And Popular Music," *Social Studies*, LXXIX (March/April 1988), pp. 53-60.

_____ "Teaching American History Through Popular Music," *AHA (American Historical Association) Newsletter*, XIV (October 1976), pp. 3-5.

Ellen K. Coughlin, "From The Great Society To The Me Decade: A Minority View Of The '60s and '70s," *The Chronicle Of Higher Education*, XXVI (June 1, 1983), pp. 29-30

R. Serge Denisoff and Mark H. Levine, "The Popular Protest Song: The Case Of 'Eve Of Destruction'", *Public Opinion Quarterly*, XXXV (Spring 1971), pp. 117-122.

Mary Ellison, "War—It's Nothing But A Heartbreak: Attitudes To War In Black Lyrics," *Popular Music And Society*, X, No. 4 (1986), pp. 29-42.

Simon Frith, "Popular Music, 1950-1980," in *Making Music: The Guide To Writing, Performing, and Recording*, edited by George Marti (London: Pan Books, 1983), pp. 18-48.

Reebee Garofalo, "Rocking Against Racism In Massachusetts," *OneTwoThreeFour: A Rock 'N' Roll Quarterly*, No. 3 (Autumn 1986), pp. 75-85.

James Goodfriend, "A Calendar Of American Music," *Stereo Review*, XXXVII (July 1976), pp. 64-69.

Charles Hamm, "Changing Patterns In Society And Music: The U.S. Since World War II," in *Contemporary Music And Music Cultures*, compiled by Charles E. Hamm, Bruno Nettl, and Ronald Byrnside (Englewood Cliffs, New Jersey: Prentice-Hall, Inc., 1975), pp. 35-70.

Peter Hesbacher and Les Waffen, "War Recordings: Incidence And Change, 1940-1980," *Popular Music And Society*, VIII. Nos. 3/4 (1982), pp. 77-101.

Paul Hirsch, John Robinson, Elizabeth Keogh Taylor, and Stephen B. Whithey, "The Changing Popular Song: An Historical Overview," *Popular Music And Society*, I (Winter 1972), pp. 83-93.

Paul Dennis Hoffmann, "Rock And Roll And J.F.K.: A Study Of Thematic Changes In Rock And Roll Lyrics Since The Assassination Of John F. Kennedy," *Popular Music And Society*, X, No. 2 (1985), pp. 59-79.

Richard Hogan, "Twenty-Five Years Of Rock 'N' Roll," in *Contemporary Music Almanac 1980/81*, compiled by Ronald Zalkind (New York: Schirmer Books, 1980), pp. 81-94.

Ralph E. Knupp, "A Time For Every Purpose Under Heaven: Rhetorical Dimensions Of Protest Music," *Southern Speech Communication Journal*, XLVI (Summer 1981), pp. 377-389.

Gene Lees, "1918-1968: From *Over There* To *Kill For Peace*," *High Fidelity*, XVIII November 1968), pp. 56-60.

———. "War Songs: Bathos And Acquiescence," *High Fidelity*, XXVIII (December 1978), pp. 41-44.

———. "War Songs II: Music Goes AWOL," *High Fidelity*, XXIX (January 1979), pp. 20-22.

Jens Lund, "Country Music Goes To War: Songs For The Red-Blooded American," *Popular Music And Society*, I (Summer 1972), pp. 210-230.

Lloyd Miller and James K. Skipper, Jr., "Sounds Of Protest: Jazz And The Militant Avant-Garde," in *Deviance: Theories, Concepts, and Research Findings*, edited by Mark Lefton, James K. Skipper, Jr., and Charles H. McCaghy (New York: Appleton-Century-Crofts, 1968), pp. 129-140.

Richard E. Miller, "The Music Of Our Sphere: Apocalyptic Visions In Popular Music For The Eighties," *Popular Music And Society*, x, No. 3 (Fall 1987), pp. 75-90.

G.P. Mohrmann and F. Eugene Scott, "Popular Music And World War II: The Rhetoric Of Continuation," *Quarterly Journal Of Speech*, LXII (February 1976), pp. 145-156.

High Mooney, "Just Before Rock: Pop Music 1950-1953 Reconsidered," *Popular Music And Society*, III, No. 2 (1974), pp. 65-108.

John P. Morgan and Thomas C. Tulloss, "The Jake Walk Blues: A Toxicological Tragedy Mirrored In American Popular Music," *JEMF Quarterly*, XIII (Autum 1977), pp. 122-126.

David E. Morse, "Avant-Rock In The Classroom," *English Journal*, LVIII (February 1969), pp. 196-200ff.

Donald K. Pickens, "The Historical Images In Republican Campaign Songs, 1860-1900," *Journal Of Popular Culture*, XV (Winter 1981), pp. 165-174.

George M. Plasketes and Julie Grace Plasketes, "From Woodstock Nation To Pepsi Generation: Reflection On Rock Culture And State Of Music, 1969 To The Present," *Popular Music And Society*, XI, No. 2 (1987), pp. 25-52.

Martin Porter, "Greatest Events In Rock 'N' Roll History," in *Contemporary Music Almanac 1980/81*, Compiled by Ronald Zalkind (New York: Schirmer Books, 1980), pp. 95-101.

Todd Postol, "Reinterpreting The Fifties: Changing Views Of A 'Dull' Decade," *Journal Of American Culture*, VIII (Summer 1985), pp. 39-45.

Fred Povey, "Important Dates In Rock 'N' Roll History," *Lexington* (Kentucky) *Herald-Leader*, (July 7, 1985), p. A13.

Robert R. Prechter, "Elvis, Frankenstein, And Andy Warhol: Using Pop Culture To Forecast The Stock Market," *Barron's LXV* (September 9, 1985), pp. 6-7, 26, 28 ff.

Robert Prechter "Popular Culture And The Stock Market," *The Elliott Wave Theorist*, (August 22, 1985), pp. 1-20.

Chuck Raasch, " '50s Seem Nifty In '80s: But Nostalgia Neglects Reality Of Cold War Era," *Battle Creek* (Michigan) *Enquirer*, (June 9, 1988), pp. B1, 2.

Harvey Rachlin. "Popular Music," in *The Encyclopedia Of The Music Business* (New York: Harper and Row, 1981), pp. 283-288.

Jonathan Rodgers, "Back To The '50s," *Newsweek*, LXXX (October 16, 1972), pp. 78-82.

Jerome L. Rodnitzky, "The Decline Of Contemporary Protest Music," *Popular Music And Society I*, (Fall 1971), pp. 44-50.

Robert A. Rosenstone, " 'The Times They Are A-Changin': The Music Of Protest," in *Old Government/New People: Readings From The New Politics*, edited by Alfred de Grazia, R. Eric Weise, and John Appel (Glenview, Illinois: Scott, Foresman and Company, 1971), pp. 96-110.

Carl Ryant, "Oral History As Popular Culture," *Journal Of Popular Culture*, XV (Spring 1982), pp. 60-66.

Steve Simels, "The All-Star No Nukes Concerts: Three Discs Of Delicious Music," *Stereo Review*, XLIV (March 1980), pp. 88-91.

Jeff Smith, "The Sixties Revisited: Reflections On The Meaning Of The Movement," *The Cresset*, XLVIII (January 1985), pp. 13-19.

Larry Stidom, "A Few Political And Topical Records From Years Past," *Goldmine*, No. 126 (May 24, 1985), p. 28.

Susan S. Tamke, "Oral History And Popular Culture: A Method For The Study Of The Experience Of Culture," *Journal Of Popular Culture*, XI (Summer 1977), pp. 267-279.

Nick Tosches, "What That Was: A Chronology Of The Coming Of Rock 'N' Roll, in *Unsung Heroes of Rock 'N' Roll: The Birth Of Rock 'N' Roll In The Dark And Wild Years Before Elvis* (New York: Charles Scribner's Sons, 1984), pp. 147-168.

Les Waffen and Peter Hesbacher, "War Songs: Hit Recordings During The Vietnam Period," *ARSC Journal*, XIII, No. 2 (1981), pp. 4-18.

Joel Whitburn, "Chronology Of Milestones In Popular Music/Recording History, 1877-1954," in *Pop Memories, 1890-1950: The History Of American Popular Music* (Menomonee Falls, Wisconsin: Record Research, Inc., 1986), pp. 11-17.

Karen J. Winkler, "Television And Film Ignored Vietnam Until The Late 1960s, Scholars Argue," *The Chronicle Of Higher Education*, XXXI (November 20, 1985), pp. 5, 9.

Charles Wolfe, "Nuclear Country: The Atomic Bomb In Country Music," *Journal Of Country Music*, (January 1978), 4-22.

Tom Wolfe, "The 'Me' Decade And The Third Great Awakening," *New York Times Magazine*, (August 23, 1976), pp. 26-40.

Unpublished Material

Robert T. Bailey, "A Study Of The Effect Of Popular Music On Achievement In And Attitude Toward Contemporary United States History" (M.Ed.: West Georgia College, 1979).

Gary Curtis Burns, "Utopia And Dystopia In Popular Song Lyrics: Rhetorical Visions In The United States, 1963-1972" (Ph.D.: Northwestern University, 1981)

Louis Cantor, "Bob Dylan And The Protest Movement Of The 1960s: The Electronic Medium Is The Apocalyptic Message," mimeographed paper presented at the 8th National Convention of The Popular Culture Association in April 1978).

David Murray Emblidge, "A Dialogue Of Energy: Rock Music And Cultural Change" (Ph.D.: University of Minnesota, 1973).

Kenneth A. Fuchsman, "Between The Garden And The Devil's Bargain: The 1960s Counter Culture In Rock Music" (mimeographed paper presented at the 6th National Convention of The American Culture Association in March 1984).

_____ "Deliver Me From The Days Of Old: Lyrical Themes In 1950s Rock And Roll" (mimeographed paper presented at the 13th National Convention of The Popular Culture Association in April 1983).

Mary Jane Johnson, "Rock Music As A Reflector Of Social Attitudes Among Youth Of The 1960s" (Ph.D.: St. Louis University, 1978).

Hugo Keesing, "Culture In The Grooves: American History At 78, 45, and 33-1/3 r.p.m." (mimeographed paper presented at the 8th National Convention of The Popular Culture Association in April 1978).

_____ "Pop Goes To War: The Music Of World War II And Vietnam" (mimeographed paper presented at the 9th National Convention Of The Popular Culture Association in April 1979).

_____ "Popular Recordings And The American Presidency: From John F. Kennedy To Ronald Reagan" (mimeographed paper presented at the 13th National Convention of The Popular Culture Association in April 1983).

_____ "Recorded Music And The Vietnam War: The First 25 Years" (mimeographed paper presented at The 17th National Convention of The Popular Cultural Association in March 1987).

_____ "Youth In Transition: A Content Analysis Of Two Decades Of Popular Music" (Ph.D.: Adelphi University, 1972).

James Petterson, "Using Popular Music To Teach Topics In American History Since 1950 For High School Students," (M.S.Ed.: University of Southern California, 1977).

Joseph D. Reading, "Tears Of Rage: A History, Theory, And Criticism Of Rock Song And Social Conflict Rhetoric, 1965-1970" (Ph.D.: University of Oregon, 1980).

James Schnell, "No Nukes: Music As A Form Of Coutercultural Communication" (mimeographed paper presented at the 15th National Convention of The Popular Culture Association in April 1985).

Selected Bibliography

Books

Albert, George, and Frank Hoffman (comps.), *The Cashbox Black Contemporary Singles Charts, 1960-1984*. Metuchen, New Jersey: Scarecrow Press, 1986.

———— *The Cashbox Country Singles Charts, 1958-1982*. Metuchen, New Jersey: Scarecrow Press, 1984.

Bane, Michael, *White Boy Singin' The Blues: The Black Roots of White Rock*. New York: Penguin Books, 1982.

Belz, Carl, *The Story Of Rock (2nd ed.)*. New York: Harper and Row, 1972.

Berry, Jason, Jonathan Foose, and Tad Jones, *Up From The Cradle Of Jazz*. Athens, Georgia: University of Georgia Press, 1986.

Betrock, Alan, *Girl Groups: The Story Of A Sound*. New York: Delilah Books, 1982.

Bianco, David (comp.), *Heat Wave: The Motown Fact Book*. Ann Arbor, Michigan: Pierian Press, 1988.

————*Who's New Wave In Music: An Illustrated Encyclopedia, 1976-1982 (The First Wave)*. Ann Arbor, Michigan: Pierian Press, 1985.

Booth, Mark W. (comp.), *American Popular Music: A Reference Guide*. Westport, Connecticut: Greenwood Press, 1983.

———— *The Experience Of Song*. New Haven, Connecticut: Yale University Press, 1981.

Brady, Barry, *Reelin' And Rockin': The Golden Age of Rock 'N' Roll Movies*. Australia: The Printing Place, Ltd., 1982.

Bronson, Fred, *The Billboard Book Of Number One Hits* (2nd ed.). New York: Billboard Books, 1988.

Broven, John, *Walking To New Orleans: The Story Of New Orleans Rhythm And Blues*. Bexhill-On-Sea Sussex: Blues Unlimited, 1974.

Busnar, Gene, *It's Rock 'N' Roll: A Musical History Of The Fabulous Fifties*. New York: Wanderer Books, 1979.

Carney, George (ed.), *The Sounds Of People And Places: Readings In The Geography Of American Folk And Popular Music*. Lanham, Maryland: University Press of American, Inc., 1979.

Chambers, Iain, *Urban Rhythms: Pop Music And Popular Culture*. New York: St. Martin's Press, 1985.

Chapple, Steve and Reebee Garofalo, *Rock 'N' Roll Is Here To Pay: The History And Politics Of The Music Industry*. Chicago: Nelson-Hall, Inc., 1977.

Charlesworth, Chris, *A-Z Of Rock Guitarists*. New York: Proteus Press, 1982.

Charters, Samuel B., *The Poetry Of The Blues*. New York: Oak Publications, 1963.

Chase, Gilbert, *America's Music: From The Pilgrims To The Present* (revised 3rd ed.). Urbana: University of Illinois Press, 1987.

Christgau, Robert, *Any Old Way You Choose It: Rock And Other Pop Music, 1967-1973*. Baltimore, Maryland: Penguin Books, Inc., 1973.

Clark, Alan (comp.), *Legends Of Sun Records*. West Covina, California: A. Clark Production, 1986.

_____ *Rock And Roll In The Movies* (3 vols.). West Covina, California: Alan Lungstrum, 1987.

_____ *Rock And Roll Memories* (2 vols.). West Covina, California: Alan Lungstrum, 1987.

_____ *Rock-A-Billy And Country Legends.* West Covina, California: A. Clark Production, 1986.

_____ *Sun Photo Album.* West Covina, California: Alan Lungstrum, 1986.

Clee, Ken (comp.), *The Directory Of American 45 R.P.M. Records: Reissue Directory.* Philadelphia, Pennsylvania: Stak-O-Wax Publications, 1984.

Cohen, Norm (with music edited by David Cohen), *Long Steel Rail: The Railroad In American Folksong.* Urbana: University of Illinois Press, 1981.

Cohen-Stratyner, Barbara (ed.), *Popular Music, 1900-1919: An Annotated Guide To American Popular Song.* Detroit, Michigan: Gale Research, Inc. 1988.

Colman, Stuart, *They Kept On Rockin': The Giants Of Rock 'N' Roll.* Poole, Dorset, England: Blandford Press, 1982.

Cooper, B. Lee, *Images Of American Society In Popular Music: A Guide To Reflective Teaching.* Chicago: Nelson-Hall, Inc., 1982.

_____ *The Popular Music Handbook: A Resource Guide For Teacher, Librarians, And Media Specialists.* Littleton, Colorado: Libraries Unlimited, Inc., 1984.

_____ "Popular Music In The Social Studies Classroom: Audio Resources For Teachers: (*How To Do It*—Series II, No. 13). Washington, D.C.: National Council For The Social Studies, 1981.

_____ *A Resource Guide To Themes In Contemporary American Song Lyrics, 1950-1985.* Westport, Connecticut: Greenwood Press, 1986.

Cotten, Lee and Howard A. DeWitt, *Jailhouse Rock: The Bootleg Records Of Elvis Presley, 1970-1983.* Ann Arbor, Michigan: Pierian Press, 1983.

Dean, Roger, and David Howells (comps.), *The Ultimate Album Cover Album.* New York: Prentice Hall Press, 1987.

Dellar, Fred (comp.), *New Musical Express Guide To Rock Cinema.* Middlesex, England: Hamlyn Paperbacks, 1981.

Denisoff, R. Serge, *Great Day Coming: Folk Music And The American Left.* Baltimore, Maryland: Penguin Books, Inc., 1971.

_____ *Sing A Song Of Social Significance* (3rd ed.). Bowling Green, Ohio: Bowling Green University Popular Press, 1983.

_____ (comp.), *Songs Of Protest, War, And Peace: A Bibliography And Discography.* Santa Barbara, California: American Bibliography Center - CLIO Press, Inc., 1973.

Denisoff, R. Serge, and Richard A. Peterson (eds.), *The Sounds Of Social Change: Studies In Popular Culture.* Chicago: Rand McNally and Company, 1972.

Denisoff, R. Serge, with William L. Schurk, *Tarnished Gold: The Record Industry Revisited.* New Brunswick, New Jersey: Transaction Books, 1986.

Dennison, Sam. *Scandalize My Name: Black Imagery In American Popular Music.* New York: Garland Publishing, Inc., 1982.

DeTurk, David A., and A. Poulin, Jr., (eds.), *The American Folk Scene: Dimensions Of The Folksong Revival.* New York: Dell Publishing Company, Inc., 1967.

Doerschuk, Bob (ed.), *Rock Keyboard.* New York: A Quill/Keyboard Book, 1985.

Doherty, Thomas, *Teenagers And Teenpics: The Juvenilization Of American Movies In The 1950s.* Winchester, Massachusetts: Unwin Hyman Books, 1988.

Duxbury, Janell R., *Rockin' The Classics And Classicizin' The Rock: A Selectively Annotated Discography.* Westport, Connecticut: Greenwood Press, 1985.

Ehrenstein, David, and Bill Reed, *Rock On Film.* New York: Delilah Books, 1982.

Eisen, Jonathan (ed.), *The Age Of Rock: Sounds Of The American Cultural Revolution.* New York: Vintage Books, 1969.

––––– (ed.), *The Age Of Rock—2: Sights And Sounds Of The American Cultural Revolution.* New York: Vintage Books, 1970.

––––– (ed.), *Altamont: The Death Of Innocence In The Woodstock Nation.* New York: Avon Books, 1970.

––––– (ed.), *Twenty-Minute Fandangos And Forever Changes: A Rock Bazaar.* New York: Vintage Books, 1971.

Elrod, Bruce C. (comp.), *Your Hit Parade And American Top Ten Hits, 1958-1984* (3rd ed.). White Rock, South Carolina: B. Elrod, 1985.

Elson, Howard, *Early Rockers.* New York: Proteus Books, 1982.

Escott, Colin, and Martin Hawkins, *Sun Records: The Brief History Of The Legendary Record Label.* New York: Quick Fox, 1980.

––––– (comps.), *Sun Records: The Discography.* Vollersode, West Germany: Bear Family Books, 1987.

Evans, David, *Big Road Blues: Tradition And Creativity In The Folk Blues.* Jersey City, New Jersey: Da Capo Press, 1987.

Ewen, David, *All The Years of American Popular Music: A Comprehensive History.* Englewood Cliffs, New Jersey: Prentice-Hall, Inc., 1977.

Flanagan, Bill, *Written In My Soul: Conversations With Rock's Great Songwriters.* Chicago: Contemporary Books, 1987.

Fong-Torres, Ben (ed.), *The Rolling Stone Rock 'N' Roll Reader.* New York: Bantam Books, Inc., 1974.

––––– (comp.), *What's That Sound: The Contemporary Music Scene From The Pages of Rolling Stone.* Garden City, New York: Doubleday Anchor Books, 1976.

Fox, Ted, *In The Groove: The Men Behind The Music.* New York: St. Martin's Press, 1986.

Frith, Simon, *Sound Effects: Youth, Leisure, And The Politics Of Rock 'N' Roll.* New York: Pantheon Books, 1981.

Gardner, Carl (ed.), *Media, Politics, And Culture: A Socialist View.* Atlantic Highlands, New Jersey: Humanities Press, 1979.

Garon, Paul, *Blues And The Poetic Spirit.* London: Eddison Press, 1975.

Gart, Galen, *First Pressings—1948-1952: Rock History As Chronicled In Billboard Magazine* (2 vols.). Milford, New Hampshire: Big Nickel Publications, 1986.

Gelt, Andrew L. (comp.). *Index To Alcohol, Drugs, And Intoxicants In Music.* Albuquerque, New Mexico: A.L. Gelt, 1982.

George, Nelson, *The Death Of Rhythm And Blues.* New York: Pantheon Books, 1988.

––––– *Top Of The Charts—The Most Complete Listing Ever: The Top 10 Records And Albums For Every Week Of Every Year From 1970.* Piscataway, New Jersey: New Century Publishers, 1983.

––––– *Where Did Our Love Go: The Rise And Fall Of The Motown Sound.* New York: St. Martin's Press, 1985.

Gillett, Charlie, *The Sound of The City: The Rise Of Rock And Roll* (revised ed.). New York: Pantheon Books, 1983.

Green, Jeff (comp.), *The 1987 Green Book: Songs Classified By Subject.* Altadena, California: Professional Desk Reference, Inc., 1986.

Grissim, John, *Country Music: White Man's Blues.* New York: Paperback Library, 1970.

Groia, Philip, *They All Sang On The Corner: A Second Look At New York City's Rhythm And Blues Vocal Groups* (revised ed.). West Hempstead, New York: Phillie Dee Enterprises, 1984.

Grushkin, Paul D., *The Art Of Rock: Posters From Presley To Punk*. New York: Abbeville Press, 1987.

Guralnick, Peter, *Feel Like Going Home: Portraits In Blues And Rock 'N' Roll*. New York: Outerbridge and Dienstfrey, 1971.

——— *Listener's Guide To The Blues*. New York: Facts on File, 1982.

——— *Lost Highway: Journeys And Arrivals Of American Musicians*. Boston: David R. Godine, 1979.

——— *Sweet Soul Music: Rhythm And Blues And The Southern Dream Of Freedom*. New York: Harper and Row, 1986.

Hagensen, Rick (comp.), *Strictly Instrumental*. New Westminster, British Columbia, Canada: R. Hagensen, 1986.

Hamm, Charles, Bruno Nettl, and Ronald Byrnside, *Contemporary Music And Music Cultures*. Englewood Cliffs, New Jersey: Prentice-Hall, Inc., 1975.

Hamm, Charles, *Music In The New World*. New York: W.W. Norton and Company, Inc., 1983.

——— *Yesterdays: Popular Song In America*. New York: W.W. Norton and Company, Inc., 1979.

Hanel, Ed (comp.), *The Essential Guide To Rock Books*. London: Omnibus Books, 1983.

Hannusch, Jeff (a.k.a. Almost Slim), *I Hear You Knockin': The Sound Of New Orleans Rhythm And Blues*. Ville Platte, Louisiana: Swallow Publications, 1985.

Haralambos, Michael, *Right On: From Blues To Soul In Black America*. New York: Drake Publishers, Inc., 1975.

Hardy, Phil and Dave Laing (comps.), *Encyclopedia Of Rock, 1955-1975*. London: Aquarius Books, 1977.

Harker, Dave, *One For The Money: Politics And The Popular Song*. London: Hutchinson and Company, Ltd., 1980.

Harris, Sheldon (comp.), *Blues Who's Who: A Biographical Dictionary Of Blues Singers*. New Rochelle, New York: Arlington House, 1979.

Hatch, David, and Stephen Millward, *From Blues To Rock: An Analytical History Of Pop Music*. Manchester, England: Manchester University Press, 1987.

Heilbut, Tony, *The Gospel Sound: Good News And Bad Times (revised ed.)*. New York: Limelight Editions, 1985.

Helander, Brock (comp.), *The Rock Who's Who*. New York: Schirmer Books, 1982.

Hendler, Herb, *Year By Year In The Rock Era; Events And Conditions Shaping The Rock Generations That Reshaped American*. Westport, Connecticut: Greenwood Press, 1983.

Herbst, Peter (ed.), *The Rolling Stone Interviews: Talking With The Legends Of Rock And Roll, 1967-1980*. New York: St. Martin's Press/Rolling Stone Press, 1981.

Hibbard, Don J., and Carol Kaleialoha, *The Role of Rock*. Englewood Cliffs, New Jersey: Prentice-Hall, Inc., 1983.

Hirshey, Gerri, *Nowhere To Run: The Story Of Soul Music*. New York: Times Books, 1984.

Hoare, Ian, Tony Cummings, Clive Anderson, and Simon Frith, *The Soul Book*. New York: Dell publishing Company, Inc., 1976.

Hoffmann, Frank, and George Albert, with Lee Ann Hoffmann (comps.), *The Cashbox Album Charts, 1955-1974*. Metuchen, New Jersey: Scarecrow Press, Inc., 1988.

——— (comps.), *The Cashbox Album Charts, 1975-1985*. Metuchen, New Jersey: Scarecrow Press, 1983.

Hoffmann, Frank (comp.), *The Cash Box Singles Charts, 1950-1981*. Metuchen, New Jersey: Scarecrow Press, Inc., 1983.

_____ (comp.), *The Literature Of Rock, 1954-1978*. Metuchen, New Jersey: Scarecrow Press, Inc., 1981.

Hoffmann, Frank, and B. Lee Cooper (comps.), *The Literature Of Rock II, 1979-1983* (2 vols.). Metuchen, New Jersey: Scarecrow Press, Inc., 1986.

Horn, David (comp.), *The Literature Of American Music In Books And Folk Music Collections: A Fully Annotated Bibliography*. Metuchen, New Jersey: Scarecrow Press, Inc., 1977.

Horstman, Dorothy, *Sing Your Heart Out, Country Boy* (revised ed.). Nashville, Tennessee: Country Music Foundation, 1986.

Hoskyns, Barney, *Say It One Time For The Broken Hearted: The Country Side of Southern Soul*. London: Fontana Books, 1987.

Hounsome, Terry (comp.), *Rock Record: A Collectors' Directory Of Rock Albums And Musicians* (revised ed.). New York: Facts on File Publications, 1987.

Inge, M. Thomas (ed.), *Concise Histories Of American Popular Culture*. Westport, Connecticut: Greenwood Press, 1982.

Iwaschkin, Roman (comp.), *Popular Music: A Reference Guide*. New York: Garland Publishing, Inc., 1986.

Jahn, Mike, *Rock: From Elvis Presley To The Rolling Stones*. New York: Quadrangle Books, 1973.

Jenkinson, Philip, and Alan Warner, *Celluloid Rock: Twenty Years Of Movie Rock*. London: Lorrimer Publishing, 1974.

Kaplan, E. Ann, *Rocking Around The Clock: Music Television, Postmodernism, And Consumer Culture*. New York: Methuen, Inc., 1987.

Keil, Charles, *Urban Blues*, Chicago: University of Chicago Press, 1966.

Kinder, Bob, *The Best of The First: The Early Days Of Rock And Roll*. Chicago: Adams Press, 1986.

Kingman, Daniel, *American Music: A Panarama*. New York: Schirmer Books, 1979.

Kocandrle, Mirek (comp.), *The History Of Rock And Roll: A Selective Discography*. Boston: Massachusetts: G.K. Hall, 1988.

Landau, Jon, *It's Too Late To Stop Now: A Rock And Roll Journal*. San Francisco, California: Straight Arrow Books, 1972.

Lax, Roger, and Frederick Smith (comps.), *The Great Song Thesaurus* (updated edition). New York: Oxford University Press, 1988.

Levine, Lawrence W., *Black Culture And Black Consciousness: Afro-American Folk Thought From Slavery To Freedom*. New York: Oxford University Press, 1977.

Lewis, George H. (ed.), *Side-Saddle On The Golden Calf: Social Structure And Popular Music In America*. Pacific Palisades, California: Goodyear Publishing Company, Inc., 1972.

Lydon, Michael, and Ellen Mandel, *Boogie Lightning: How Music Became Electric* (2nd ed.). New York: Da Capo Press, 1980.

Lydon, Michael, *Rock Folk: Portraits From The Rock 'N' Roll Pantheon*. New York: Dial Press, 1971.

Macken, Bob, Peter Fornatale, and Bill Ayres, *The Rock Music Source Book*. Garden City, New York: Doubleday and Company, Inc., 1980.

Malone, Bill C., *Country Music U.S.A.* (revised ed.). Austin: University of Texas Press, 1985.

_____ *Southern Music/American Music*. Lexington: University Press of Kentucky, 1979.

Marcus, Greil, *Mystery Train: Images Of America In Rock 'N' Roll Music* (revised edition). New York: E.P. Dutton and Company, Inc., 1982.

Marsh, Dave, with Lee Ballinger, Sandra Choron, Wendy Smith, and Daniel Wolff, *The First Rock And Roll Confidential Report: Inside The Real World Of Rock And Roll*. New York: Pantheon Books, 1985.

Marsh, Dave, *Fortunate Son*. New York: Random House, 1985.

Martin, George (ed.), *Making Music: The Guide To Writing, Performing, And Recording*. London: Pan Books, 1983.

Mawhinney, Paul C. (comp.), *MusicMaster: The 45 R.P.M. Record Directory, 1947 to 1982* (two volumes). Allison Park, Pennsylvania: Record-Rama, 1983.

McKee, Margaret and Fred Chisenhall, *Beale Black And Blue: Life And Music On Black America's Main Street*. Baton Rouge, Louisiana: Louisiana State University Press, 1981.

McNutt, Randy, *We Wanna Boogie: An Illustrated History Of The American Rockabilly Movement*, Fairfield, Ohio: Hamilton Hobby Press, 1987.

Meeker, David, *Jazz In The Movies (revised edition)*. New York: Da Capo Press, 1982.

Melhuish, Martin, *Heart Of Gold: 30 Years Of Canadian Pop Music*. Toronto, Ontario, Canada: Canadian Broadcasting Corporation, 1983.

Mellers, Wilfrid, *Angels Of The Night: Popular Female Singers Of Our Time*. New York: Basil Blackwell, Inc., 1986.

Middleton, Richard, *Pop Music And The Blues: A Study Of The Relationship And Its Significance*. London: Victor Gollancz, Ltd., 1972.

Middleton, Richard, and David Horn (eds.), *Popular Music: Folk Or Popular? Distinction, Influences, Continuities*. Cambridge University Press, 1981.

———— (eds.), *Popular Music 2: Theory And Method*. Cambridge: Cambridge University Press, 1982.

———— (eds.), *Popular Music 3: Producers And Markets*. Cambridge: Cambridge university Press, 1983.

———— (eds.), *Popular Music 4: Performer And Audiences*. Cambridge: Cambridge University Press, 1984.

Miles, Daniel J., Betty T. Miles, and Martin J. Miles (comps.), *The Miles Chart Display, Volume I: Top 100, 1955-1970*. Boulder, Colorado: Convex Industries, 1973.

———— (comps.). *The Miles Chart Display Of Popular Music, Volume II: Top 100, 1971-1975*. New York: Arno Press, 1977.

Miller, Jim (ed.), *The Rolling Stone Illustrated History Of Rock And Roll*. New York: Random House/Rolling Stone Press, 1976.

———— (ed.), *The Rolling Stone Illustrated History Of Rock And Roll (revised edition)*. New York: Random House/Rolling Stone Press Book, 1980.

Moore, MacDonald Smith, *Yankee Blues: Musical Culture And American Identity*. Bloomington: Indiana University Press, 1985.

Morthland, John, *The Best Of Country Music: A Critical And Historical Guide To The 750 Greatest Albums*. Garden City, New York: Dolphin/Doubleday and Company, Inc., 1984.

Murrells, Joseph, *Million Selling Records From The 1900s To The 1980s: An Illustrated Directory*. London: Batsford Press, 1986.

Music/Records/200: Billboard's July 4, 1976 Spotlight On American. New York: Billboard Publications, Inc., 1976.

Nachbar, Jack, Deborah Weiser, and John L. Wright (comps.), *The Popular Culture Reader*. Bowling Green, Ohio: Bowling Green University Popular Press, 1978.

Naha, Ed (comp.), *Lillian Roxon's Rock Encyclopedia (revised edition)*. New York: Grosset and Dunlap, 1978.

Neises, Charles P. (ed.), *The Beatles Reader: A Selection Of Contemporary Views, News, And Reviews Of The Beatles In Their Heyday*. Ann Arbor, Michigan: Pierian Press, 1984.

Nite, Norm N. (comp.), *Rock On: The Illustrated Encyclopedia Of Rock 'N' Roll—Volume One: The Solid Gold Years* (revised edition). New York: Harper and Row, 1982.

Nite, Norm N., with Ralph M. Newman (comps.), *Rock On: The Illustrated Encyclopedia Of Rock 'N' Roll—Volume Two: The Years Of Change, 1964-1978* (revised edition). New York: Harper and Row, 1984.

Nite, Norm N., with Charles Crespo (comps.), *Rock On: The Illustrated Encyclopedia Of Rock 'N' Roll—Volume Three: The Video Revolution, 1978 To The Present*. New York: Harper and Row, 1985.

Norman, Philip. *The Road Goes On Forever: Portraits From A Journey Through Contemporary Music*. New York: Fireside Book, 1982.

———— *Shout! The Beatles In Their Generation*. New York: Simon and Schuster, 1981.

Nugent, Stephen, and Charlie Gillet, (comps.), *Rock Almanac: Top Twenty American And British Singles And Albums Of The '50s, '60s, And '70s*. Garden City, New York: Anchor Press/Doubleday, 1976.

Nye, Russel, *The Unembarrassed Muse: The Popular Arts In America*. New York: Dial Press, 1970.

Oakley, Giles, *The Devil's Music: A History Of The Blues*. New York: Harcourt Brace Jovanovich, 1978.

Obst, Lynda R. (ed.), *The Sixties: The Decade Remembered Now, By The People Who Lived It Then*. New York: Random House/Rolling Stone Press, 1977.

Obermann, Robert K., and Douglas B. Green, *The Listener's Guide To Country Music*. New York: Facts on File, 1983.

Oliver, Paul, *The Meaning Of The Blues*. New York: Collier Books, 1972.

Orman, John, *The Politics Of Rock Music*. Chicago: Nelson-Hall, Inc., 1984.

Osborne, Jerry, and Bruce Hamilton (comps.), *Blues/Rhythm And Blues/Soul: Original Record Collectors Price Guide*. Phoenix, Arizona: O'Sullivan, Woodside and Company, 1980.

Osborne, Jerry (comp.), *Our Best To You—From Record Digest*. Prescott, Arizona: Record Digest, 1979.

———— *Soundtracks And Original Cast Recordings Price Guide*. Phoenix, Arizona: O'Sullivan, Woodside and Company, 1981.

Palmer, Robert, *Baby, That Was Rock And Roll: The Legendary Leiber And Stoller*. New York: Harcourt Brace Jovanovich, 1978.

———— *Deep Blues*. New York: Viking Press, 1981.

Pareles, Jon, and Patricia Romanowski (eds), *The Rolling Stone Encyclopedia Of Rock And Roll*. New York: Rolling Stone Press/Summit Books, 1983.

Pavletich, Aida, *Sirens of Song: The Popular Female Vocalist In America*. New York: Da Capo Press, Inc., 1980.

Pavlow, Al (comp.), *Big Al Pavlow's The R & B Book: A Disc-History Of Rhythm And Blues*. Providence, Rhode Island: Music House Publishing, 1983.

Philbin, Marianne (ed.), *Give Peace A Chance: Music And The Struggle For Peace*, Chicago: Chicago Review Press, 1983.

Pichaske, David, *Beowulf To Beatles And Beyond: The Varieties Of Poetry*. New York: Macmillan Publishing Company, Inc., 1981.

———— *A Generation In Motion: Popular Music And Culture In The Sixties*. New York: Schirmer, 1979.

———— *The Poetry Of Rock: The Golden years*. Peoria, Illinois: Ellis Press, 1981.

Pielke, Robert G., *You Say You Want A Revolution: Rock Music In American Culture*. Chicago: Nelson-Hall, Inc., 1986.

Podell, Janet (ed.), *Rock Music In America*. New York: The H.W. Wilson Company, 1987.

Pollock, Bruce, *In Their Own Words: Twenty Successful Song Writers Tell How They Write Their Songs*. New York: Collier Books, 1975.

———— (ed.), *Popular Music, 1980-1984—Volume 9*. Detroit, Michigan: Gale Research Company, 1986.

———— (ed.), *Popular Music 1985—Volume 10*. Detroit, Michigan: Gale Research Company, 1986.

———— (ed.), *Popular Music 1986—Volume 11*. Detroit, Michigan: Gale Research Company, 1987.

———— (ed.), *Popular Music 1987—Volume 12*. Detroit, Michigan: Gale Research Company, 1988.

———— *When The Music Mattered: Rock in The 1960s*. New York: Holt, Rinehart and Winston, 1983.

———— *When Rock Was Young: A Nostalgic Review Of The Top 40 Era*. New York: Holt, Rinehart and Winston, 1981.

Prakel, David, *Rock 'N' Roll On Compact Disc: A Critical Guide To The Best Recordings*. New York: Harmony Books, 1987.

Quirin, Jim, and Barry Cohen (comps.), *Chartmasters' Rock 100: An Authoritative Ranking of The 100 Most Popular Songs For Each year, 1956 Through 1986* (Supplements for 1987, 1988. . .are also available.). Covington, Louisiana: Chartmasters, 1987.

Rachlin, Harvey (comp.), *The Encyclopedia Of The Music Business*. New York: Harper And Row, 1981.

Redd, Lawrence N., *Rock Is Rhythm And Blues: The Impact Of Mass Media*. East Lansing: Michigan State University Press, 1974.

Rees, Tony, *Rare Rock: A Collectors' Guide*. Poole, Dorset, England: Blandford Press, 1985.

Reid, Robert, *"Music And Social Problems: A Poster Series."* Portland, Maine: J. Eston Walch, Publisher, 1971.

Reinhart, Charles, *You Can't Do That: Beatles' Bootlegs And Novelty Records, 1963-1980*. Ann Arbor, Michigan: Pierian Press, 1981.

Rimler, Walter, *Not Fade Away: A Comparison Of Jazz Age With Rock Era Pop Song Composers*. Ann Arbor, Michigan: Pierian Press, 1984.

Riswick, Don (comp.), *Nothin' But Instrumental: A Compendium Of Rock Instrumentals*. Virginia Beach, Virginia: D. Riswick, 1985.

Robbins, Ira A. (ed.), *The New Trouser Press Record Guide* (2nd edition). New York: Charles Scribner's Sons, 1985.

Robinson, Red, and Peggy Hodgins, *Rockbound: Rock 'N' Roll Encounters, 1955-1969*. Surrey, British Columbia, Canada: Hancock House Publishers, Ltd., 1983.

Rodnitzky, Jerome L., *Minstrels Of The Dawn: The Folk-Protest Singer As A Cultural Hero*. Chicago: Nelson-Hall, Inc., 1976.

Rogers, Dave, *Rock 'N' Roll*. London: Routledge and Kegan Paul, 1982.

Rogers, Jimmie N., *The Country Music Message: All About Lovin' and Livin'*. Englewood Cliffs, New Jersey: Prentice-Hall, Inc., 1983.

Root, Jr., Robert L., *The Rhetorics Of Popular Culture: Advertising, Advocacy, And Entertainment*. Westport, Connecticut: Greenwood Press, 1987.

Rowe, Mike, *Chicago Blues: The City And The Music*. New York: Da Capo Press, 1981.

Ruppli, Michel (comp.), *Atlantic Records: A Discography* (4 volumes). Westport, Connecticut: Greenwood Press, 1979.

———— (comp.), *The Chess Labels: A Discography* (2 volumes). Westport, Connecticut: Greenwood Press, 1983.

———— (comp.), *The King Labels: A Discography* (2 volumes). Westport, Connecticut: Greenwood Press, 1985.

Ryan, John, *The Production Of Culture In The Music Industry: The ASCAP-BMI Controversy*. Lanham, Maryland: University of America, Inc., 1985.

Sandahl, Linda J. (comp.), *Rock Films: A Viewer's Guide To Three Decades Of Musicals, Concerts, Documentaries, And Soundtracks, 1955-1986*. New York: Facts on File Publications, 1987.

Sander, Ellen, *Trips: Rock Life in The Sixties*. New York: Charles Scribner's Sons, 1973.

Sanjek, Russell, *American Popular Music And Its Business—The First Four Hundred Years: Volume Three, 1900-1984*. New York: Oxford University Press, 1988.

Santelli, Robert, *Sixties Rock: A Listener's Guide*. Chicago: Contemporary Books, 1985.

Sarlin, Bob, *Turn It Up (I Can't Hear The Words): The Best Of The New Singer/Song Writers*. New York: Simon and Schuster, 1973.

Savage, Jr., William W., *Singing Cowboys And All That Jazz: A Short History Of Popular Music In Oklahoma*. Norman: University of Oklahoma Press, 1982.

Schaffner, Nicholas, *The British Invasion: From The First Wave To The New Wave*. New York: McGraw Hill Book Company, 1982.

Schroeder, Fred E.H. (ed.), *Twentieth-Century Popular Culture In Museums And Libraries*. Bowling Green, Ohio: Bowling Green University Popular Press, 1981.

Schultheiss, Tom (comp.), *The Beatles—A Day In The Life: A Day-By-Day Diary, 1960-1970*. New York: Quick Fox, 1981.

Scott, John Anthony, *The Ballad Of America: The History Of The United States In Song And Story*. Carbondale: Southern Illinois University Press, 1983.

Sculatti, Gene, and Davin Seay, *San Francisco Nights: The Psychedelic Music Trip, 1965-1968*. New York: St. Martin's Press, 1985.

Shannon, Bob, and John Javna, *Behind The Hits: Inside Stories Of Classic Pop And Rock And Roll*. New York: Warner Books, 1986.

Shapiro, Nat, and Bruce Pollock (comps.), *Popular Music, 1920-1979—A Revised Compilation* (3 vols.). Detroit, Michigan: Gale Research Company, 1985.

Shaw, Arnold, *Black Popular Music In America: From The Spirituals, Minstrels, And Ragtime To Soul, Disco, And Hip-Hop*. New York: Schirmer Books, 1986.

———— *Honkers And Shouters: The Golden Years Of Rhythm And Blues*. New York: Collier Books, 1978.

———— *The Rockin' 50s: The Decade That Transformed The Pop Music Scene*. New York: Hawthorn Books, Inc., 1974.

Shore, Michael (comp.), *Music Video: A Consumer's Guide*. New York: Ballantine Books, 1987.

Simels, Steve, *Gender Chameleons: Androgeny In Rock 'N' Roll*. New York: Arbor House, 1985.

Stacy, Jan, and Ryder Syvertsen, *Rockin' Reels: An Illustrated History Of Rock And Roll Movies*. Chicago: Contemporary Books, Inc., 1984.

Stambler, Irwin (comp.), *Encyclopedia Of Pop, Rock, And Soul*. New York: St. Martin's Press, 1974.

Stecheson, Anthony, and Anne Stecheson (comps.), *The Stecheson Classified Song Directory*. Hollywood, California: The Music Industry Press, 1961.

Szatmary, David P., *Rockin' In Time: A Social History Of Rock And Roll*. Englewood Cliffs, New Jersey: Prentice-Hall, Inc., 1987.

Taraborrelli, J. Randy, *Motown: Hot Wax, City Cool, And Solid Gold*. Garden City, New York: Dolphin/Doubleday and Company, Inc., 1986.

Taylor, Paul (comp.), *Popular Music Since 1955: A Critical Guide To The Literature*. New York: Mansell Publishing, Ltd., 1985.

Terry, Carol D. (comp.), *Sequins And Shades: The Michael Jackson Reference Guide*. Ann Arbor, Michigan: Pierian press, 1987.

Tharpe, Jac L. (ed.), *Elvis: Images And Fancies*. Jackson: University Press of Mississippi, 1979.

Titon, Jeff Todd, *Early Downhome Blues: A Musical And Cultural Analysis*. Urbana: University of Illinois Press, 1977.

Tobler, John, and Stuart Grundy, *The Record Producers*. New York: St. Martin's press, 1983.

Tosches, Nick, *Country: Living Legends And Dying Metaphors In America's Biggest Music* (revised edition). New York: Charles Scribner's Sons, 1985.

———— *Hellfire: The Jerry Lee Lewis Story*. New York: Dell Publishing Company, Inc., 1982.

———— *Unsung Heroes of Rock 'N' Roll: The Birth Of Rock 'N' Roll in The Dark And Wild Years Before Elvis*. New York: Charles Scribner's Songs, 1984.

Tudor, Dean (comp.), *Popular Music: An Annotated Guide To Recordings*. Littleton, Colorado: Libraries Unlimited, Inc., 1983.

Uslan, Michael, and Bruce Solomon, *Dick Clark's The First 25 Years Of Rock And Roll*. New York: Delacorte Press, 1981.

Vassal, Jacques, *Electric Children: Roots And Branches Of Modern Folkrock*. New York: Taplinger Publishing Company, 1976.

Vulliamy, Graham, and Edward Lee, *Popular Music: A Teacher's Guide*. London: Routledge and Kegan Paul, 1982.

———— *Pop, Rock, And Ethnic Music In School*. Cambridge: Cambridge University Press, 1982.

Ward, Ed, Geoffrey Stokes, and Ken Tucker, *Rock Of Ages: The Rolling Stone History Of Rock And Roll*. New York: Rolling Stone Press/Summit Books, 1986.

Weinberg, Max, with Robert Santelli, *The Big Beat: Conversations With Rock's Great Drummers*. Chicago: Contemporary Books, 1984.

Westcott, Steven D. (comp.), *A Comprehensive Bibliography Of Music For Film And Television*. Detroit, Michigan: Information Coordinators, 1985.

Whetmore, Edward Jay, *Mediamerica: Form, Content, And Consequence Of Mass Communication* (3rd edition). Belmont, California: Wadsworth Publishing Company, 1987.

Whitburn, Joel (comp.), *The Billboard Book Of Top 40 Albums: The Complete Chart Guide To Every Album In The Top 40 Since 1955*. New York: Billboard Books, 1987.

———— (comp.), *The Billboard Book Of Top 40 Hits* (3rd edition). New York: Billboard Books, 1987.

———— (comp.), *Billboard's Top 10 Charts: A Week-By-Week History of The Hottest Of The Hot 100, 1958-1988*. Menomonee Falls, Wisconsin: Record Research, Inc., 1988.

———— (comp.), *Billboard's Top 3,000 +, 1955-1987: A Ranking Of Every Top 10 hit of The Rock Era*. Menomonee Falls, Wisconsin: Record Research, Inc., 1988.

———— (comp.), *Bubbling Under The Hot 100, 1959-1981*. Menomonee Falls, Wisconsin: Record Research, Inc., 1982.

——— (comp.), *Music And Video Yearbook 1987*. Menomonee Falls, Wisconsin: Record Research, Inc., 1988.

——— (comp.), *Music And Video Yearbook 1988*. Menomonee Falls, Wisconsin: Record Research, Inc., 1989.

——— (comp.), *Pop Memories, 1890-1954: The History Of American Popular Music*. Menomonee Falls, Wisconsin: Record Research, Inc., 1986.

——— (comp.), *Pop Singles Annual, 1955-1986*. Menomonee Falls, Wisconsin: Record Research, Inc. 1987.

——— (comp.), *Top Rhythm And Blues Singles, 1942-1988*. Menomonee Falls, Wisconsin: Record Research, Inc., 1988.

Whitcomb, Ian, *After The Ball: Pop Music From Rag To Rock*. Baltimore: Penguin Books, Inc., 1972.

——— *Rock Odyssey: A Musician's Guide To The Sixties*. Garden City, New York: Dolphin Books, 1983.

——— *Whole Lotta Shakin': A Rock 'N' Roll Scrapbook*. London: Arrow Books, Ltd., 1982.

White, Timothy, *Rock Stars*. New York: Stewart, Tabori, and Chang, 1984.

Wiegand, Wayne A. (ed.), *Popular Culture And The Library: Current Issues Symposium II*. Lexington: College of Library Science at the University of Kentucky, 1978.

Williams, Paul, *Outlaw Blues: A Book Of Rock Music*. New York: E.P. Dutton, 1969.

Worth, Fred L., *Rock Facts*. New York: Facts On File, 1986.

York, William, *Who's Who in Rock Music* (revised edition). New York: Charles Scribner's Sons, 1982.

Yorke, Ritchie, *Axes, Chops, And Hot Licks: The Canadian Rock Music Scene*. Edmonton, Alberta, Canada: M.G. Hurtig, Publisher, 1971.

Zalkind, Ronald (comp.), *Contemporary Music Almanac 1980/81*. New York: Schrimer Books, 1980.

Articles

Anderson, T.J., and Lois Fields Anderson, "Images Of Blacks In Instrumental Music And Song," in *Images Of Blacks In American Culture: A Reference Guide To Information Sources*, edited by Jessie Carney Smith (Westport, Connecticut: Greenwood Press, 1988), pp. 119-137.

Auslander, H. Ben, " 'If Ya Wanna End War And Stuff, You Gotta Sing Loud': A Survey Of Vietnam-Related Protest Music," *Journal of American Culture*, IV (Summer 1981), pp. 108-113.

Baker, Glenn A., "Recording The Right," *Goldmine*, No. 66 (November 1981), pp. 176-178.

——— "Rock's Angry Voice," *Goldmine*, No. 75 (July 1982), pp. 10-11.

Burns, Gary, "Film And Popular Music," in *Film And The Arts In Symbiosis: A Resource Guide*, edited by Gary R. Edgerton (Westport, Connecticut: Greenwood Press, 1988), pp. 217-242.

——— "Trends In Lyrics In The Annual Top Twenty Songs in The United States, 1963-1972," *Popular Music And Society*, IX (1983), pp. 25-39.

Carey, James T., "Changing Courtship Patterns In The Popular Song," *American Journal Of Sociology*, LXXIV (May 1969), pp. 720-731.

Carney, George O., "Music And Dance," in *This Remarkable Continent: An Atlas of United States and Canadian Society and Cultures*, edited by John F. Rooney, Jr., Wilbur Zelinsky, and Dean R. Louder (College Station, Texas: For the Society for the North American Cultural Survey by Texas A & M University Press, 1982), pp. 234-253.

Chenoweth, Lawrence, "The Rhetoric Of Hope And Despair: A Study Of The Jimi Hendrix Experience And The Jefferson Airplane," *American Quarterly*, XXIII (Spring 1981), pp. 25-45.

Cobb, James M., "From Muskogee To Luckenbach: Country Music And The Southernization Of America," *Journal of Popular Culture*, XVI (Winter 1982), pp. 81-91.

Cole, Richard, "Top Songs Of The Sixties: A Content Analysis Of Popular Lyrics," *American Behavioral Scientist*, XIV (January-February 1971).

Cooper, B. Lee, "Audio Images Of The City," *Social Studies*, LXXII (May/June 1981), pp. 129-136.

_____ "Examining A Decade Of Rock Bibliographies, 1970-1979," *JEMF Quarterly*, XVII (Summer 1981), pp. 95-101.

_____ "Exploring The Future Through Popular Music," *Media And Methods*, XII (April 1976), pp. 32-35ff.

_____ "The Fats Domino Decades, 1950-1969," *R.P.M.*, No, 5 (May 1984), pp. 56-58, 71.

_____ "Huntin' For Discs With Wild Bill: William L. Schurk—Sound Recordings Archivist," *ARSC Journal*, XIV, No. 3 (1982), pp. 9-19.

_____ "Information Services, Popular Culture, And The Librarian: Promoting A Contemporary Learning Perspective," *Drexel Library Quarterly* XVI (July 1980), pp. 24-42.

_____ "Just Let Me Hear Some Of That...: Discographies Of Fifty Classic Rock Era Performers," *JEMF Quarterly*, No. 74 (Fall 1983/Winter 1984), pp. 100-116.

_____ "Les McCann, Elvis Presley, Linda Ronstadt, And Buddy Holly: Focusing On The Lives Of Contemporary Singers," *Social Education*, XLIV (March 1980), pp. 217-221.

_____ "Music And The Metropolis: Lyrical Images Of Life In American Cities, 1950-1980," *Teaching History: A Journal of Methods*, VI (Fall 1981), pp. 72-84.

Cooper, B. Lee, Frank W. Hoffman, and William L. Schurk, "The Music Magazine Reader's 'Hot 100': Popular Music Periodicals, 1950-1982", *JEMF Quarterly*, XIX (Spring 1983), pp. 32-48.

Cooper, B. Lee, "Popular Music In The Classroom: A Bibliography Of Teaching Techniques And Instructional Resources," *International Journal of Instructional Media*, X, No. 1 (1982-83), pp. 71-87.

Cooper, B. Lee, and James A. Creeth, "Present At The Creation: The Legend Of Jerry Lee Lewis On Record, 1956-1963," *JEMF Quarterly*, XIX (Summer 1983), pp. 122-129.

Cooper, B. Lee, "Recorded Resources For Teaching The History Of Contemporary Music, 1950-1985: A Discography Of Musical Styles And Recording Artists," *International Journal Of Instructional Media*, XIV, No. 1 (1987), pp. 63-81.

_____ "Review Of *Work's Many Voices*—Volumes One and Two (JEMF 110/111) compiled by Archie Green," *Popular Music And Society*, XII (Spring 1988), pp. 77-79.

_____ "Rock Discographies: Exploring The Iceberg's Tip," *JEMF Quarterly*, XV (Summer 1979), pp. 115-120.

_____ "Rock Discographies Revisited," *JEMF Quarterly*, XVI (Summer 1980), pp. 89-94.

_____ "Rock Music And Religious Education: A Proposed Synthesis," *Religious Education*, LXX (May/June 1975), pp. 289-299.

―――― "Sounds Of The City: Popular Music Perspectives On Urban Life," *International Journal Of Instructional Media*, V III (1980/81), pp. 241-254.

―――― "Women's Studies And Popular Music: Using Audio Resources In Social Studies Instruction," *The History And Social Science Teacher*, XIV (Fall 1978), pp. 29-40.

Denisoff, R. Serge, and John Bridges,"The Battered And Neglected Orphan: Popular Music Research And Books," *Popular Music And Society*, VIII (1981), pp. 43-59.

Denisoff, R. Serge, "Folk-Rock: Folk Music, Protest, Or Commericalism?" *Journal Of Popular Culture*, III (Fall 1969), pp. 214-230.

Denisoff, R. Serge, and David Fandray, " 'Hey, Hey Woody Guthrie I Wrote You A Song': The Political Side Of Bob Dylan," *Popular Music and Society*, V (1977), pp. 31-42.

Denisoff, R. Serge, and Mark H. Levine, "The Popular Protest Song: The Case of 'Eve Of Destruction'," *Public Opinion Quarterly*, XXXV (Spring 1971) pp. 117-122.

Denisoff, R. Serge, "Protest Songs: Those On The Top Forty And Those On The Street," *American Quarterly*, XXII (Winter 1970), pp. 807-823.

Denisoff, R. Serge, and Richard A. Peterson, "Theories Of Culture, Music, And Society," in *The Sounds Of Social Change: Studies In Popular Culture* (Chicago: Rand McNally and Company, 1972), pp. 1-12.

Dimaggio, Paul, Richard A. Peterson, and Jack Esco, Jr., "Country Music: Ballad Of The Silent Majority," in *The Sounds Of Social Change: Studies in Popular Culture*, edited by R. Serge Denisoff and Richard A. Peterson (Chicago: Rand McNally and Company, 1972), pp. 38-55.

Friedlander, Paul, "The Rock Window: A Systematic Approach To An Understanding Of Rock Music," *Tracking: Popular Music Studies*, I (Spring 1988), pp. 42-51.

Frith, Simon, "'The Magic That Can Set You Free;: The Ideology of Folk And The Myth Of The Rock Community," in *Popular Music I: Folk Or Popular? Distinction, Influences, Continuities*, edited by Richard Middleton and David Horn Cambridge: Cambridge University Press, 1981), pp. 159-168.

―――― "Popular Music, 1950-1980," in *Making Music: The Guide To Writing, Performing, And Recording*, edited by George Martin (London: Pan Books, 1983), pp. 18-48.

Fryer, Paul, "Can You Blame The Colored Man?: The Topical Song In Black American Popular Music," *Popular Music And Society*, VIII (1981), pp. 19-31.

Garofalo, Reebee, and Steve Chapple, "From ASCAP To Alan Freed: The Pre-History Of Rock 'N' Roll," *Popular Music And Society*, VI (1978), pp. 72-80.

Gritzner, Charles F., "Country Music: A Reflection Of Popular Culture," *Journal Of Popular Culture*, XI (Fall 1978), pp. 857-864.

Harmon, James E., "Meaning in Rock Music: Notes Toward A Theory Of Communication," *Popular Music And Society*, II (Fall 1972), pp. 18-32.

―――― "The New Music And Counter-Culture Values," *Youth And Society*, IV (September 1972), pp. 61-82.

Heckman, Don, "Black Music And White America," in *Black America*, edited by John F, Szwed (New York: Basic Books, Inc., 1970), pp. 158-170.

Hellmann, John M. Jr., " 'I'm A Monkey': The Influence Of The Black American Blues Argot On The Rolling Stones," *Journal Of American Folklore*, LXXXVI (October/December 1973), pp. 367-373.

Henderson, Floyd M., "The Image Of New York City in American Popular Music of 1890-1970," *New York Folklore Quarterly*, XXX (December 1974), pp. 267-278.

Hesbacher, Peter, and Les Waffen, "War Recordings: Incidence And Change, 1940-1980," *Popular Music And Society*, VIII (1982), pp. 77-101.

Hey, Kenneth R., "I Feel A Change Comin' On: The Counter-Cultural Image Of The South in Southern Rock 'N' Roll," *Popular Music And Society*, V (1977), pp. 93-99.

Hirsch, Paul, John Robinson, Elizabeth Keogh Taylor, and Stephen B. Withey, "The Changing Popular Song: An Historical Overview," *Popular Music And Society*, I (Winter 1972), pp. 83-93.

Hirsch, Paul M., "Sociological Approaches To The Pop Music Phenomenon," *American Behavioral Scientist*, XIV (January-February 1971), XIV (January-February 1971), pp. 371-388.

Horton, Donald, "The Dialogue Of Courtship In Popular Songs," *American Journal Of Sociology*, LXII (May 1957), pp. 569-578.

Hugunin, Marc, "ASCAP, BMI, And The Democratization Of American Popular Music," *Popular Music And Society*, VII (1979), pp. 8-17.

Kamin, Jonathan, "Parallels In The Social Reactions to Jazz And Rock," *Journal Of Jazz Studies*, II (December 1974), pp. 95-125.

_____ "Taking The Roll Out Of Rock 'N' Roll: Reverse Acculturation," *Popular Music And Society*, II (Fall 1972), pp. 1-17.

_____ "The White R & B Audience And The Music Industry, 1952-1956," *Popular Music And Society*, IV (1975), pp. 170-187.

Kelly, William P., "Running on Empty: Reimaging Rock And Roll," *Journal Of American Culture*, IV (Winter 1981), pp. 152-159.

King, Florence, "Rednecks, White Socks, And Blue-Ribbon Fear: The Nashville Sound of Discontent," *Harper's Magazine*, CCXLIX (July 1974), pp. 30-34.

Levine, Mark H., and Thomas J. Harig, "The Role Of Rock: A Review And Critique Of Alternative Perspectives On The Impact Of Rock Music," *Popular Music And Society*, IV (1975), pp. 195-207.

Lewis, George H., "Country Music Lyrics," *Journal of Communication XXVI* (Autumn 1976), pp. 37-40.

_____ "Social Protest And Self Awareness In Black Popular Music," *Popular Music And Society*, II (Summer 1973), pp. 327-333.

_____ "The Sociology Of Popular Music: A Selected And Annotated Bibliography," *Popular Music And Society*, VII (1979), pp. 57-68.

Lund, Jens, "Country Music Goes To War: Songs For The Red-Blooded American," *Popular Music And Society*, I (Summer 1972), pp. 210-230.

Lund, Jens, and R. Serge Denisoff, "The Folk Music Revival And The Counter Culture," *Journal Of American Folklore*, LXXXIV (October/December 1971), pp. 394-405.

Lund, Jens, "Fundamentalism, Racism, And Political Reaction In Country Music," in *The Sounds Of Social Change: Studies In Popular Culture*, edited by R. Serge Denisoff and Richard A. Peterson (Chicago: Rand McNally and Company, 1972), pp. 79-91.

Marcus, Greil, "Rock Films," in *The Rolling Stone Illustrated History Of Rock And Roll*, edited by Jim Miller (New York: Random House, 1976), pp. 350-357.

Maultsby, Portia K., "Soul Music: Its Sociological And Political Significance In American Popular Culture," *Journal Of Popular Culture*, XVII (Fall 1983), pp. 51-65.

McCarthy, John D., Richard A. Peterson, and William L. Yancey, "Singing Along With The Silent Majority," in *Popular Culture: Mirror Of American Life*, edited by David Manning White and John Pendleton (Del Mar, California: Publisher's Inc., 1977), pp. 169-173.

McCourt, Tom, "Bright Lights, Big City: A Brief History Of Rhythm And Blues, 1945-1957," *Popular Music And Society*, IX (1983), pp. 1-18.

Mooney, Hughson F., "Commercial 'Country' Music In The 1970s: Some Special And Historical Perspectives," *Popular Music And Society*, VII (1980), pp. 208-213.

———— "Just Before Rock: Pop Music 1950-1953 Reconsidered," *Popular Music And Society*, III (1974), pp. 65-108.

———— "Popular Music Since The 1920s: The Significance Of Shifting Taste," *Popular Music And Society*, I (Spring 1972), pp. 129-143.

———— "Twilight Of The Age Of Aquarius? Popular Music In The 1970s, *Popular Music And Society*, VII (1980), pp. 182-198.

———— "Years Of Strain And Stress: 1917-1929 In The Whitburn Record Charts," *Popular Music And Society* XII (Summer 1988), pp. 1-20.

Morgan, John P., and Thomas C. Tulloss, "The Jake Walk Blues: A Toxicologic Tragedy Mirrored In American Popular Music," *Annals Of Internal Medicine*, LXXXV (December 1976), pp. 804-808.

Peterson, Richard A., and David G. Berger, "Cycles In Symbol Production: The Case Of Popular Music," *American Sociological Review*, XL (April 1975), pp. 158-173.

Peterson, Richard A., "Disco!" *The Chronicle Review*, XVIII (October 2, 1978), pp. R 26-27.

———— "The Production Of Cultural Change: The Case Of Contemporary Country Music," *Social Research*, XLV (Summer 1978), pp. 292-314.

———— "Taking Popular Music Too Seriously," *Journal Of Popular Culture*, IV (Winter 1971), pp. 590-594.

———— "The Unnatural History Of Rock Festivals: An Instance Of Media Facilitation," *Popular Music And Society*, II (Winter 1973), pp. 97-123.

Prechter, Robert R., "Elvis, Frankenstein, And Andy Warhol: Using Pop Culture To Forecast The Stock Market," *Barron's LXV* (September 9, 1985), pp. 6-7, 26, 28 ff.

———— "Popular Culture And The Stock Market," *The Elliott Wave Theorist*, (August 22, 1985), pp. 1-20.

Reinartz, Kay, "The Paper Doll: Images Of American Women In Popular Songs, in *Women: A Feminist Perspective*, edited by Jo Freeman (Palo Alto, California: Mayfield Publishing Company, 1975), pp. 293-308.

Rice, Ronald E., "The Content Of Popular Recordings," *Popular Music And Society*, VII (1980), pp. 140-158.

Robinson, John P., Robert Pilskaln, and Paul Hirsch, "Protest Rock And Drugs," *Journal Of Communication*, XXVI (Autumn 1976), pp. 125-136.

Rodnitzky, Jerome, "Also Born In The U.S.A.: Bob Dylan's Outlaw Heroes And The Real Bob Dylan," *Popular Music And Society*, XII (Summer 1988), pp. 37-43.

Rollin, Roger B., "Beowulf To Batman: The Epic Hero And Pop Culture," *College English*, XXXI (February 1970), pp. 431-449.

Romanowski, William D., and R. Serge Denisoff, "Money For Nothin' And The Charts For Free: Rock And The Movies," *Journal Of Popular Culture*, XXI (Winter 1987), pp. 63-78.

Root, Jr., Robert L., "A Listener's Guide To The Rhetoric Of Popular Music," *Journal Of Popular Culture*, XX (Summer 1986), pp. 15-26.

Rosenstone, Richard A., " 'The Times They Are A'Changin'": The Music Of Protest," *The Annals of The American Academy Of Political And Social Science*, CCCLXXXI (March 1969), pp. 131-144.

Schilling, James Von, "Records And The Record Industry," in *Handbook Of American Popular Culture—Volume Three*, edited by M. Thomas Inge (Westport, Connecticut: Greenwood Press, 1981), pp. 385-411.

Seidman, Laurence I., " 'Get On The Raft With Taft' And Other Musical Treats," *Social Education*, XL (October 1976), pp. 436-437.

_____ "Teaching About The American Revolution Through Its Folk Songs," *Social Education*, XXXVIII (November 1973), pp. 654-664.

Stevenson, Gordon, "Popular Culture And The Public Library," in *Advances In Librarianship—Vol. VII*, edited by Melvin J. Voight and Michael H. Harris (New York: Academic Press, 1977), pp. 177-229.

_____ "Race Records: Victims Of Benign Neglect In Libraries," *Wilson Library Bulletin*, L (November 1975), pp. 224-232.

_____ "The Wayward Scholar: Resources And Research In Popular Culture," *Library Trends*, XXV (April 1977), pp. 779-818.

Tamarkin, Jeff, "White House Funnies: Presidential Satire Records," *Goldmine*, No. 217 (November 18, 1988), pp. 26-27, 83-85.

Thorpe, Peter, "I'm Movin' On: The Escape Theme In Country And Western Music," *Western Humanities Review*, XXIV (Autumn 1970), pp. 307-318.

Wells, John, "Bent Out Of Shape From Society's Pliers: A Sociological Study Of The Grotesque in The Songs Of Bob Dylan," *Popular Music And Society*, VI (1978), pp. 27-38.

Unpublished Materials

Berger, David G., "The Unchanging Popular Tune Lyric, 1910-1955." Ph.D. Dissertation: Columbia University, 1966.

Burns, Gary, "Utopia And Dystopia In Popular Song Lyrics: Rhetorical Visions In The United States, 1963-1972." Ph.D. Dissertation: Northwestern University, 1981.

Butchart, Ronald E., and B. Lee Cooper, " 'Teacher, Leave Them Kids Alone!': Perception Of Schooling And Education In American Popular Music" (mimeographed paper presented at the Annual Convention of The American Education Studies Association in November 1981).

Cooper, B. Lee, "I'm A Hog For You Baby: Problems Of Thematic Classification In Popular Music" (mimeographed paper presented at the Annual Convention of The Music Library Association in February 1988).

Dewitt, Howard A., "Using Popular History In The American Survey: Rock And Roll As An Expression Of American Culture In The 1950s" (mimeographed paper presented at the 7th Annual Convention of The Popular Culture Association in April 1977).

Harmon, James Elmer, "The New Music And The American Youth Subculture." Ph.D. Dissertation: United States International University, 1971.

Johnson, Mary Jane Carle, "Rock Music As A Reflector Of Social Attitudes Among Youth Of The 1960s." Ph.D. Dissertation: St. Louis University, 1978.

Kamin, Jonathan, "Rhythm And Blues In White America: Rock and Roll As Acculturation And Perceptual Learning." Ph.D. Dissertation: Princeton University, 1976.

Keesing, Hugo A., "Youth In Transition: A Content Analysis Of Two Decades of Popular Music." Ph.D. Dissertation: Adelphi University, 1972.

Reading, Joseph D., "Tears Of Rage: A History, Theory, And Criticism Of Rock Song And Social Conflict Rhetoric, 1965-1970" Ph.D. Dissertation: University of Oregon, 1980.

Redd, Lawrence N., "The Impact Of Radio, Motion Pictures, And Blues, On Rock And Roll Music" M.A. Thesis: Michigan State University, 1971.

Slater, Thomas J., "Rock Music, Youth, And Society: The Uses Of Rock Music In The Movies, 1955-1981" (mimeographed paper presented at the 12th National Convention of the Popular Culture Association in April 1982).

Wanzenried, John Werner, "Extentional And Intentional Orientations of Rock And Roll Song Lyrics, 1955-1972: A Content Analysis." Ph.D. Dissertation: University of Nebraska, 1974.

Weller, Donald J., "Rock Music: Its Role And Political Significance As A Channel of Communication." Ph.D. Dissertation: University of Hawaii, 1971.

Index